The Touch of the Present

SUNY series, Transforming Subjects: Psychoanalysis, Culture, and Studies in Education
———————
Deborah P. Britzman, editor

The Touch of the Present

*Educational Encounters, Aesthetics,
and the Politics of the Senses*

Sharon Todd

SUNY PRESS

Cover art: Copyright Sharon Todd, *Becoming, Wound Healing*, 2021.

Published by State University of New York Press, Albany

© 2023 State University of New York

All rights reserved

Printed in the United States of America

No part of this book may be used or reproduced in any manner whatsoever without written permission. No part of this book may be stored in a retrieval system or transmitted in any form or by any means including electronic, electrostatic, magnetic tape, mechanical, photocopying, recording, or otherwise without the prior permission in writing of the publisher.

For information, contact State University of New York Press, Albany, NY
www.sunypress.edu

Library of Congress Cataloging-in-Publication Data

Name: Todd, Sharon, 1962– author.
Title: The touch of the present : educational encounters, aesthetics, and the politics of the senses / Sharon Todd.
Description: Albany : State University of New York Press, 2023. | Series: SUNY series, Transforming subjects : psychoanalysis, culture, and studies in education | Includes bibliographical references and index.
Identifiers: LCCN 2022025288 | ISBN 9781438492179 (hardcover : alk. paper) | ISBN 9781438492193 (ebook) | ISBN 9781438492186 (pbk. : alk. paper)
Subjects: LCSH: Human body in education. | Learning, Psychology of. | Senses and sensation. | Spatial behavior. | Intersubjectivity. | Liminality.
Classification: LCC LA135 .T64 2023 | DDC 370—dc23/eng/20220713
LC record available at https://lccn.loc.gov/2022025288

10 9 8 7 6 5 4 3 2 1

For all those who have helped me travel that slow journey of being of the world and not just in it.

If the aesthetic dimension and not the economic was governing society, and if tactile perception was valued as highly as the rational, then how would you teach?

—Sisters Hope, *Sisters Academy: Education for the Future*

Contents

ACKNOWLEDGMENTS   xi

INTRODUCTION
Why Encounters?   1

Part One: Theoretical Framings

CHAPTER ONE
The Present Tense Incarnate: Education as Encounters/Encounters as Education   19

CHAPTER TWO
Senses of Encounter   45

CHAPTER THREE
Enculturation, Regimes of Perception, and the Politics of the Senses   75

CHAPTER FOUR
Forms and Formations of Encounters   99

CHAPTER FIVE
Becoming as a Time of Unfolding   123

Part Two: Encounters in/of Education

CHAPTER SIX
Digital Encounters: Online Education and the Space-Time of the Virtual   151

CHAPTER SEVEN
Encounters with Climate Change: Teaching in the Presence
of Climate Sorrow   169

AFTERWORD
The Touch of the Present and Education *as* Social Justice   187

NOTES   191

REFERENCES   199

INDEX   209

Acknowledgments

I always have this sense when beginning a book that *this* one is going to somehow capture my thinking, ideas, and puzzlements in a more exhaustive way than ever before. This hubris of the representational power of the text makes the books I write necessarily a tad disappointing. Unable to hide behind the genre-imposed limitations of articles, essays, or self-contained chapters, I imagine books on the contrary to be expansive worlds—they open up encounters for the writer as much as for the reader. And as such I still imagine them to hold something magical, emerging from the alchemy of place, thought, and style; and it is this amazing coming together—even more amazing than my sourdough bread—that makes the faint feeling of disappointment bearable—along with, of course, the encouragement and support I have been so fortunate to receive from others, personally as well as academically. So a few remarks of gratitude are in order.

First, a very warm thanks to Deborah Britzman for inviting me to contribute to her series. She has been an intellectual mentor, champion, and friend, and I'm honored to be part of what she has created here. A huge thanks to Rebecca Colesworthy at SUNY Press who has been most supportive and patient throughout a turbulent few years, and to the three reviewers for their careful readings and thoughtful feedback. Also thank you to David Howes for hosting me through the auspices of both the Centre for Sensory Studies and the Centre for Interdisciplinary Studies in Society and Culture (where I in fact wrote my PhD in 1996!) at Concordia University in Montréal during the fall of 2019. While there, I was also able to partake of some activities hosted by the SenseLab. Erin Manning has created a vibrant international community around her and Brian Massumi's work there. Thanks also to Sisters Hope, whose pedagogical installations have made me rethink the place of the body in education over the past number of years.

Thanks also to my colleagues at Maynooth University in Ireland, which has been my wonderful home now for eight years. I've particularly enjoyed and learned from the conversations about philosophy and existence I've had with Aislinn O'Donnell since meeting her in Colombia in 2010; they have contributed to my thinking enormously. Special thanks go to Juliette Bertoldo, Seán Henry, and Angela Rickard who took the time to read various chapters, and whose spirited conversations have contributed in many ways to making me a better scholar, person, walker, and bread baker! I am also grateful to my sisters in arms, Lovisa Bergdahl and Elisabet Langmann, for our continued conversations about embodiment and feminism. Our current project with the Swedish Research Council on "Forms of Formation" (grant no. 987-3.2.2-2020) has contributed invaluably to making this book a reality. Thanks also to Marit Honerød Hoveid for her passion and understanding (and dog-mushing capabilities!) to spearhead a special issue with me and Elisabet Langmann on "Education and the Senses" for *Studies in Philosophy and Education*.

Although I had been hoping to present aspects of this work in person at conferences and other fora, most of those plans were canceled due to the pandemic. I was fortunate, however, to present some of the initial thinking of this work at the Philosophy of Education Society 2020 meeting in Pittsburgh, just before Europe, the US, and Canada closed their borders. And many thanks to Lisa Farley for inviting me to present online for York University in Toronto in September 2020.

I am indebted to Vanessa Machado de Oliveira Andreotti's conversations about coloniality, indigenous thought, and life itself, and also for her invitation to participate in the Gesturing Toward Decolonial Futures collective, whose online seminars really spurred on my thinking. Thanks also to Dougald Hine's online gathering, The Climate Sessions, as part of the School Called Home initiative in Sweden. As well, I want to thank the master's and doctoral students in my Social Justice Perspectives in Education class for sharing their passion and commitment—that class taught me a great deal about what can be achieved in online education (and thanks again to Vanessa as well for allowing us to read a manuscript text of *Hospicing Modernity*).

Thanks also are due to Jenny Mooney who has taught me so much about transformation and trauma. The influence of Buddhism is apparent in these pages, and I want to give thanks to Bhante Bodhidhamma for his teachings for almost a decade, and to the sangha at Zen Buddhism Ireland led by Myozan Kodo for sharing what it means to live a life with Dōgen, still all very new to me. I also owe a huge thanks to Zoom for keeping me connected with friends, family, and sangha members both near and far.

This book, along with so much else in my life, would not be what it is without Carl Anders Säfström. Your love is the touch that moves me to become other than what I thought I could be.

Parts of various chapters have been published previously and have been reworked here with kind permission from the publishers:

Parts of chapter 2 appeared in Todd, Sharon. 2021. "Education, Contact and the Vitality of Touch; Membranes, Morphologies, Movements." *Studies in Philosophy and Education* 40: 249–260. Sections of chapter 2, 3, and 5 appeared in Todd, Sharon. 2020. "The Touch of the Present: Educational Encounters and Processes of Becoming." *Philosophy of Education* 76 3: 61–74. https://www.philofed.org/issue-3. Parts of chapter 4 appear in Todd, Sharon. 2021. "Teaching as Bodily Enactment: Relational Formations of Touch and Movement." *Discourse: Studies in the Cultural Politics of Education*, https://doi.org/10.1080/01596306.2021.1978698. Chapter 7 originally appeared in slightly altered form as Todd, Sharon. 2020. "Creating Aesthetic Encounters *of* the World, or Teaching in the Presence of Climate Sorrow." *Journal of Philosophy of Education*. 54(4): 110–125.

Introduction

Why Encounters?

In October 2017 I became a student again—at a boarding school. Not the usual kind. This one was in a public art space in the center of Copenhagen. Sisters Hope, a feminist art collective, is known for creating installations based on enacting a "sensuous pedagogy" as part of a larger project entitled Sisters Academy (www.sistershope.dk). The one I attended for forty-eight hours as a student-researcher was, in fact, eponymously named the *The Boarding School*. The transformed space was dreamlike, both in its setup and in the intensity of sensation it evoked. Its soundscapes, soft furnishings, velvet draperies, and dimmed lighting were utterly enveloping, folding in and out and at the edges of experience, like a Möbius strip moving through time and space. A journal entry from breakfast the first morning speaks to this feeling, prompted no less by a serendipitous encounter I had with a pat of butter:

> The mind is tricky. Black butter on the table. Had all kinds of narratives flash through my head about what it should be; took some time to become aware of what it is. It's taken a good long time to begin to do that with myself. Like butter once it is in the mouth, so my self melts into the environment and yet not "at one" with it precisely, but in connection, reaching to fill the outer corners of the space and returning to my own deep recesses. I do not become butter but am definitely related to it as it is—now.

This kind of meandering and quite non-commonsensical reflection was a regular occurrence during my time there. The aesthetic practices that

Sisters Hope curate are both rooted in and occasion a sense of self that is porous and liminal.[1] At *The Boarding School*, the encounters staged with various artist-teachers were the relational spaces that allowed for a flow of experience and a transformation of both body and materials. Each artist-teacher curated experimental synesthetic spaces in their own "classes," as well as in the dining hall and the dorms we slept in, sometimes playfully at other times troublingly. Prior to entering *The Boarding School*, I had been interested in aesthetic practices for the way they challenged conventional ways of seeing and being in the world (see Todd 2015a, 2018). However, participating in these sensory encounters made me realize how what passes for familiar and normal perceptions in regular educational settings are also very much part of a sense-scape that intersects deeply and inextricably with our everyday educational experiences.

In fact, the inextricability between our sensory and educational experiences makes it difficult sometimes to distinguish between them. Each of us is continually touched by and touches the world, and what we come to know about it cannot be divorced from our living in/with/through it. Learning to multiply numbers as a child is bound up with the smooth surface of my math textbook, my hunched shoulders over my school desk, and the feel of my pencil between my fingers as I worked on problems; learning cursive writing is intricately connected with the sound of my fountain pen scratching across the paper and the shape of words as they appeared in liquid form through each stroke of my hand; learning the history of early European "explorers" is inseparable from the musty smell of the colonial wall maps with their fading colors, as well as from the deeply disturbing portrayals of First Nations in our textbooks and the grotesque images of so-called Christian martyrs. Through touching and being touched by the world, associations were made that connected some sense of "me" to the curriculum, or rather *created* a sense of "me" through my relation to it, generating a sense-scape that was and continues to be intimate with what I now see to be the work of education. There were also a host of other sensations not directly connected to the official curriculum at all—the heavy, guilt-laden silences following an act of witnessed cruelty, the eruptive bouts of loud laughter that threatened all order, the sharp odors of other bodies, the fresh scent of pencil shavings, and the dank smell of frozen mittens thawing on the radiators during a typical Montréal winter morning. These sensations nonetheless also permeated my understanding of the world, the knowledge we were learning about it, and my and others' place within it. Encounters with, in, and through things and people are the very stuff out of which not only education, but ourselves and the world are made.

The recent years of the pandemic, however, have brought certain questions about our encounters to the fore: What kind of encounters and sense-scapes have educators been able to create for and with students within the constraints of contagion? How has the move to online education shaped the ways we think about encounters more generally? And, more broadly still, how has our planetary interconnection so evidenced by the virus's disregard for species borders impacted how we understand ourselves in relation with the more-than-human world? While this book was born out of a "boarding school" experience which would not have been possible to stage during the lockdowns, precautionary measures, and institutional closures that hit the globe with such force in the past few years, the bodily insights gleaned from that experience have enabled me to see that encounters take form through all kinds of circumstances. That is, teachers still stage them and students still participate in them in whichever conditions prevail, even if they do so very differently than the ways we are used to. Encounters, while constrained and limited, nonetheless still *happen*. And they, too, give rise to the world and ourselves in the process, even within the restrictions we face.

Encounters. The word is often used by educators, artists, and activists to talk about a significant aspect of the work they do. They stage, create, and make certain encounters *happen*; it is part of their planned practice, whether this takes place in schools or other educational sites. They act as introducers of things, events, and happenings through lectures, seminars, activities, performances, and protests. They create encounters with artifacts, such as books and maps, plants and stones, texts and numbers. Through these encounters their aim is to create an alternative way of seeing, experiencing, and perhaps ultimately being and living with others—an alternative to what students, participants, and audiences already take for granted as commonplace. In this way, education, like art and politics, offers an occasion for *becoming* that opens students up to new ways of thinking, doing, and living; encounters, as Maxine Greene would put it, that have the power to make the familiar strange.

But the demands made upon educators' practices are significantly different to those made upon artists and activists in the sense that education is bound not only to ideas of transformation, change, and freedom but is also burdened with a certain amount of transmission, concerning the inheritance of ideas, norms, and social codes. Society tasks educators, particularly those who work with children and youth (whether in schools, preschools, museums, community centers, or in face-to-face or online settings) with ensuring that the young not only learn *about* or *from* their environments, but also *inhabit* those environments in particular ways. On this view, educators are thought to play an important role in shaping a young person's embodied understanding of themselves and their social and cultural environment. This raises a huge problem, however, of how these normative demands have worked in deleterious ways, which have at times contributed to outright forms of violence and abuse, as well as to the creation of unjust and unwelcoming spaces for neurodiverse, disabled, working-class, indigenous, LGBTQ, and minority students. Indeed decades of critical multicultural, anti-normative, and decolonial projects in education have focused precisely on the need to recognize that there are multiple ways environments are inhabited across social and cultural differences and how injurious it has been to individuals and communities to erase these differences. In this, there is a tension that all educators need to face between participating in this social and cultural work with its risk of reproducing what might be harmful, on the one side, and the transformative potential that education aspires to, on the other.

Reflecting on my time as an educator for well over thirty years, first in an elementary school then in various universities in Canada, Sweden, and Ireland where I have taught both teachers and student-teachers, I feel those tensions deeply still. My professional life has been infused with a genuine (if not always successful) attempt to create encounters with and for others that optimally could be transformative for students, enabling them to become more expansive versions of themselves, opening them up to new ways of seeing and being in their own intimate corners of the world. There has been an overarching sense that such encounters can assist students in living and leading lives worth living with others. This has often taken the form of exposing students to ideas that bring to the fore issues of social justice. And yet, I have always felt an enormous responsibility to acknowledge students as being also good enough as they are—without me and my pedagogical interventions—that they are subjects of value and worth in their own right, living complex lives, coming to class from a range of different and unique experiences. Questions have gathered over the years, like heavy clouds at times, settling in and around the work I do: Who am I to teach someone else? What kinds of being or becoming do I make possible or limit through the encounters I stage as a teacher? How do I create spaces for students' becoming someone different in a gesture of affirmation and acceptance for who they are right here and now? What does my teaching *do* to my students—and myself? These are not mere academic queries, but haunting existential questions for me. But stage encounters I must, for that is what I do as a teacher and as a professional committed to equality and justice. However, I do so now, more so than I was able in those early years, with a fuller sense of the fine line I walk with students between hubris and humility, between critical change and affirmation. Admittedly, though, the walking itself is just as demanding as it always was, and perhaps that is as it should be.

Such questions concerning the relationality of teaching and the affect, ethics, and embodied nature of it, has informed a great deal of my scholarly work (see Todd 2003, 2009, and 2016b in particular) and continues to shape the angle I take in this book, which is primarily from the point of view of the pedagogical relation and the act of teaching and educating. In this way, my being a student again at *The Boarding School* prompted me to face those persistent questions I've had as a teacher, to face more directly the practices of encounter that shape pedagogical engagement, and to face the ways the boundaries between subject/object (and sometimes subject/subject) become blurred—like that pat of black butter. That is, I began to understand—to *feel* even!—how the encounters I stage as a teacher are living, bodily forms of contact with various things, people, and other living beings. And I began to wonder about the complex entanglements encounters always engender and in which sense they are educational.

Strangely, from a scholarly point of view, while encounters appear to be somewhat foundational to what is *done* in the name of education, they are little theorized and conceptually underdeveloped. A body of work that is promising for remedying this occlusion and for paying attention to the way bodies interact with the materiality of educational settings can be found in the turn to "new materialism,"[2] represented through materialist and vitalist frameworks (Ringrose et al. 2020; Hickey-Moody 2016; O'Donnell 2018), sociobiology (Youdell 2017) and posthumanism (Mikulan and Rudder 2019; Taylor and Pacini-Ketchabaw 2015). This work has been instrumental in highlighting the generative aspect of these interactions in engendering bodies, their surfaces, borders, and fleshly substance. Moving beyond the discursive constitution of bodies, this focus on embodiment in education has enabled a significant shift toward viewing the centrality of the physical, material dimensions of educational practices.³

Specifically, they place an emphasis on nondualist thinking, which has drawn together—in not so easy fashion at times—scholars of Spinoza and Deleuze, those concerned with the sciences and technology, and those who write on ecology and posthumanism. Collectively, their work represents a turn to ontology as being rooted in the complex interplay of relationality that makes it difficult to distinguish the boundaries and borders between things—both human and more-than-human alike. It is a *relational ontology* that recognizes the centrality of the interdependence of all life, which is also represented by numerous indigenous thinkers (Ahenakew et al. 2011; Cajete 1994; Mika 2017) along with those interested in questions of the planetary crisis (Braidotti and Bignall 2019; Haraway 2016; Latour 2017). With respect to education, relational ontology shifts our understanding of spaces and places from being the context *in* which educational stuff happens, to being an active player in the processes of education itself.

Yet, knowing how certain encounters have also worked to further injustices, Sara Ahmed (2008) cautions against what she sees as the "fetish of matter" in some works of feminist new materialism. For her, this work does not account sufficiently for culture, language, and discourse, which translates into an attention on matter that is somewhat skewed and ahistorical.⁴ More recently, Rosi Braidotti (2019) has echoed a similar point in her critique of the nihilist tendencies within new materialist thinking when it is cut off from processes of racialization, capitalism, and colonialism. While seeking to build on the ideas of nonduality and relationality that have been discussed within new materialist work, I also seek to look at the complexity of relational encounters in ways that do not always sit firmly within this materialist approach. Indeed the focus on attending to the physical and material conditions of materialization leaves aside important questions concerning culture, the senses, and affective experience, which constitute my own focus here. That is, what tends to be undertheorized within certain new materialist frameworks is how our interactions and interdependence with things, plant life, humans, and other animals are both inflected by and generate complex matrices of sensations, affects, and attachments. In this way, this volume is rooted within a relational ontological framework that is not solely concerned with the material.

However, it is also important to signal that the senses and experience are often theorized as something bodies *have* as opposed to what bodies *do* and have been traditionally associated with the fields of phenomenology and psychology, where some scholars have noted a tendency to abstract living physical bodies into categories that remain oddly dematerialized. This is perhaps why it is not entirely surprising that some new materialist scholars have largely stayed clear of the senses and experience. Moreover, as Ahmed (2000) points out, this dematerializing move of abstraction has often erased the fundamentally different ways bodies both create and are created by the world around them as racialized and sexualized subjects. My focus on the senses here seeks to avoid the pitfalls of replicating an abstract, white-washed, desexualized (and hence depoliticized) notion of *the* body (in the singular), while also understanding that sensory experience and not only materiality is part of the space and time of bodily encounters. I do this primarily by referring to bodies in the plural and by focusing on the specifically *political* and *aesthetic* dimensions of the senses in educational encounters. Each brings bodies into conversation with their environments in complementary ways, and each helps to chart a course for educators between the poles of social norms and transformation mentioned above.

First, with respect to the political dimension, sensory encounters are deeply involved in the ways bodies come to be embedded within what Jacques Rancière (2006, 46) refers to as "regimes of perception." That is, what is taken to be common sense, appropriate forms of sensation, and proper affective expression are experienced and felt in particular ways by particular subjects. This has been borne out by a range of scholars, from early postcolonial writers such as Frantz Fanon and Aimé Césaire to later feminists of color such as Audre Lorde, Sylvia Winter, and Sara Ahmed, who have all depicted how colonial and racist regimes of perception not only categorize or imprint themselves upon bodies, but how they come to be blended with one's own sensations and experiences of oneself. On this view, becoming racialized (as well as gendered and sexualized) is a relational process that involves both the inner self and outer social realities, a process which is never fully complete or deterministic.

In line with this, decolonial educational scholars, such as Vanessa (Andreotti) Machado de Oliveira (2021),[5] call for a radical understanding of undoing the terms of "modernity/coloniality" (Mignolo and Walsh 2018) through working at the self's borders of inner and outer. Machado de Oliveira calls this work a "non-western psychoanalysis," one that faces how our bodily affects and sensibilities are interlaced with modern/colonial forms of desire—and the harmful relationalities to self and other they are based on—in order to begin the difficult work of self and social transformation. While affects and sensibilities may be experienced singularly and at varying levels of intensity, they are communal in how they play out as well as in how they can be unraveled. Machado de Oliveira sees this double move of facing and undoing as a process of social, psychological, and affective "decluttering:" a process of taking stock in order to activate change. While the adage that the personal is political is fitting here, what Machado de Oliveira (see also Andreotti 2021b) underscores is that this "depth education" is not only political but also requires collective aesthetic practices that can offer new sources of imagination and new opportunities for re-sensing the world, what Rancière (2009) would see as creating new "communities of sense."

Secondly, seeing encounters also through an aesthetic lens allows for an exploration of the ways in which bodily encounters can create new relational (and political) formations. Although often conceived as a branch of philosophy having to do with art, aesthetics has its roots in the Greek understanding of perception. Aristotle refers to aesthetics as a sensory faculty and Seremetakis (1994) notes the complex and rich etymological associations aesthetics carries: "The word for senses is *aesthísis*; emotion-feeling and aesthetics are respectively *asthima* and *aesthitikí*. They all derive from the *aesthánome* or *aesthínome* meaning I feel or sense, I understand, grasp, learn or receive news or information, and I have an accurate sense of good and evil, that is I judge correctly. *Aesthísis* is defined as action or power through the medium of the senses, and the media or the *semía* (points, tracks, marks) by which one senses" (4–5).

Accordingly, aesthetics is fundamentally a term of encounter that captures its multiplicity, where the borders between feeling, perception, affect, understanding, and art are constantly shifting in relation to whatever it is I am encountering. The aesthetic dimensions of educational encounters thus do not only pertain to whether or not they are creating some kind of art form, but rather *how* the encounters can be seen as (artistic) formations of sensory experience. As I discuss in chapter 4, this way of understanding the aesthetic dimensions of encounters lends itself to a consideration of how we stage, curate, and design encounters as educators. Attending to the senses thus means to attend to the forms and formations of educational practice.

Through these lenses, my intent is not to tell educators (or artists or activists or anyone else for that matter) what they/I should be doing, but to open up questions that might inform what encounters can become in educational settings, what they can lead to, and how they form a central element in any educational practice. In this, I am not interested in offering a theory of encounter (in the singular) that can then be *applied* to education, but to take seriously what *transpires in* and *through* encounters (in the plural) in order to better understand what education is capable of.

The Touch of the Present, or What's in a Title?

The current pandemic has occasioned some deep reflection about the significance of touch in our everyday lives, how desperately it was longed for by those living alone, how strangely it was absent from children's and youth's regular interactions, and how teachers suddenly needed to shift from physical places to online spaces to do their work. The lack of physical touch and existential feelings of isolation went hand in hand, one might say. And while this book is very much about physical bodies, touch, as I understand it here, and as I develop more explicitly in chapter 2, is not simply one of the senses, but is the primary way we experience the world through all our senses: each sense is a form of touch, a form of encounter. So, even during the pandemic—albeit through different encounters than conventional face-to-face ones—we continue/d to touch and be touched by things and people around us. Circumstances only change the *kinds* of the encounters we have; they do not stop encounters altogether. Encounters are a marker of our interconnection with whatever and whomever we are in contact.

Thus I use the idiom *touching and being touched by* throughout the book in order to call attention to that interconnection and to the anticipatory and transitive state of touch; the *by* is open to what is about to approach, it implies a something or someone on the other side of the act of touching. So a hand, eye, or ear is always encountering some*thing*, and that something, in the very moment of contact, is also touching a hand, eye, or ear. Together they generate an encounter. Following Brian Massumi (2002), I treat touch primarily as an "event" of contact and sensation that is not only *in* but *of* the present. In this sense, touch conveys a liminal space and time: the dynamic of "touching and being touched by" transpires at the threshold of here and now, a transient moment that arises and passes. However, as I explore in chapter 5, this transient time of the present is also complex—not simply a passing between past and future, but an opening through which bodily acts of "presencing" bring past and future into conversation.

Since contact is not an abstraction, but a concrete relation that arises when (at least) two things come together, it is important not to use language that tugs us back into overgeneralizations and away from the particularities I am seeking to hold onto here, even while recognizing words themselves have a tendency to do just that. One prevalent way of speaking of contact is to say that we encounter the *world*; but this I feel, despite its poetic intimations, conjures an image of a great amorphous form that does not address *what* it is we are actually encountering and entangled with. So, instead of the *world* which erases the particular in its shorthand, I have chosen the perhaps less elegant phrase "elements of the environment" to indicate that our encounters are always with something more intimate in our immediate surroundings than the *world* can convey and to remind us of that very specificity. Elements can range from tangible objects to the air we breathe, from words or ideas to animate beings, from human to more-than-human entities. The book is committed to understanding the educational significance of the imminent, immediate, and sometimes irreverent ways encounters are practiced, on the ground, through our daily encounters with these elements. In this sense, what I am calling the touch of the present is an attempt to work through the ways in which encounters create, as Erin Manning (2007) remarks, "spaced times and timed spaces" of interdependence and how those events speak in very concrete ways to educational processes of enculturation and becoming.

I am especially concerned in this book with directly enhancing our educational commitments to these educational processes (which are given full attention in chapter 1), particularly at this critical time where they are so desperately needed, for two reasons. The first is the rise of digital educational experiences, especially prevalent since the pandemic, which challenge us to think about bodily relationality and its educational significance differently. The second is the increasing difficulties of teaching youth who are deeply affected by the climate emergency, which challenge us to question the kinds of relationality that have led to ecological collapse in the first place and how education can respond with new approaches. As Rosi Braidotti (2019) suggests, shifts in modes of subjectivity have been ushered in by the decentering of the human through biotechnological developments and environmental crises, and this requires different kinds of education, aesthetics, and politics—ones that do not simply seek to reinstate a noncritical humanism, but that take a thoroughly affirmative stance to confront the effects of these transformations. To this end, facing the planetary crisis and posthuman modes of digital relationality are central to understanding educational encounters at this point in the twenty-first century. These two contexts, to me, are defining the very shape of how we interact across times, spaces, devices, and species, and they link in complex ways to ongoing issues of equality and social justice across multiple subjectivities. My intent throughout the volume is to provide new vocabularies, forms, and images for thinking through the significance of educational practices of enculturation and becoming, and the final two chapters of the book bring these directly into conversation with these contexts.

My Approach

Approach. It is a very bodily word, implying as it does a movement or style, the act of drawing near or sidling up to something. Approaching encounters from the perspective of practices means exploring that what we do and how we do it actually matter in constructing these new vocabularies, forms, and images mentioned above. Taking my cue from Isabelle Stengers (2005), this book proposes viewing education *as* and *through* an ecology of practices. For Stengers, an ecology of practices is a tool for thinking which "aims at the construction of new 'practical identities' for practices, that is, new possibilities for them to be present, or in other words to connect" (186). This means seeing educational encounters not simply as objects of analysis, but as interrelated happenings that can tell us something vital about *what* education is doing, the claims it is making *about* what it is doing, and how it might shift our understandings of what it *could* be doing. Moreover, as it names those practices, it allows for new connections to be made, as Stengers suggests, and new terms, vocabularies, and forms to be developed. An *ecology* of practices means investigating education not as *containing* certain practices, but as being *comprised of* the interrelationship of those practices. It is neither pure description nor pure critique, but a movement of tracing the interconnections of practices to see how education might take form differently, "fostering its own force, [and] mak[ing] present what causes practitioners to think and feel and act" (195). Thus for Stengers, an ecology of practices is not simply a matter of describing practices "as they are," but "practices as they may become" (186) and the impact this has on the domain of what practitioners *do*.

Rather than approaching or drawing near to practices from a singular theoretical perspective, I have let the specific dimensions of encounters under discussion guide me. This book seeks to perform what is intimated in the title, a form of touching and being touched by as it feels its way through a number of theoretical viewpoints. My eclecticism is not intended to string together incommensurable notions, concepts, and ideas; theoretical bricolage risks creating a whole that is less than the sum of its parts. Instead, I have attempted to create more of a montage, whose integral elements inform each other through their juxtaposition and contrasts while nonetheless maintaining their singular integrity. Traversing across different philosophical, educational, aesthetic positions I have sought not to appropriate them in ways that divorce them entirely from the contexts in which they were generated, while also seeking to give them space to breathe life into a new context. In some sense, this compositional strategy is very much about creating conversations between various positions that help to highlight the particularly *educational* issues at stake in order to generate a theoretical stance that is internally diverse and multiple.

There are three major commitments that inform my choice of scholarly work here: (1) that it speaks to the relational interdependence of the body, materiality, and the senses; (2) that it considers the experiential, sensate dimensions of this interdependence; and (3) that it can address the political and aesthetic aspects of this relationality. Each chapter brings into conversation a diverse range of positions in order to think through the central ideas under study. While the project overall is informed by relational ontology (Brian Massumi, Erin Manning, Bruno Latour, Rosi Braidotti), I draw on ideas that are rooted within a phenomenological frame (Maxine Sheets-Johnstone, Sara Ahmed, David Abram). Moreover, in turning to the political-aesthetic dimensions of encounters, I draw upon ideas from art theory and political philosophy (Nicolas Bourriaud and Jacques Rancière) that have no clear alignments to either of these philosophies. The psychoanalytic work of D. W. Winnicott and Mark Epstein is discussed in relation to time and ideas from Buddhist philosophy (Nagarjuna, Dōgen) are interwoven throughout as well, particularly as they speak to the nondual aspects of relationality and interdependence I am developing here. Since my priority is to explore educational encounters through and as an ecology of practices, I believe this theoretical diversity can shed light on the complexity of educational relations through which new modes of becoming can arise.

Structure of the Book

The book is divided into two unequal parts. The first, and larger, one deals with Theoretical Framings; the second one with Encounters in/of Education. Part One is composed of five chapters that present a theoretical understanding of encounters, their relation to the senses and education. Chapters 1 and 2 are foundational, setting out the terms of education, encounter, and the senses which are used throughout the rest of the volume.

Chapter 1, "The Present Tense Incarnate: Education as Encounters/Encounters as Education," draws primarily on educational scholarship to argue for what I see to be the two cornerstones of educational encounters, namely enculturation and becoming. I contend that both of these resist the determinism embodied in the grid of social identity, positionality, and cultural background without decontextualizing education in the process. To do this, the chapter poses and responds to two interrelated questions: How is education sensually *encountered*? And, what is specifically *educational* about such encounters? In response to this latter question I show how education is not simply the work of either socialization and cultural transmission, on the one hand, or subjectification (Biesta 2010, 2014), on the other. Instead, it involves elements of cultural translation (Bergdahl and Langmann 2018a) and processes of becoming that involve living bodies of sense. In response to the first question, I turn to a critique of Masschelein and Simons's (2013) notions of "suspension" and "profanation" as a way of bracketing off students' backgrounds to suggest that the materiality of student bodies and lived realities of their contexts (as well as material relations of objects of study themselves) matter to education.

Chapter 2, "Senses of Encounter," explores the centrality of the senses to encounters, seeing touch as vital and as having a relationship to all of the senses. I begin with discussing the meaning of encounters, drawing on Sara Ahmed's (2000) work to explore how they participate in processes of racialization and colonization and then investigate how our sensory encounters with the world can also exceed these logics. To this end, I discuss Brian Massumi's understanding of encounter as an event of sensation, along with Maxine Sheets-Johnstone's understanding of encounter as the movement and interrelationality of organisms with their environment. Here I establish how the dynamic of touching and being touched by is central to both our becoming and enculturation, and can offer insight into living realities of encounters, which are marked through (and not by) our differences.

Chapter 3, "Enculturation, Regimes of Perception, and the Politics of the Senses," concerns the ways in which enculturation can enact a politics of the senses to resist dominant forms of signification and expressions of inequality through alternative sensory experiences. I begin with a challenge to "common sense" as a function of socialization and move to discuss the ways in which the senses and bodies have been theorized as central to enculturation. Here I draw on the discursive constitution of the body advanced by Judith Butler (2015) and the socially coded sensory body explored by David Howes and Constance Classen (2014) and suggest that the politics of the senses lies not simply in how the senses are policed—what Jacques Rancière (2006) refers to as a "regime of perception and intelligibility"—but also in how they exceed these normative frames. Thus, I explore the aesthetic politics of Rancière, who claims that new "communities of sense" are only made possible through a "sensible or perceptual shock." I argue that this aesthetic shaking up of common sense is the task of enculturation within our educational encounters.

Chapter 4, "Forms and Formations of Encounters," looks particularly at the aesthetics of encounters as relational, spatial formations, drawing on the relational aesthetics developed by Nicolas Bourriaud. Here, notions of spaces of becoming and enculturation are theorized in terms of the forms education takes. I focus in particular on the form of the teacher as the one who points and explore its underlying relational dynamics, or formations. Through a reading of Eve Kosofsky Sedgwick's "Pedagogy of Buddhism," I outline how this formation of pedagogy presents us with a complex relational choreography of moving bodies. I then discuss these relations through touch and movement, drawing on Erin Manning's (2007, 2012) work to show how bodies cocreate spaces of educational encounters.

Chapter 5, "Becoming as a Time of Unfolding," discusses the temporal dimension of encounters, seeing the present as a complex enactment of *presencing* that is divorced neither from past nor future, yet is not determined by them. I begin with exploring six different ways time is usually invoked within education and suggest that any transformational focus on becoming needs to think about education's relationship to time differently. Here I draw on Zen master Dōgen's notion of "being-time" to argue for the fluidity of the present through which we touch and are touched by the world. I explore the present as a *presencing* of past and future, drawing on the psychoanalytic understanding of the traumatic time of the past, through the work of Mark Epstein (2013) and D. W. Winnicott (1974), and the notion of touch as embedded within the future anterior, as discussed by Erin Manning (2007). As a living time where past coalesces with future, the present, I argue, is continually unfolding through our educational encounters.

Part Two addresses specifically educational questions of encounter from the point of view of two key issues facing education today: the climate emergency and online education. Rather than see these chapters that compose Part Two as *applying* the theoretical discussion that precedes them, I zero in on how the specific issues offer up their own nuanced understandings of educational encounters that are particular to their contexts. In this, these chapters are not meant to be empirical or analytic chapters, but ones that show how what has been discussed heretofore can inform and be informed by contemporary concerns.

Chapter 6, "Digital Encounters: Online Education and the Space-Time of the Virtual," explores how bodies and the senses can be understood as having an important role to play even within online spaces. I begin by examining the issues that have been raised with respect to online education, many of them emerging particularly with the move to digital forms of pedagogy since the pandemic. In order to address these, I suggest that our digital encounters need to become *more* not less virtual, drawing on Massumi's (2002) understanding of the virtual as potentialities and incipient tendencies which are felt by the body. Moreover, outlining distinctions between the virtual and the actual, the analog and the digital, I argue that pedagogies within the space of online education also need to be analogical in their design and execution. I suggest how curating digital encounters can both be an aesthetic act and address a decolonial project that challenges the ways students are cut off from their relations to and with the world.

Chapter 7, "Encounters with Climate Change: Teaching in the Presence of Climate Sorrow," begins by identifying a common response particularly experienced by youth in relation to the current planetary crisis, namely, overwhelming sorrow. Through this lens, I explore Olafur

Eliasson's artwork *Ice Watch* as a sensory encounter that lives in the complex time of the present, or *kairos*, as well as in chronological time. Drawing on the work of David Abram and Bruno Latour, I discuss educational encounters that can open up the sensual dimension of our interconnectedness to the elements of the environment, seeing how we are not just in relation to the environment, but are fundamentally *of* the environment. I argue that climate sorrow can be explored through educational encounters that take this aesthetic dimension seriously.

In the afterword, I offer some thoughts on how the touch of the present can act as a way of bringing the aesthetic and political dimensions of our educational encounters together to reframe the work we do as social justice, forever mindful of our own implication in the world we share with others. The aspiration behind this book as a whole is to contribute to new ways of thinking that frame what we do as educators as times and spaces that expand our vistas of what education can offer, right here and right now.

PART ONE

Theoretical Framings

Chapter One

The Present Tense Incarnate

Education as Encounters/Encounters as Education

> Learning requires the invention of a special kind of tense. The *present tense incarnate*, for example. Here I am, in this class, and I understand, at last. I've got it. My brain is reaching out to the rest of my body: the word is *being made flesh*. . . . When this isn't the case, when I don't understand anything, I crumble on the spot, I disintegrate as time stands still, I collapse in the dust, and the slightest breath scatters me. . . . For knowledge to have a chance of being embodied in the present tense of a lesson, we need to stop brandishing the past as something shameful and the future as a punishment.
>
> —Daniel Pennac, *School Blues*

In his book *School Blues*, French author Daniel Pennac (2010) sets out to chart, through his own initial experience as a proclaimed "dunce" and then as a schoolteacher of so-called disadvantaged youth in the French *banlieux*, the kinds of encounters that enable students to become—not some*thing* in terms of an end position or profession, but some*one* who is able to exist, without being crushed by either expectation or background. The encounters he so eloquently depicts are not about teacherly performance, but about practices of being present in the classroom, in both mind and body. For Pennac, being present entails teachers and students "paying attention," which is not only a mindful act but involves a change in bodily engagement, where one's presence is felt and experienced as such. But being in the present, he observes, is not easy for the students he teaches, when their futures cannot be fathomed: "If you can't picture a future for yourself, then you can't settle in the present either. You're sitting on your chair but you're somewhere else, prisoner in some dreadful limbo, a place where time stands still, a kind of perpetuity, and you feel as if you're being tortured, and you want to make somebody pay for this, it doesn't matter who, as long as someone does" (993).[1]

As a teacher, he investigates ways in which to bring students' bodies, with all their despair, frustration, and sadness, into the classroom, not in order to psychologize or pathologize them or to "cater to their individual needs" as we so often hear in education, but in order to fully embrace and attend to what is happening at the moment: their relation to the novel, the poem, the equation. Buddhist-like at times, he does this not by denying students' bodies and their feelings, but by allowing them space to be present in the encounter with the said novel, poem, or equation. His message is that by being present, students' feelings of frustration ease off or even dissipate—at least for the moment, perhaps only to return again, necessitating the repetition of the process the next day, the next lesson. However, rather than being caught in some hell of infinite repetition, there is always the possibility of something else happening and catching fire, something in the encounter that generates other kinds of feelings, igniting a student's change of perception about herself, who she is, and who she might become.[2] For Pennac (2010), paying attention is to *inhabit* our encounters. "Knowledge is in the first instance, carnal. Our ears and eyes capture it, our mouths transmit it. Yes, it comes to us from books, but those books come out of us. A thought makes noise, and the taste for reading is born of the need to speak" (1324). Capturing the sensual aspects of encounters, the invention of a "present tense *incarnate*" is a call for understanding that bodies and educational encounters are deeply connected through the "now" of educational experience.[3]

This understanding of the corporeal dimensions of the present raises two interrelated questions for me that I believe are instructive to pursue so as to frame how I am understanding education throughout the rest of this book: How is education sensually *encountered*? And what is specifically *educational* about such encounters? The first question might seem obvious if we are thinking about the sites with which education is usually associated (such as schools, preschools, community centers, and universities), but the "how" of my question has more to do with the specific bodily practices that constitute education itself and how bodies participate, engage, and emerge in and through encounters. The second question involves thinking about encounters as embodying something in particular that we call educational, as opposed to say artistic, political, or ethical. This gets to the heart of a very tangled set of assumptions and conceptions about what constitutes "education proper" and what exactly we are referring to when we refer to education.

In response, I first address myself to what constitutes ideas of education proper and navigate through two aspects of education that have become the Scylla and Charybdis of modern educational thought (and through which other educational theorists have charted numerous if difficult courses ahead of me): namely, the relation between education and socialization, on the one hand; and education and subjectification/emancipation, on the other hand. Here, I suggest that what is educational about encounters needs to move beyond these polarizations (particularly when we look at encounters in an embodied way) if we are to understand more fully how education both interrupts and instantiates different ways of being for different bodies. Secondly, to investigate how education is sensually encountered, I delve into how "encounter" has been reimagined as a relation between students and objects of study. Through this I question the place of the body given in these accounts and argue how the senses are not only intimately involved *in* educational encounters but can be considered to be a fundamental part of what is educational about them in the first place. Before continuing, I wish to take a slight detour here to better situate the trajectory of my argument.

Change and Bodies

I set a course below that embraces the necessity of change as central to what education *does* through its bodily practices, through its encounters. As I mean it here, change is not to be seen merely in terms of adaptation, development, or fulfilment, which are so often markers of "educational" achievement—and indeed of socialization. Instead, as Brian Massumi (2002) puts it, change necessarily involves an open-endedness to our practices, inviting an unpredictable and unknown quality to our encounters. While his object of concern is the dominant way in which the subject is framed in cultural theory and philosophy, I think his comments nonetheless fit well with what I will be developing in terms of encounters and education below.

Writing against theories that seek to understand subject formation in terms of the structural "production" or the discursive "positionality" of body-subjects, whereby a body-subject corresponds to a discrete site (or sites) on a grid of "culturally constructed significations" (Massumi 2002, 2) (for example, the white body, the woman's body, the lesbian body), Massumi seeks instead to frame subjectivity as material encounters that are generative of transformation, of becoming, in ways that transverse and transfigure cultural scripts. He views bodies as central to any theory of change, since it is in and through corporeal movement and felt sensation in engagement with elements of the environment—and not through one's positionality—that change becomes possible for the subject (I discuss this in more detail in chapter 2). More importantly, without a theory of change that compels us to face the sheer embodiedness of becoming, we are caught, as Massumi says, in a "gridlock" (3), forever condemned to theories that either "critique" or "support" positionality itself (for example, theories of reproduction or intersectionality). Massumi notes that it is not as if there isn't movement around the grid (the working-class student who gets a middle-class job after university is one such example), but there is no qualitative transformation of either the subject or the grid itself in such movement: the subject remains defined in terms of its location(s) on the grid (even as negation), and the grid becomes a determinant feature of all subjectivity.

To some degree, this is familiar territory for education as well. It is precisely this grip on the student-subject that Pennac, as teacher, seeks to loosen in insisting on the importance of the present moment. Breaking the gridlock for students from certain backgrounds who have low expectations placed on them does not entail a strategy framed in terms of students' positionality, but in terms of how their engagement in the present can initiate (embodied) change and new becomings beyond those positionalities. However, Pennac's strategy is a rarity in dominant views about education. First, there are those who hold a deeply rooted attachment between education and its cultural role in enabling the young to flourish in society. Although not perhaps defined theoretically in terms of subject "positions," there are roles, behaviors, and expectations about disposition, comportment, and the future itself that are visited upon the young. To this end, the goal of education is conceived in terms of its socialization function in enabling certain students to attain certain positions, adopt certain habits, and fulfil certain social expectations. Secondly, for many educators concerned with social justice issues—who would disagree with the previous insistence on socialization as a goal for education, arguing instead from an emancipatory paradigm—the subject has also been framed largely through social positioning. For example, programs are set up to create better access to education for those currently underrepresented, and success, we could say, is determined by someone's movement on the grid. While such programs are perhaps necessary within the current structures of educational systems, and their critique of how certain subject positions on the grid are excluded from educational opportunity is warranted, students are still caught within the "frame" of the grid and frequently students' bodies (with all their cultural significations) are perceived as simply being reflective of such positionality, usually defined by class, race, ethnicity, disability, sexuality, gender, and combinations thereof. So, in order to begin to think of education as something other than the vehicle through which positionalities, roles, and expectations are either shifted or fulfilled, we need to be able to conceive of change in Massumi's sense, attending to what our encounters are *doing* and how their embodiment creates potential for becoming beyond the grid entirely.[4]

What Is Educational?

To ask why education matters, or what education is for, is to give a very specific direction and shape to what one thinks the purpose of education is. Recent educational theory has rightly been critical of the overly instrumental and narrow definitions lent to the name of education, across policy development, public discourse, and funding (Biesta 2014; Lewis 2017; Masschelein and Simons 2013; Todd 2016a). Within this, there has been specific attention paid to reframing teaching, schooling, and the purpose of education itself from a range of philosophical perspectives (drawing on, though by no means reducible to, the work of Arendt, Rancière, Levinas, Deleuze, and Agamben). These scholars also often manifest overlapping concerns about the public, subjectification, and democracy. While concerned to distinguish education proper not only from instrumentalism, but also from notions of socialization as central to education's purpose, there remains a significant issue to face regarding how to think about the prominent role education plays in the *passing on* and *taking up* of traditions, cultural significations, values, and social codes, particularly since this includes not only "positive" ones such as democracy, but also those attached to histories of, for example, colonization, racism and sexism which fundamentally impact how education is practiced. How might this other side of education be considered as being part of what counts as "educational" without losing sight of the ways educational encounters entail new becomings beyond given social orders, beyond socialization?

Jane Roland Martin (2011), for one, advocates seeing education *as* encounter, and for this reason, her work is important to consider here. However, unlike my own understanding of encounters as sensual contact with elements of the environment, between bodies and other bodies and objects, Martin sees encounter more along the lines of a person's encounter with an item of "cultural stock." Martin's idea is that for too long educational thinking has been concerned with the individual as the "basic educational unit" (7). For her, this view "involves an encounter between an individual and something external and that this encounter brings about change" (9). This can sometimes lead to believing that individual change is the way of making changes to society at a broader level. Thus, involving education in the project of establishing democracy or abolishing racial inequalities, the question often posed is: "What do individual people need to learn so that the problem can be solved?" (8). In Martin's view, this is problematic, since it not only implies that individuals are the entities that need to change, but also that "the idea that the encounter might be a two-way interactive affair and that both parties to it might change [is] not entertained" (9).

Martin seeks a unified theory of education, one that takes account of both individual learning and the continuation of culture itself. On the surface at least, such a project seems to make eminent sense. In fact, she proposes that every educational encounter is composed both of an individual and an element from our cultural environment (she also includes "natural" entities, such as animals and plants since our *knowledge* about them is part of our cultural landscape) and in so doing acknowledges the importance of interaction between them. However, her description of what this encounter looks like is ultimately troubling—and for this reason is instructive. Specifically, an educational encounter comes about through the "yoking" of one or more capacities of the individual (curiosity, attention, wonder, interest) with an "item of cultural stock" (such as a poem, piece of music, or knowledge about the natural world). It is this "yoking" which produces the "character" of education. Giving the example of the well-known sociobiologist E. O. Wilson's childhood encounter with a jellyfish, which led to hours of observation and absorption in the animal's ways, Martin claims that he "had some idea what he was looking at" and through hours of observation was acquiring a "burning desire to know more about jellyfish and other living things." She continues: "Here we have an educational encounter. The desire for knowledge about jellyfish and other creatures is not something human beings are born with or that automatically develops as we mature. It is an item of cultural stock and in Ed Wilson's case it became yoked to his already existing capacity of wonder" (16). In trying to illustrate why Wilson's encounter is educational, she juxtaposes his story with an imaginary example: a boy who also encounters a jellyfish on the beach, who stops and looks at it but "does not know what he is looking at . . . and does not find it interesting" (16). His mother calls him for ice cream and he runs off.

What becomes clear is that what is deemed educational by Martin is rendered in terms not only of capacity, but in each case whether the child was already familiar with something which is assumed to be the reason for the spark in interest. Presumably both (indeed all) children have a *capacity* for wonder, and why or how that develops into interest is here linked to prior knowledge, or at least an acquaintance with something. This surely is problematic from an educational point of view, since encounters, particularly for young children (as Wilson and the imaginary boy are), routinely involve unfamiliar or unknown "items of a culture's stock." And, presumably, Martin would want to say that developing interest or "yoking" one's capacities to these items is education's purpose.

> The existence of an encounter—be it between an individual and a jellyfish, a mountain, an animal, a book, another person, the square root of two, or the idea of God—is no guarantee, therefore, that an educational event has occurred. Our theory holds that education only occurs if there is an encounter between an individual and a culture in which one or more of the individual's capacities and one or more items of a culture's stock become yoked together; or, if they do not in fact become yoked together, it is intended that they do. (16–17)

This intentionality now brings the "encounter" into another frame, whereby it is not so much the actual yoking that matters—the individual interest that matters—but the way in which encounters are set up so that items of cultural stock are kept alive and passed on from generation to generation. For Martin, this cultural point of view is important since it "represents education as an interactive process in which both individuals and cultures change" (23). The child learning its first language entails a coupling that gives that language a "new lease on life" (23), and with each new cultural invention there is a yoking that needs to take place in order for certain technological revolutions to take hold in the population at large (e.g., the telephone or the computer). For Martin, then, "the theory of education as encounter makes it clear that whenever and wherever education occurs, it is at one and the same time an instance of individual learning and a case of cultural transmission" (22).

While I acknowledge Martin's attempt to provide a unified theory is a way of challenging the individualism which often works perniciously against a communal, democratic, and public understanding of education, I find the language of encounter as tied to "capacity" and "stock" quite limiting for thinking about education in the end. For me there is an unresolved tension between cultural transmission and cultural change operating here. Martin seems to imply that when cultures do change through education it is because individuals have "learned" to use things (languages, technologies), and they do so because they have certain "capacities" that these things "tap into" or "draw out" (my words). But if we think of how multidimensional and multisensorial our encounters with any object, idea, animal, or language are, surely there is more at stake than any internal or psychological "capacity" can account for? Whose languages or technologies actually count here? And to what degree is cultural change connected with cultural transmission? It is unclear why encounters, in order to be educational, always need to be about transmission; in fact, I would suggest that Martin's unequivocal stance regarding all educational encounters as embodying transmission does not allow for change at all but is really describing a very narrow view not only of education but of enculturation itself.

What is more at stake from my point of view is how to think about education in terms of the "passing on" and the "taking up" of culture and our places within it not through the language of transmission and capacity, but through inheritance, translation, and change.[5] David Hansen (2008) claims that education is not to be conflated with socialization. Yet, "education depends on it, on [one] having entered a way of life and become part of it" (298). Its role in inheritance is to provide a purposive practice through which a student can be confronted with various artifacts as objects of study. For Hansen, "Socialization is entirely functional: its aim is to sustain culture. Education is purposive as well as functional: its aim is to contribute to culture understood in its anthropological, artistic, and individual senses" (298). What Hansen makes clear is that there is doubleness to education, in terms of function and purpose, which makes its deep connections to processes of socialization necessary to the projects of criticality and of exercising freedom. Thus for Hansen,

> new forms of understanding, undergoing, and moving in the world . . . may be in accord with processes of socialization, but they do not simply replicate them. They typically accompany socialization and may be hard to distinguish from the latter. The differences between them can create tensions and difficulties when the requirements of socialization butt up against the impulses of education. At all times education is a standing back as well as standing in. . . . In contrast, socialization is a marvelously well-rehearsed if evolving system of inhabiting the known and the familiar. (298)

Unlike Martin, this view claims that education is never about cultural transmission, even when it is dealing directly with aspects of cultural inheritance. Moreover, in contrast to Martin's "items of cultural stock" to which one is coupled or yoked, Hansen sees the dynamic quality of inheritance itself, in a way that separates education from socialization:

> Thus in an educational context an inheritance takes on a different character than in socialization, even if the vehicle may at first glance be the same. That is, the vehicle in both cases can take the shape of what we call books, methods, equipment, exercises, activities, and so forth. . . . [Inheritance is] not like being bequeathed a piece of property or a cache of goods. . . . In education an inheritance is a dynamic amalgam of convictions, values, ideas, practices, doubts, and even hopes and yearnings. To assimilate an inheritance educationally constitutes a process whose shape and substance are always in motion. That process encompasses thinking, imagining, questioning, inquiring, contemplating, studying, and deciding. Students *participate* in an educational inheritance rather than merely ingest it or glance at it like a museum visitor idly strolling by one object after another. (298–299)

Rightly, in my view, Hansen moves away from static notions of culture and into the terrain of studying and deciding, of dynamically creating a relationship with cultural artifacts that cannot entirely be separated from the artifacts themselves, producing new meanings, new understandings, and new significations. This, to my mind, lends another quality that I see as belonging to *enculturation*, which is participatory and contested, separate from any oversimplified renderings of socialization or cultural transmission.

Taking this dynamic along a more radical path and in a direction that further untangles enculturation from socialization, Bergdahl and Langmann (2018a) point to the ways in which inheritance is not just about, in Hansen's words, "assimilating an inheritance educationally," neither do they see that socialization needs to happen prior to an engagement with cultural values; instead, they view inheritance as also intimately tied to the present in "radically conservative" ways. They write: "One way of responding to these questions is to use Arendt's distinction between two different ways of relating to the past: as a continuity handed down from generation to generation across centuries, or as a fragmentation that nevertheless can be retrieved and collected to give 'some assurance in confronting specific questions' in our present situation [Arendt 1962, p. 15]" (Bergdahl and Langmann 2018a, 377–378). Thus a fragmentary cultural inheritance entails the study of cultural values and traditions in the present, and through this these values and traditions end up becoming not an entirely decidable, stable unity of signification, but are in turn messy and remain fragmentary in their plurality. In this view, enculturation is neither about "transmission" nor about a subject inhabiting a predetermined set of significations; neither does it mean occupying a specific position, attitude, or disposition on the "grid" of subjectivity which would correspond to a particular tradition (e.g., an Islamic body-subject, a democratic body-subject, or an indigenous body-subject). Instead, enculturation is in this account about the multiple ways in which pasts are "taken up," resignified, and made into the stuff of current concern. Moreover, this is inevitable from Bergdahl and Langmann's perspective because in European contexts "every tradition already is marked by heterogeneity and multiplicity as well as by what it leaves out and forgets (e.g. the non-West)" (378).

What Bergdahl and Langmann's work makes clear are two interconnected characteristics of enculturation: first, because traditions are lived and negotiated practices, they can never easily map onto or determine the subject; second, because of their inherent partiality, traditions can never simply be transmitted *in toto*. From an educational point of view, Bergdahl and Langmann propose that: "As a way of studying the tradition by choosing from a fragmented past, the notion of translation becomes helpful, particularly if one wants to move beyond the ideal of the autonomous liberal subject in values education and, instead, recognize the essentially relational and fragmented character of human existence" (378). Translation is thus a mode of encounter that sees the possibility for becoming beyond socialization, beyond transmission, without doing away with cultural signification—and a subject's embeddedness in and connectedness to that signification—altogether. "Making values common in and through education turns teachers and students into critical translators of traditions but also into subjects in translation" (379). That is, students and teachers are not only socialized into traditions but also *become enculturated subjects* through their translations.

To my mind, translation gives us another way of thinking about enculturation beyond the fixed social scripts usually associated with socialization. This means that enculturation no longer neatly maps onto socialization but concerns a more dynamic and negotiated way of viewing how students take up traditions, roles, and values in ways that conceptually avoid the traps of socialization. That is, what Bergman and Langmann's work demonstrates is that we do not have to think of enculturation as always embodying "what is given" in culture, rather it is about *embodying a relation to culture*. This shift is important since it does not assume that all encounters with cultural artifacts, practices, and their significations lead to or are in any way dependent upon socialization, as Hansen claims; neither does it automatically lead to transmission of culture, as Martin holds. Thus education can have a powerful role to play in both shaping and inhabiting traditions, understanding that both traditions and subjects are always on the move. With respect to what constitutes education proper, then, an emphasis on translation and relationality allows us to think about how subjectivity emerges in ways that are not entirely co-opted by the social *even as it* becomes embodied through histories of cultural significations. I will return to this point below.

Finally, I want to consider how this meshes with the important ideas of subjectification (Biesta 2010, 2014; Ruitenberg 2013) and emancipation (Biesta 2014; Lewis 2012; Säfström 2021) which many scholars identify as what is "educational" about education beyond socialization. Is there a way of thinking about subjectification that does not forego the educational significance of enculturation outlined above? Gert Biesta is perhaps the most well-known proponent of subjectification in education, and his work has consistently revolved around seeing it as linked to freedom and emancipation. Biesta (2010, 2015) proposes viewing education in terms of its threefold function:[6] qualification, socialization, and subjectification. While recognizing that education embodies all three, sometimes in overlapping ways, Biesta avers that both *qualification*, in terms of passing exams, demonstrating skills, and obtaining degrees, and *socialization,* as a process of equipping the young to assume their places within the given social order, are *not specifically* what makes education educational. Not only are these functions not limited to the sphere of education, but more importantly, simply because they depict aspects of what happens in various sites of education does not mean that they should be conflated with the actual purpose of education itself. He writes: "What matters more, however, and here we need to shift the discussion from questions about the actual functions of education to questions about the aims, ends and purposes of education, is the 'quality' of subjectification, i.e., the kind of subjectivity—or kinds of subjectivity—that are made possible as a result of particular educational arrangements and configurations" (Biesta 2010, 21). Not wishing to give content to what subjectivity ought to be, or to offer one particular theory about how subjectivity emerges (2014, 18), Biesta instead focuses on the idea that "coming into presence" for a student-subject entails a process through which that subject enacts its own freedom. Moreover, subjectification then becomes the very thing that makes education *educational*; "any education worthy of its name should always contribute to processes of subjectification that allow those educated to become more autonomous and independent in their thinking and acting" (2010, 21). This call for autonomy and independence, while nuanced in terms of how it is moves away from the Enlightenment tradition, nonetheless reveals the importance the singular subject has for Biesta. He also writes, "Those at whom our educational efforts are directed are not to be seen as objects but as subjects in their own right; subjects of action and responsibility" (2010, 80). Thus his views should not be seen as a repetition of the individualism that has haunted modern education, and which Martin has critiqued (and inadvertently in the end represented), but as embracing the singular subject in terms of the Arendtian idea of uniqueness within plurality. For Biesta, the uniqueness of each subject stands as a bulwark against becoming fully subsumed within a given social order. Hence it is a source of freedom to decide, to plan, and to lead one's life project, without falling into positions, roles, and identities that socialization demands.

However, subjectification is not simply a description of what education *does*, in Biesta's terms:

> It is also meant as a normative statement expressing the belief that education becomes uneducational if it only focuses on socialization—i.e., on the insertion of "newcomers" into existing sociocultural and political orders—and has no interest in the ways in which newcomers can, in some way, gain independence from such orders as well. Education, in other words, should always also have an interest in human freedom, and this is what lies behind my insistence on the importance of the subjectification dimension of education. (Biesta 2010, 75)

Biesta's position therefore relies on a clear distinction between socialization and subjectification because we need to be able to judge why education is worthy of pursuit. Unlike Martin, he does not see that subjectification should ever be involved in processes of cultural transmission, and unlike Hansen, he does not see that education "depends" on socialization in order to provide the initial ground from which one can critique existing cultural practices. Biesta is unequivocal about this:

> It is important to see that subjectification and socialization are not the same—and one of the important challenges for contemporary education is how we can actually articulate the distinction between the two. . . . Socialization has to do with how we become part of existing orders, how we identify with such orders and thus obtain an identity; subjectification, in contrast, is always about how we can exist "outside" of such orders, so to speak. With a relatively "old" but still crucially important concept, we can say that subjectification has to do with the question of human freedom—which, of course, then raises further questions about how we should understand human freedom. (Biesta 2014, 129)

Articulating the distinction between socialization and subjectification seems relatively straightforward here since, to return to Massumi's formulation, socialization is about positioning people on a grid and subjectification is about the freedom to become outside of the grid. "Subjectification is about the appearance—the 'coming into presence,' as I have called it elsewhere (Biesta 2006a)—of a way of being that had no place and no part in the existing order of things" (Biesta 2014, 84). In this, Biesta's views are in accord with the idea of change I proposed earlier—that of becoming in ways that exceed cultural significations.

However, I want to raise two issues from the vantage of bodily encounters. One has to do with what socialization stands for in his argument, and the other has to do with the idea of freedom. First, in light of my previous discussion on translation in the context of Bergdahl and Langmann's work, socialization on Biesta's account does not fully address how student bodies are enculturated in ways that do not necessarily involve "inserting" students into predetermined orders but that also see them "taking up" traditions and values through acts of translation. While one might be tempted to say that this translation entails subjectification, to my mind this process of enculturation is part of neither socialization nor subjectification. I see there is more room for nuance about how our educational practices might invite enculturation in terms of generating a relation between the subject and culture (traditions, codes, significations, languages) without entailing either "freedom" from social orders or insertion into them. That is, my argument is that there is a view of enculturation that does not fall into the purposes or functions of socialization, qualification, or subjectification and which, in my view, educational theorizing needs to take account of, particularly if we are concerned with the idea of change in education. Thus, to be clear, while I agree that Biesta's definition of socialization does not concern education proper, I propose that subjectification alone does not fully capture what is educational about education either.

In my view, education's relationship to and with cultural signification is important, not because it supports or depends upon socialization—quite the contrary—but because, through its embodied practices, it continually stages encounters with the manifold nature of cultural traditions and views culture as a living practice as opposed to a fixed set of determinant points on a grid. These encounters do *more* than socialize students into an order while nonetheless ensuring cultural intelligibility; and they also do *less* than subjectification while nonetheless creating cultural horizons and senses of emplacement and inhabitation for students that are not entirely of one's choosing. As subjects who are themselves translated, students not only come to *understand* themselves in particular ways, but also *physically* belong to certain communities, embody certain traditional practices, and materially enact their beliefs, values, and perspectives through routine, ritual, performance, comportment, and disposition. They become translators also of inherited systems of racism, homophobia, sexism, and colonialism, and form complicated relationships to these violent forms of cultural practice that can never be easily captured within certain identities or subject positions on the grid. While *socialization* might be about insertion into and compliance with society and dominant forms of culture, *enculturation* does not have to be. Although socialization acts as a powerful foil to subjectification, it does not fully get at what is educationally at stake in how legacies of thought, histories of custom, ceremony, and everyday routine become embodied for the singular subject. And this brings me to my second point.

Subjectification is a well developed and, to my mind, necessary aspect of education. It is understood by Biesta and others, particularly those influenced by Jacques Rancière's work, to be linked to notions of emancipation and freedom (Galloway 2012; Säfström 2011; Vlieghe 2018). While freedom can be understood as both a freedom *from* insertion into the social order as well as a freedom *to* act, judge, and decide one's life's project, emancipation is of a slightly different order. Understanding emancipation from a Rancièrean perspective also entails understanding how subjectification is about the *enactment* of equality and is not just about freedom from or freedom to. In Biesta's words: "If 'traditional' emancipation starts from the assumption of inequality and sees emancipation as the act through which someone is made equal through a 'powerful intervention' from the outside, Rancière conceives of emancipation as something that people do for themselves. For this they do not have to wait until someone explains their objective condition to them. Emancipation 'simply' means to act on the basis of the presupposition—or 'axiom'—of equality" (Biesta 2014, 90). Both these trajectories of freedom and emancipation entail an *enactment* that, for Rancière, has also to do with changing our *sensible* perceptions of the world, beyond what he refers to as the current "regime of perception" (Rancière 2006, 46). In fact, he is clear that acting on the supposition of equality, which interrupts the logic of perception, is not simply a conceptual or hermeneutic shift in understanding but involves a "sensible or perceptual shock caused . . . by that which resists signification" (59)—beyond the grid. While I discuss the politics of the senses more thoroughly in chapter 3, the point I wish to raise at this juncture is that enacting emancipatory acts of equality entails a body that feels, senses, and moves.[7] Taking this embodied approach to questions of freedom and emancipation is central, in my view, since, from the point of view of educational encounters, it means that emancipation not only *manifests* itself *through* bodies, but bodies *enact* emancipation *through* their becoming. That is, there is no body-subject prior to the encounter that generates an act of emancipation. That act, or event, is itself the becoming of the body-subject. While becoming is not part of the Rancièrean lexicon, I use this term to indicate that there is something more than subjectification at stake: there is a living sensate body that lies at the heart of any event of freedom, any assertion of equality. By this I mean that calling for education to be oriented toward freedom/emancipation needs to recognize that movement, sensation, and physicality are necessary for its enaction, its materialization, and its emergence. Subjectification, if it is to be something that makes its appearance through education, cannot avoid the sheer physicality of becoming and the sensory elements so necessary to that becoming. Thus, while I agree that subjectification is central to what constitutes education proper, it needs to incorporate a view of change rooted in the material, physical conditions of becoming itself.

Thus, my response to what is educational about education from the perspective of the encounters it engages in requires a double move: first, shifting from socialization and cultural transmission to *enculturation*; and secondly, supplementing subjectification and emancipation with *becoming*. Both moves enhance our understanding of what is educational through the "present tense incarnate." The latter acknowledges that freedom can only be enacted through (not *by*) bodies in the present; becoming is not simply a way of "being *in* the world" but is continually generated through, with, and of the world. Moreover, as we have seen in the discussion of translation above, that students translate themselves in the here and now of encountering fragmented traditions means that they inhabit those traditions in a variety of ways that do not conform to the demands of socialization. As such, education proper entails an inevitable doubleness. As I develop further below, seeing both enculturation and becoming *as* educational means attending to the surprising alchemy of culture and bodies in our actual encounters.

How Is Education Encountered?

To respond to my second question requires exploring the ways both enculturation and becoming are made possible through educational practices. There is a current trajectory of thought that seeks to open up the "educational encounter" to what is distinctive and particular to its own dynamic. For the most part, parallel to my discussion above, these conceptions are attempts to decouple instrumentality, socialization, and functionalism from education proper by positioning the encounter as central to educational practice. While some have focused explicitly on the nature of teaching (Biesta 2017; Säfström 2014; Vlieghe and Zamojski 2019), others have focused more on the idea of encounter itself (Masschelein and Simons 2013; Lewis 2017; Ford 2013). Masschelein and Simons offer what is perhaps the most well-cited position, which I focus on here since it speaks directly to the time of the present and also builds on references to Daniel Pennac's account of his teaching practice.

In their book, *In Defence of the School: A Public Issue*, Masschelein and Simons (2013) offer an innovative challenge to commonsense views of schools and education more broadly conceived. Rooting their ideas in the ancient Greek *scholé*, they reconfigure school as a place of "free time," where the time of production, labor, and work are kept outside of the classroom. Contending that the *scholé* was configured so that "goodness and wisdom were detached from one's origin, race and nature" (27) they then assert that the very "making" of school "is about the suspension of a so-called natural unequal order" (27).[8] This portrayal of the school provides a frame for understanding students' encounters with knowledge, with subject matter, as that which is free from the demands of use-value, production, and socialization, which are so often geared toward the future and are used to justify current systems of education; instead the school is occupied with the time of the present, in the free time of scholastic practices. "Free time" does not refer to relaxation or leisure, as in the sense of hobbies, tourism, or physical activities. Instead,

> the school . . . arises as the concrete materialisation and spatialisation of time that literally separates or lifts schoolchildren out of the (unequal) social and economic order (the order of the family, but also the order of society as a whole) and into the luxury of an egalitarian time. It was the Greek school that gave concrete shape to this kind of time. This means that this—and not, for instance, knowledge transfer or talent development—is the form of free time through which schoolchildren could be lifted out of their social position. (Masschelein and Simons 2013, 29)

While one might question how the *actual* "concrete materialization" of the Greek school functioned, since it barred access to girls, slaves, and others who were not deemed citizens of the polis, the idea of "free time" it initiated, in Masschelein and Simons's account, means that school *could* serve as the form through which egalitarianism was practiced (at least for free Athenians). And this is the case, for Masschelein and Simons, since the backgrounds of children ceased to *matter*, ceased to be the stuff that determined one's place in the social order through the school. They refer to this bracketing off of background in the free time of the school as "suspension," and this works in two ways that are important for how education is encountered.

First, schools offer students the opportunity to "leave their past and family background behind and to become a student just like everyone else" (32), at least for the time being. In Masschelein and Simons's account, this is entirely freeing; no longer weighed down by low expectations, questionable futures, or the burden of "background" (be this depicted through poverty, race, ability, talent, family function, etc.), students get to become, simply, students. Moreover, they get to "decouple" themselves from their positions on the grid in order to experience themselves beyond what the social scripts demand. This means being able to act, participate, and attend to subject matter in the present and to do so in a way that is not predefined by a teacher's or a society's expectations. In this, suspension offers a perspective for seeing students' lives beyond the limited ways the social order has depicted them. It offers, in other words, a space of becoming beyond cultural and social scripts.

> Thus, the school is the time and space where students can let go of all kinds of sociological, economic, familiar and culture-related rules and expectations. In other words, giving form to the school—making school—has to do with a kind of suspension of the weight of these rules. A suspension, for instance, of the rules that dictate or explain why someone—and his or her whole family or group—falls on a certain rung of the social ladder. Or of the rule that says that children from housing projects or from other environments have no interest in mathematics, or that students in vocational education are put off by painting, or that sons of industrialists would rather not study cooking. (35)

Secondly, suspension also pertains to the subject matter; that is, its ties to cultural significations and the logic of production are temporarily suspended from their normal uses and meanings. Through subject matter, knowledge and skills are detached from their applications, and students are free to study for the sake of it. Thus in this view subject matter is qualitatively different from the kind of knowledge that is presented in terms of its social applicability and relevance. Through subject matter, knowledge and skills are "thus liberated, that is, detached from the conventional, societal uses assigned as appropriate for them. . . . Or put differently: the material dealt with in a school is no longer in the hands of one particular societal group or generation and there is no talk of appropriation; the material has been removed—liberated—from regular circulation" (32). Moreover, Masschelein and Simons introduce the notion of "profanation" as a way of thinking about subject matter that is not only about *removing* it from its social and cultural meanings but also about its potentiality in contributing to freedom. They write: "Students are drawn from their world and made to enter a new one. Thus, on one side of the coin there is a suspension, that is, a rendering inoperable, a liberation. On the other, there is a positive movement: the school as present tense and middle ground, a place and time for possibilities and freedom. For this, we would like to introduce the term *profanation*" (38). Significantly here, profanation echoes suspension insofar as it refers "to something that is detached from regular use, no longer sacred or occupied by a specific meaning, and so something in the world that is both accessible to all and subject to (re)appropriating meaning . . . in other words, something that has become public" (38). For Masschelein and Simons, profanation not only suspends the cultural signification of subject matter, but also claims it is a public *thing* that is "confronted": "The typical scholastic experience . . . is exactly that confrontation with public things are made available for free and novel use" (38). Indeed, referring to Pennac, they draw attention to how there is "always *something* on the table" which a student encounters in a form of suspension and which is placed there in an act of profanation.

Linking their views to freedom, Masschelein and Simons see that the becoming of students (my terminology) is a fundamental part of the encounter with the subject matter in the present. This encounter is characterized by the students' emergence into a new form: a new "I" comes into being through the encounter with the some*thing* of subject matter, through its study, free from social use and conventional meaning. From the point of view of what this encounter looks like concretely, Masschelein and Simons see that the technologies of the classroom (the chalkboard, desks, paper, books, etc.) "assert control over the student and teacher": "Sitting down at a desk is not only a physical state; it also calms and focuses attention: a place to sit and be at ease. The chalkboard keeps the teacher grounded. Step by step, a world is made to unfold before the eyes of the students . . . their strength hangs together with an approach, a method of application and concrete acts" (50–51).

On the surface, the idea of school presented here offers us a way to think about encounter that echoes Biesta's ideas of subjectification: the encounter lends itself to exploration of objects of study in ways that are neither determined by nor contribute to socialization. While I am in full agreement with the ways in which students need to be able to simply be students, without the expectations, orders, codes, and rules imposed on them from outside, I do wonder about the consequences of asserting that suspension (and the linked notion of profanation) actually speak to the way flesh and blood bodies participate in complex ways through encounters in the plural. Indeed, even the simple suggestion that sitting down at a desk calms and focuses attention doesn't speak to what many students actually feel and experience. Thus I want to raise a few concerns about their conceptualization of encounter that push against what I see is a tendency toward decontextualization and disembodiment.

Calling for suspension and freedom from the constraints of social positioning and the deleterious practices these often lead to is not my issue. In fact, based on my discussion in the previous section, it is clear that locking students onto a grid of positions, replete with their low expectations and narrow prejudices, can never be *educational*. Rather it is to see that students' backgrounds in terms of family, feelings of belonging, and traditions are not simply negative forces or indicative of positions within a social order. They also involve complex processes of translation and contextualization. Backgrounds, from the point of view of enculturation described above, are also corporeal translations that are lived through bodies in ways that are unique, in ways that do not easily align themselves with points on the grid in the first place. Becoming a student therefore might be about suspending some aspects of one's social identity (such as a particular point of view, an attitude, or disposition), but one's suspension of the relational and corporeal horizons that contextualize one's life in very particular ways is neither possible nor desirable from an educational—or embodied—point of view.

Presumably, when a student encounters subject matter in the present, the point is not that their background is suspended (although it might well be), but that there is a *relation* in the present that is made to the subject matter that is not *predetermined* by that background. And it is this relationship, whether conceived as enculturation or becoming that is significant for education. So while Masschelein and Simons are correct in claiming that there is freedom from social expectations in attending to subject matter, they miss, I think, a more subtle point: that the very movement of "becoming inter-ested" (of becoming "between") is made both within and in excess of cultural horizons that are never neutral, even if they are "liberated" from their social use value. To what degree, then, is attending to the present about suspension and the profanation of subject matter and to what degree is it about enabling the conditions through which students' bodies can begin to inhabit knowledge, to make knowledge carnal, as Pennac puts it?

Take the example of one of Pennac's students, Jocelyne. She is distraught, distracted, full of grief due to her parents' difficult relationship. She cannot settle in the classroom, is anxious, and in tears. After a self-acknowledged failed attempt on Pennac's part to assuage her feelings, he decides in a burst of inspiration to introduce her to Maisie Farange from Henry James's *What Maisie Knew*. After reading the novel over the course of the next few weeks "inspired by the familiar terrain of conjugal battle" (1033), Jocelyne one day remarks to Pennac that her parents "are arguing just like the Faranges, sir!" (1033). From a "suspension" perspective, one might claim that what has transpired is that she was able to leave her troubles aside to study the text. But from the perspective of embodied encounter, she herself attests to the relation she makes between the novel and her context—although not in any determinant way. Moreover, she is able not simply to see the novel as a reflection of her situation but sees her parents' fighting from the perspective of the novel. This, to me, is an act of translation; the novel does not simply begin to hold new meaning because it is "free" from her background, but actually affects who she is becoming, and how she sees herself and the world in relation to it.[9]

Moreover, for Masschelein and Simons, "confronting" things in the classroom with others, sharing in their commonality, is "an act of de-privatisation [and] de-appropriation" whereby the meaning of the objects of study in the world outside the classroom is detached from the encounter itself. This assumes two things. First, that students themselves, as students, disconnect themselves from what they already know, how they already live, and things they give value to, which are not simply contained in their minds, but are very much part of their bodily ways of being in the world (such disconnect can be instigated, from a pedagogical point of view, as benignly as challenging their preconceptions and as violently as not giving any validity to cultural modes of expression that emerge through their bodies). Secondly, it assumes that objects themselves are not connected to contested histories of representation whose meaning cannot ever be fully neutralized for "free and novel use." While I understand the impetus here is to allow for freedom to study, freedom from the burdens of past and future, freedom to become someone other than a point on a grid, and freedom from seeing subject matter only through the lens of its production value, the problem is that things and objects become dehistoricized and decontextualized in such a manner that does not allow for the *educational* investigation of what is actually being experienced by the students who encounter them in the present. That is, their experiences are not solely conceptual, cognitive, or hermeneutic elements of the "past"; they are felt, lived, sensed, and perceived on, in, and through the body in the present. As such, any encounter with subject matter occasions the possibility of sensations linked to an embeddedness within practices, movements, rituals, performances, and gestures, triggering connections to feelings, memories, and thoughts that are very much part of one's background without necessarily being part of one's social positionality. Perhaps suspension is easier to imagine when the object is an equilateral triangle or an equation (and even then I'm not so sure); but when it comes to historical statements in texts, language use, images of certain peoples, and maps of nations and territories, the tenability of profanation and suspension seems not to be able to address the complexity of students' experiences as legitimately educational. It is not that I want to say that students "carry with them" baggage that then either determines what they think or determines what is under study, but failure to see that students' bodies sense and feel their world and translate that world in multifaceted and fragmented ways is to ignore a large part of what the "present tense incarnate" can offer.

Take the example of learning to read a map in mainstream schools in Canada. This is neither an innocent nor neutral exercise—never has been, never will be. The entire narrative of cartographic reality caught within the single object of the map is bound up with colonization, disputes about legitimation, apocryphal stories of "discovery," centuries of violent oppression, genocide, and loss. For me, suspension doesn't adequately address the complexity of the educational encounter for a First Nations student who through their singularity might (or *might not*) engage with the map through a sensory reality rooted not in their *identity* as a First Nations person, but in the variety and multiplicity of cultural fragments which form their background: stories they've heard at home and through the community, feelings of place and belonging, languages spoken and heard, bodily habits ingrained over the course of their upbringing. And this is the case for all students in the classroom; equal as students but different in background experiences and embodied modes of knowledge, communication, and expression. The educational point, as I've stated earlier, is not about suspension or profanation (this only gets at one side of the educational coin), but about the open relationship to culture (the thing, the object of study) as a singular act of translation, beyond socialization. Bodies are not just what students *bring into* the classroom, or *bring to* the object on the table, they are formed, transformed, and made through these very encounters. But those bodies cannot be suspended from their contexts since their very existence, their very physicality also *takes form* through the cultural horizons of experiencing the world that exists outside of their school time. Map reading thereby becomes part of a singularity of embodied experience through which histories, legacies, values, prejudices may be negotiated, through which students translate themselves. And this does not make the encounter any less educational.

Calling for a "pedagogy of place," Lars Løvlie (2007) insists that students are always "implaced" and "situated." Differentiating between spaces and places, he writes: "Place . . . refers to actions and person in their actualizations. Spatially distributed individuals are defined by formal positions; implaced individuals are inscribed in the contexts of the bodily and material existence. Or to put it this way: individuals have a position, only persons are situated" (34). Thus in claiming that situation or background is educationally significant does not mean that an object of study is encountered from the vantage of a student's subject position; indeed, I agree with Masschelein and Simons that freedom from positionality is a necessary feature of educational encounters. However, I think suspension undermines how student bodies actually are sources of newness as well as conformity to a social order and how they are intimately and physically involved in acts of enculturation as translation. Moreover, as I hope I have made clear, one can never claim categorically that objects of study themselves can be (or ought to be) placed outside of the contestation and circulation of cultural meaning and representation in the classroom (even if they might be outside of production or use value); and this is because they potentially touch students differently: resonating, vibrating, pushing with more or less intensity across their bodies. It is not for us (as teachers or theorists) to decide whether an object is "neutral" when its "vibrancy" is encountered differently through different bodies and different students. And when some objects enact more vibrancy than others, their very materiality poses challenges to students in ways teachers cannot fathom but nonetheless need to appreciate.

Concluding Thoughts

My position is that we need to hold onto the doubleness of education in terms of seeing how it is encountered through bodies. This means viewing not only the *present tense* of the encounter as important, but also its *incarnation*: the way the encounter moves through bodies and the way bodies are necessary for those encounters to happen in the first place. Indeed, as Biesta and Masschelein and Simons capture so well, how students' bodies can become "free" from social positioning and the constricted pasts and narrow expectations a position gives rise to, is key to unlocking the grid-like view of subjectivity that prevails in education. Encountering education on this understanding brings to the fore the change that becoming entails: freedom to become someone beyond socialization. Importantly, however, this becoming is dependent on bodies who feel, who sense, who move. Moreover, as we have seen, encountering education entails a translation and a relationship between students and cultural significations that also exist beyond socialization. In this respect, neither suspension nor socialization captures the nuanced ways student bodies encounter the world through objects of study. That is, enculturation is something *more* than socialization and *less* than subjectification. Perhaps we can suspend our beliefs, ideas, or attitudes, but we cannot suspend our sensory and felt relations to cultural practices; they can change as result of educational encounters, but this is different than saying they can be suspended and not "matter" to the very materiality that make up those encounters. Moreover, the stuff of subject matter and the contestation around various objects cannot entirely be erased by claiming they are free from productive value since contestation itself is carried on, in, and through bodies. Bodies are enfleshments, if you will, of custom, traditions, and values. It is my contention that through seeing what is educational about encounters, and encounters as educational, we, as educators, are better equipped to deal with what is most productive and perhaps also messy about education and to become aware of how what we *do* in the classroom has bodily effects that are generative of education itself, both as enculturation and becoming.

Chapter Two

Senses of Encounter

Am I already here
Before I see and taste and feel?
If not, how could I see and taste and feel?
How can I know if I'm already here or not?
If I were here without them,
They could be here without me.
I reveal them and they reveal me.
How can I be here without them?
How can they be here without me?
I am not already here
Before experience as such:
Seeing reveals just the seer,
Tasting just the taster,
Feeling just the feeler.
If I'm not already here before them all,
Could I be here before each one?
Can the seer taste?
Can the taster feel?
Were they different,
I would be legion.
Nor am I tucked inside the elements
Whence seeing and tasting and feeling unfold.
If I to whom these things belong
Cannot be found,
How can they be found?
I do not precede them.
Nor am I with them.
Nor do I follow them.
Let go of "I am"
Let go of "I am not"

—Nagarjuna, "Already"[1]

In the poem above, the third-century Buddhist monk, Nagarjuna, draws our attention to the paradoxical nature of experience and perception. On the one hand, there is someone who experiences: a feeler who feels, a seer who sees, a taster who tastes; on the other hand, there is no one: no feeler, seer, taster that is outside or prior to the experience of touch, sight, taste generated in any particular moment. Prefiguring some of the major concerns of twentieth-century phenomenology, new materialism, process philosophy, and feminist theorizing of the body, Nagarjuna holds that the encounter with things and persons in the world is what reveals each of us to be an "I," an emergent self. We do not exist prior to these bodily experiences of seeing, tasting, feeling (and one could, of course, add on all our other sensory capacities). Coupled with this is the understanding that while experiences generate the subject, they are composed not simply through our passive receipt of the world, but also through our engagement with it. Each of us becomes a seer, a taster, a feeler in the bodily *enactment* of seeing, tasting, feeling some*thing*. What Nagarjuna opens up is a way of viewing sensory encounters as an ongoing unfolding, a meeting of elements that shapes the very contours of how we experience our own existence.

What is important about Nagarjuna's insights for education has to do with how encounters are not only meetings between an already existing subject and an object of study (or another person, such as a teacher), but also how they can engender complex sensations that say something about who we think we are and who we think we can become. While in the previous chapter I discussed education from the point of view of bodily encounters, and how these contribute to a complex understanding of education as being about both enculturation and becoming, I said little about how I understand the specific qualities of encounters themselves in terms of their bodily dynamics and the sensory experiences they engender: *How do encounters work in, on, and through bodies, and what does this tell us about the links between education and sensory experiences?* As a response to this question, this chapter outlines an understanding of encounters as events of contact, of touch, exploring the dynamics of perception, sensation, and movement and how these play out in ways that are germane to educational processes of becoming and enculturation. In particular, I explore the ways living bodies are *of* encounters with the environment and are not merely *in* them. This chapter then turns to understanding the significance touching and being touched by has for subjectivity as a mode of thinking about encounters across a range of sensory experiences. Through this I identify key aspects of encounters that inform the chapters that follow. Indeed, the specific idea that our bodies are *of* the environment is something I return to in more detail when discussing online education and educational responses to the climate crisis in chapters 6 and 7, respectively. Before turning to this any in detail, I first examine the term *encounter* itself, troubling some of its legacies in order to situate better my overall argument.

Troubling Encounters

Discourses within education are rife with appeals to creating encounters: with nature, with art, with language and poetry, with digital and screen technologies, as well as with people across cultures and faiths. Encounters are also frequently used in relation to intercultural or cross-cultural community work where they signal face-to-face meetings that presume some form of difference in worldviews, beliefs, or values. And in another context entirely, various forms of performance, installation, and socially engaged art practices all enact some form of encounter for either the viewing public, the participants in the practice, or both.[2] Etymologically, the word *encounter* refers to the meeting of adversaries; however, usage has become *both* more anodyne in terms of denoting simply a "meeting" or having direct "contact" with someone (where the adversarial aspects *seem* to have all but disappeared) *and* more malignant in terms of reference to "colonial contact" as well as to "encountering" acts of racism, homophobia, and sexism. As geographer Helen Wilson (2017) has noted, encounter is, to say the least, a "conceptually charged construct" (451) and, I would add, how it has been used in various contexts raises questions as to its professed innocence.

Encounter carries with it historical codes, and the spatial concepts that are used when speaking of cultural encounters, such as "border" "boundary" and "margin," all derive from particular geographies of colonialism (Wilson 2017, 452). Wilson also discusses that in a variety of usages of encounter in postcolonial, urban, and animal geographies, an implicit opposition, conflict, prejudice, or unease permeates throughout. This is particularly true when thinking of multicultural or multiethnic encounters, as well as encounters that seek to engage positions across class, religions, and sexualities—all of which have also concerned many educational scholars (Wilson 2017, 454). Thus, Wilson's insights are important not just from within geography, but speak to the ways linguistic associations, ideological assumptions, and philosophical commitments frame our understanding of encounter. Key to Wilson's analysis across the various domains of geography—and I believe one can see this in education as well—is the understanding that "encounter" is premised on "difference"; it is not only involved at the borders of difference but is also instrumental in creating those borders in the first place (456). Moreover, she suggests that a further element of difference is evident in encounters: they "are not only about the coming together of different bodies but are about meetings that also make (a) difference" (464). Wilson's exploration of encounter as being imbued with a strong sense of difference linking it to legacies of imperial thought and cultural contestation gives rise to the question of how we might invite a framing of encounter that troubles its colonial usage, without falling into the trap of neutralizing encounter, as though face-to-face or other forms of encounter do not pose their own strangeness or challenges to one's senses—and possibly to one's being. Moreover, how might encounter be troubled further in seeing it in the plural, in order not to lose sight of its multiple singularities? That is, how might encounters be understood conceptually in ways that move beyond both the colonial and the universalizing gaze?

One way of proceeding with this task is presented in Sara Ahmed's 2000 volume, *Strange Encounters*, which takes an explicitly sociological-phenomenological stance to problematize the ofttimes perceived innocence of encounters. While Ahmed's account ultimately underscores encounters as being always already imbued with social positioning and identities, a language this book in general distances itself from, I nonetheless think her work is invaluable for its reworking of encounters through the lenses of race and coloniality, to follow more fully the thread of Wilson's work above.

Writing with and against the grain of some the key texts in feminist theories of embodiment,[3] Ahmed seeks to challenge the ways "others" have been framed within colonial imaginaries and how they have been experienced as "strangers." Ahmed explores how bodily encounters, in the plural, both constitute and are constituted by social relations with others. Her focus is primarily on encounters that occur between people differentially positioned within society and not on encounters one has with ideas, matter, or things. Encounters, for Ahmed, are largely about bodies and identities and are always mediated; they "presuppose other faces, other encounters of facing, other bodies, other spaces and other times" (2000, 7). Thus encounters, for Ahmed, are never simply neutral face-to-face meetings; they are always simultaneously infused with larger power dynamics of sociality, including the dynamics of racism, colonialism, and sexism. In this sense, she is interested in exploring

> how the particular encounter both informs and is informed by the general: encounters between embodied subjects always hesitate between the domain of the particular—the face to face of this encounter—and the general—the framing of the encounter by broader relationships of power and antagonism. The particular encounter always carries *traces* of those broader relationships. Differences, as markers of power, are not determined in the "space" of the particular *or* the general, but in the very determination of their historical relation (a determination that is never final or complete, as it involves strange encounters). (8–9)

What is noteworthy here is that Ahmed's conception of encounters is framed within a sociological understanding of relations of power and not an ontological understanding of difference, such as one finds in other phenomenologically informed philosophers such Levinas and Merleau-Ponty with whom she also engages. Bodies themselves are scripted upon in ways that shape identities and that come to define one's positionality even if this definition resists "final or complete" determination. Difference itself here is not an ontological condition but an effect of power and as such any face one meets is inflected by that power. Moreover, differences (in the plural) manifest themselves not because singular bodies are in and of themselves "different" from each other as a condition of their existence, but because of their differential relation to other bodies *in the social*: "Bodies become differentiated not only *from each other* or *the other*, but also through differentiating *between others*, who have a different function in establishing the permeability of bodily space. . . . Difference is not simply found in the body, but is established as a relation between bodies: *this suggests that the particular body carries traces of the differences that are registered in the bodies of others*" (44). What all this means, for Ahmed, is that the body is social in a way that it bears markers of social differentiation through its engagement/encounters with other bodies (bodies which also carry these traces of difference). This carrying of bodily traces is the mechanism through which we can understand how systems of oppression, denigration, strangerhood, and exclusion are felt in the body and through other bodies. Ahmed also argues that the skin of our bodies is not only that which acts to contain us but is involved in a process of "materialization" that occasions "an affective opening out of bodies to other bodies, in the sense that the skin registers how bodies are touched by others" (45).

Not wishing to champion any kind of determinism (for example, that a "lesbian body" in relation with a "straight body" will always produce a felt sense of exclusion, enacting an embodied social heteronormativity through the encounter), Ahmed sees that encounters always carry within them elements of surprise as well as conflict. She asks, "How does identity itself become instituted through encounters with others that surprise, that shift the boundaries of the familiar, of what we assume that we know?" (7). However, this surprising capacity for shifting boundaries is ultimately limited by the nature of conflict that social power relations carry with them. Ahmed suggests, for instance, that "bodies are touched by some bodies differently from other bodies" (48) and that bodies are racialized, sexualized, and classified as other through that very touch. She makes the important point: "We could consider how some forms of touch have been means of subjecting others, or of forming the other as a place of vulnerability and fear (colonial and sexual histories of touch as appropriation, violation and possession). We could also begin to deal with the relationship of touch implicit in the very fear of touching some others: such a refusal of touch is also a means of forming and de-forming some bodies in relationship to other bodies" (49). While I think Ahmed is right to question how bodies *become* bodies through complex processes of racialization and sexualization that operate at the nexus of encounters—at the nexus of the general and the particular as she sees it—I think her tendency to link bodies to positionalities or identities does not allow her to explore more fully how the *processes* of encounter can also actually challenge existing modes of identity and the bodies associated with them. To take the case of racialization, "racial difference" itself can become destabilized through bodily practices. As Paul Gilroy (2000) notes, black bodies produce an "anxiety" about the inherited borders of race by shifting the terms of signification through clothing style and body art; no longer easily "seen" as "black," difference materializes differently and not merely as a mirrored "effect" of coloniality or othering (22). Race, racism, and the "difference" they are based upon are always shifting.

Moreover, in terms of my own aims in this book of putting living bodies at the center of educational encounters, what exactly happens to bodies in these "strange encounters" in terms of their materiality, their movement, and specific sensations beyond their explicitly *social significations of difference*? I ask this question, not to dismiss Ahmed's concerns with troubling encounters; quite the contrary, since I see how encounters can indeed perpetuate, sustain, and maintain social orders, a point I discuss in detail in chapter 3. Rather, I pose this question here at this juncture in order to open up the question of *difference* itself to bodily sensation, perception, and movement—all of which act to *confound* and not merely sustain borders and differentiation through singular encounters with things, objects, ideas, as well as others. Although Ahmed is concerned with the singularity of encounters, the fact that she ties them to general relations of power and antagonism axiologically means that there is little sense of the "outside" or "more" to dynamics of social inscription; encounters transpire *within* the given—following Ahmed's logic here (even as they might contribute to reconstituting that given)—and bodies are *social* bodies, not because they emerge *in relation* to others (although they do that too), but because they bear traces of the social order itself.

I'm left wondering, though, about the sheer *contact* of singular encounters. As Richard Shusterman (2012) writes, "When we get down to it—to cells, membranes, to responses to form and sensitivity—we are singular" (29). Is there something in this utter singularity, in this sensual responsivity, that is *not* always already *filtered* through markers of social power? At the moment when my skin touches yours, before you or I can *register* pleasure or distaste—before we can place value on it—something happens that matters for "difference" in light of that singularity. That is, I'm wondering how what William James calls a "pure experience," a contact that has yet to be classified into a *kind* of experience or signification (1912, 29), comes to matter in processes of differentiation. So, while encounters are emplaced and transpire through social and historical contexts, this does not make them representative of those contexts, or *necessarily and transparently* marked by them (besides, by which processes do they come to be marked in the first place?); there is a danger of slipping too easily into equating encounters with that which mirrors in some way *existing* dynamics of power or even existing cultural dynamics of feeling, without sufficiently taking into account a host of other contexts including tendencies of impression, expression, attunement, disposition, and attention that also factor into singular encounters. Thus, while encounters between bodies do indeed bear traces of social difference, my point is that they are also something *else*; and I think that it is this elseness that gives us a glimpse into how encounters might be understood as *events of contact that exist in excess of our social scripts*, whilst also saying something to us about how differences come into being through those encounters. Thus what I am proposing here is shifting away from viewing *social* bodies at the center of encounters, to *living* bodies in order to see how encounters bear not only traces of social relations of power but, more to the point, are animate, fleshy, tactile, and "creatural," to use Marjorie O'Loughlin's (2006) apt term, in ways that exist on another register from specifically *social* differences. How might we see encounters when *living* and not *social* bodies are at stake without falling back into a naïve view of encounters themselves? How can we honor the proliferation of becoming bodies *beyond* the grid of identity positions while recognizing the perniciousness of the social systems which we know can also be sustained through bodies, as Ahmed's work captures so well?

From the point of view of education, these are crucial questions to ask, since they speak against viewing encounters as merely innocuous meetings, while at the same time also seeing them as events of potential becoming (and subjectification). If we fail to see encounters as educational, and merely as *either* sociological *or* psychological entities, I worry that we miss out on the very ways in which sensory encounters generate differences that matter to enculturation and becoming. First, *becoming* is thwarted when educational encounters are seen solely as informing and being informed by social relations of power—for what is explicitly *educational* about them risks becoming lost in practices of reproduction and socialization. What I seek to show below is how becoming is predicated on attending to the dynamics of sensory contact as ways of opening up possibilities beyond these very frames. This does not mean returning to the innocuous meeting view of encounters, however; and this brings me to my second point: claiming that educational encounters have nothing to do with the larger world of power also leads to ignoring the significance emplacement, bodies, and context have for education itself—this is especially important for processes of enculturation. Heeding both of these issues, I suggest that encounters are in no way reducible to the effects of the social even when, following Ahmed, they *play a role* in encounters. My point is that from an educational point of view, encounters do not simply bear traces of power relations, but more complicatedly participate in acts of translation between subjects and legacies of thought, values, and beliefs through the senses in ways that take up, discard, or ignore these traces. While enculturation will be explored in more detail in chapter 3 in terms of what I am calling the politics of the senses, suffice for now to note that in what follows I seek to trouble encounters as being *either* sociological mechanisms that police the senses *or* psychological ones that merely individualize and thereby neutralize them. Instead, I turn to ideas that help us make sense of *educational* encounters as living bodily events of contact that move beyond these polarities altogether.

Living Bodies *of* Encounters

It might seem obvious to claim that we become (human) subjects through *living*—that is, through our bodies and through our senses. Infants explore their world primarily through touch, smell, and taste, as well as more culturally dominant modes of vision and hearing—and as Maxine Sheets-Johnstone (2011) has written extensively about, through movement as animate organisms as well. As sensible creatures we come to form impressions and make relationships with, between, and to things; we become oriented to the world in particular ways, forming feelings and affects as "we" encounter our environment, or more accurately perhaps, as the elements of an environment encounter each other. After all, as Nagarjuna put it "I" am not "tucked inside the elements" but arise from a sensory experience of those elements.

The senses are so central to subjectivity that indeed depriving children of sensory contact results in developmental challenges that can last a lifetime, and sensory deprivation when used as a technique of torture for incarcerated adults results in a devastating loss of all sense of identity and subjecthood. Subjectivity itself is predicated upon sensory encounters. Sensory contact concerns not only perception in the narrow sense of the word, including individual sense experience and percepts, but also concerns sensations, feelings, and affects. Together they constitute a reality without which we cannot survive. Seeing encounters through *living* bodies (and not simply *the* body, in the abstract) means thinking through the fullness of that living. Rather than provide an encyclopedic overview of the conceptual histories of perception, sensation, and affect, I instead discuss below a select range of ideas that give shape to understanding living bodies as organisms that are not simply situated in encounters but are *of* encounters, *of* contact with elements of the environment.

Contact as I'm suggesting here is another word for a specific kind of relation that bodies have in encounters with other elements of a given situation; unlike relations of contiguity, juxtaposition, or proximity, encounters engender relations of *connection*. Drawing on Buddhist philosophy, as well as cognitive- and neuroscience, Francesco Varela and his colleagues (1993) identify contact as a "relational property" through which a self emerges; it "is a form of rapport between the senses and their objects, a matching of sensitivity between a sense and an object in the sense field" (199). This "matching of sensitivity" is a way of signaling that bodies are not only subject to sensory input but also actively reach toward elements of the environment—importantly, however, without a predetermined self that orchestrates that movement. Having a rapport with objects means that the senses are actively engaged with what is being encountered. Bodies thereby enact the world and do not simply passively receive it. Although coming at the question of the senses from a wholly different angle, James Gibson's work is nonetheless in agreement with Varela on this point (and perhaps on this point alone). In his classic theory of perceptual systems,[4] Gibson (1966) is adamant that senses are not only passive receptors of the body but are also active and exploratory. They are central in "detecting" information as part of complex systems. Moreover, he writes about the "affordances" given in the environment: "The environment consists of *opportunities* for perception, of *available* information, of *potential* stimuli" (23). This means that together, perceptual systems and their environments engage in a mutual dance, where some opportunities are taken and where other potentialities are left aside.

However, there is good reason to be cautious here about associating encounters with perceptual contact along Gibson's lines. Gibson's understanding of perception as systems also entails seeing encounters primarily as information-gathering functions and not as affective, sensate occurrences or happenings. That is, he is interested in how perceptual systems generate information about our surroundings, not about how we necessarily *live* in and through those surroundings. Thus, from an educational point of view, we need to be careful about what kind of encounters we would be advocating if we were to build those encounters on a theory of perceptual systems. Educational encounters are not about information gathering, but about living processes of becoming and enculturation. This is not to suggest that perceptual information is not crucial to living, but that the senses are also involved in other, complex formations central to it, such as feelings and sensations. While it might be the case that the senses can detect something without having a sensation or a feeling attached to it (as Gibson writes, "there can be sensationless perception, but not informationless perception" [2]), there is nonetheless something about sensation that factors significantly into how we come to know, make a relationship with, and orient ourselves in our surroundings. In a curious statement, Gibson insists that infants obtain information from the world through perception but not necessarily felt sensation (5). But perceptions surely are more complicated than this, unless one is already subjecting to classification *what* one encounters solely in terms of previously attained informational data, with no accompanying feeling. The senses, however, are not simply about information, but bring into being a host of other aspects of and qualities in living a life. As Ashley Montagu (1986) has shockingly pointed out in his classic work *Touching*, even infants whose biological needs are being met can die from a lack of sensation, specifically a lack of touch—a point echoed in Tiffany Field's (2001) work on touch and infants; presumably these infants could "perceive" the world in Gibson's terms (that is, gather information about it through other senses), but perish because they did not experience those sensations needed for existence itself, garnered primarily through touch. Seeing our perceptual contact with the world as a form of data gathering is seeing only one part of what the senses *do*. A living body needs not only to detect information, but to feel and to be felt in the world.

William James (1912) has written extensively on the idea of "pure experience" as a way of thinking about the primacy of sensation in the living force of encounters. That is, before we can name some*thing* or some*one* as part of the circuit of perception, a sensation arises in a relation between them. To cite a well-known passage: "This 'pen,' for example, is, in the first instance, a bald that, a datum, fact, phenomenon, content, or whatever other neutral or ambiguous name you may prefer to apply. I called it . . . a 'pure experience.' To get classed either as a physical pen or as someone's percept of a pen, it must assume a function, and that can only happen in a more complicated world" (James 1912, 123). James's intent is not to say that our lives solely take place in a world of pure experience, excised from the world of thought and consciousness; that would be impossible since we do indeed live in a "more complicated world." Rather, it is that sensations arise through relational encounters with our environment that cannot be captured within categories of experience, such as perception, or directly into categories of subject and object. He admits that "purity" is a "relative term, meaning the proportional amount of unverbalized sensation which it [i.e., experience] still embodies" (94). That is, he recognizes that we do not as adults, or even as children beyond infancy, encounter the world entirely new each and every time, but that there remains nonetheless a sensation, a feeling, that accompanies experience which exists beyond our social codes, cultural scripts, and scientific classifications. This allows him to reflect on how pure experience is neither mental nor physical but is instead a *felt* process of living. "'Pure experience' is the name I gave to the immediate flux of life which furnishes the material to our later reflection with its conceptual categories" (93).

Thus, this *feeling* of the flux of life, while not technically a perception, involves sensory connections and impulses rooted in our bodily relation to things. Drawing on James's notion of pure experience (as well as Deleuze and Spinoza), Brian Massumi (2015) discusses how the subject emerges out of a relational field, whereby the body "always affects and is affected in encounters; which is to say, through events" (ix). Events are moments of affective contacts that "strike the body as immediately as they stir the mind" (x) and cut across categories of experience, including perception and experiences of social difference. Indeed, because they are not tied to an "information gathering" view of the senses, encounters are moments of affect, moments of feeling (rather than emotion), that arise through the body's relation to its situation in ways that neither confirm nor deny a social or conceptual category, nor operate within already ordered meaning. Instead, they exist "transversally," offering a way of sensing the world that is not containable within our conceptual frameworks, since they involve bodies directly in the flux of living, in the movement from one moment to another, from one condition to another. That is, bodies *feel* (through the senses) before conceptualization, classification, and categorization happen; that is before we can think, reflect, or act.

In Massumi's (2015) understanding, it is not that "subjects" are free or suspended from memories, instincts, thoughts, and inclinations in an encounter. On the contrary. The point is to think about how this complexity moves into a "new constitution, the constitution of a becoming" (52). This is important, for on the one hand without something to break with habit, convention, or tradition, we are caught in a logic of determination, condemned to seeing subjectivity as merely a series of cause-effect relations, traceable back to a source of instinct, memory, or social identity. We need a theory of bodily change that has the potential to usher in something new. On the other hand, we cannot deny that these sources of identity might arise in encounters (sometimes weakly, sometimes powerfully, sometimes not at all); encounters do not begin from scratch: "everything re-begins, in a very crowded overpopulated world" of sources, but which ones participate in the constitution of becoming are not predetermined (51). So rather than say that encounters are already embedded in, reproduce, or represent colonial, racist, or sexist contexts, we can say that encounters are *dynamic events of contact* that resist collapsing into the given while nonetheless understanding that there are myriad forces operating through any particular situation in a particular moment that are not predetermined. This, to my mind, expresses a far more educational sense of encounter since it is concerned with moving beyond social prescription while also allowing for newness to emerge in and with the world. Massumi sees that relational events—moments of affective contact—offer something in excess of these sources of social identity, memory, or instinct that enables subjects to emerge and reemerge, like waves of becoming. Moreover, unlike theories of becoming bound to notions of intersubjectivity, such events exist beyond the coming together of two already distinct subjects (or subject and object). It is worth quoting him at length:

> Calling affect, or that felt moment of bodily moving on, calling that intersubjective is misleading if intersubjective is taken to mean that we start from a world in which there are already subjects that are preconstituted, or a pregiven structure of positions ready for subjects to come occupy. What is in question is precisely the emergence of the subject, its primary constitution, or its re-emergence and reconstitution. The subject of an experience emerges from a field of conditions which are not that subject yet, where it is just coming into itself. Those conditions are not yet necessarily even subjective in any normal sense. Before the subject, there's an in-mixing, a field of budding relation too crowded and heterogeneous to call intersubjective. It's not at a level where things have settled into categories like subject and object. It's the level of what William James called pure experience. When I say that it all comes back to the body, I don't mean the body as a thing apart from the self or subject. I mean that the body

is that region of in-mixing from which subjectivity emerges. It is the coming together of the world, for experience, in a here-and-now prior to any possibility of assigning categories like subject or object. (Massumi 2015, 52)

Bodies are therefore regions or territories through which the subject or self emerges. Their sensory elements are neither receiving nor detecting information for a subject who is already defined; instead they enable a felt sense of the world that is then attributed to "me" after the fact, after this in-mixing.

We can see this happening on a daily basis with what Deleuze would call "tiny perceptions" or "microperceptions"⁵—that is, those perceptions that are unconsciously experienced and "felt without registering consciously" (Massumi 2015, 53); they are imperceptible, though central, in encounters. I might, for example, experience a sudden tension when walking into a classroom before I even recognize the reasons why or am conscious that it is "me" who is the subject of the feeling. I then might seek to identify its source and decide how to respond to it. It is at this point that I own it as "my" feeling. Then and only then does this feeling belong to "me" and become part of my personal landscape; "but in the instant of the affective hit, there is no content yet" (Massumi 2015, 54). Significantly, this is accompanied by bodily sensation and movement: my stomach clenches, my breath becomes shallow, my jaw muscles tighten. These are not simply bodily *effects* of tension—this would entail that "I" experience tension, and as a result of this experience the body responds in a particular way. This is a conventional way we have of thinking about feeling: through a modality of identification and possession. Instead, bodily movement *is* the feeling that is *then* identified (with) as "mine"—that is, bodily sensations are felt and subsequently characterized as a tension belonging to me. In this way we proclaim that *I* am tense, *I* feel tension; the *I* becomes the center of feeling.⁶ But tension is nothing if not that bodily movement of clenching, tightening, or hyperventilating. Sensations are simply forces of intensity, to put it in Deleuzian (1993, 2003) terms, that act upon the nervous system; they only find a home in "my" body, in "my" history, in "my" memory after some form of reflection upon which we impose a self, a subject, an I. As James writes: "Our body itself is the palmary instance of the ambiguous. Sometimes I treat my body purely as a part of outer nature. Sometimes, again, I think of it as 'mine,' I sort it with the 'me,' and then certain local changes and determinations in it pass for spiritual happenings. Its breathing is my 'thinking,' its sensorial adjustments are my 'attention,' its kinesthetic alterations are my 'efforts,' its visceral perturbations are my 'emotions'" (James 1912, 153).[7] In this way, there is a strange echo with Nagarjuna here: there is an unsettled ambiguity between subjectivity and the body since the I does not exist prior to its emergence through sensation yet it nonetheless proclaims the body as "mine." For Massumi (2015), the encounter provides *bodies* with "sensation" and "affect"[8] prior to one's constitution as subject. This means that bodies themselves are not completely differentiated from other elements of the environment, at least at the moment of contact. The differentiation—the categorization, classification, and identification of what that sensation as a series of bodily movements means—into subject and object has not yet come about. Its identification hasn't yet been propelled along the route of social signification either, which enables those of us in Western cultures to unequivocally identify certain bodily movements, contractions, and extensions *as* tension. Being touched by the environment in a way that has no content, however fleetingly, means that bodies are not entirely separated from the environments they are part of.

However, this does not mean bodies are *identical* to the environment or to the stuff of encounters. To affect and be affected by through an event, for Massumi, means also that bodies are in a continual process of individuation and becoming in relation to other bodies and things they encounter. It is not so much that they start off from a position of "distinction" (the identity position, the position on the grid of social difference, or the enduring self); rather they become distinct *with and through* others (other things, elements, people) in relation. And here is where we can say that *difference is relational but not entirely social*; difference does not only work as a social marker of value that is produced through power but works as a field of relationality where social power is but one, if extremely significant, element. Seeing difference in this way opens up our understanding of encounters to be not merely sites for reproduction and socialization, but as complex relational entities through which bodies can experience intensities beyond the oppressive demands of the social, outside of the demeaning ways the social reads race, sexuality, class, (dis)ability, and gender.

With this reading of encounters, bodies are not so much carriers or bearers of social difference *in* encounters or even *through* encounters, as they are essentially *of* encounters, *of* relation. A subject emerges as an individuated body from *moments* of affective contact, blending aspects of new sensations that are not yet categorized into subject-object or into perception as information. What is significant here is that bodies on these terms enact a potentiality for change, for alteration and becoming beyond the social scripts we have inherited. That is, because bodies through their sensory modalities encounter streams and flows of *living* in the moment, they create conditions for initiating new continuities, new streams, and new potentialities.

Encounters as Touching and Being Touched By

But how are we to understand these possibilities more concretely, beyond the relatively abstract conceptual framework sketched above? Thus far, I have explored encounters in terms of the dynamics of sensation in order to suggest that *educational* encounters might be best understood in terms of a network of sensory relations and intensities that give rise to subjectivity. For without an understanding of this relational quality of subjectivity, we miss out on the significant ways educational practices can offer conditions of possibility for becoming and enculturation—without replicating conditions of coloniality and racialized othering. However, before going into the educational significance of this in any detail, and in order to drill down into what these dynamics might look like for singular living bodies, I turn now to explore the corporeal dimensions of these relations and intensities further. In other words, how are intensities experienced somatically, and what significance does contact have at the level of skin, flesh, and membrane? As Richard Shusterman has noted, "The term 'soma' indicates a living, feeling, sentient body rather than a mere physical body that could be devoid of life and sensation" (2008, 1). As such my task here is to outline the significance this living, feeling, sentient body has for a relational quality of subjectivity that relies on touch and the senses more generally. As suggested above, touch encapsulates the dynamism and movement of living bodies: sensation, perception, or affect cannot arise without touching and being touched by the elements of the environment, even as this touching occurs without a firmly established, preexisting sense of a subject or self.

More importantly, as I briefly mentioned above with respect to infants' sensate experiences, touch has been identified as the prime sense modality needed for survival. As early as Aristotle, it has been seen to be essential to our very existence as animate creatures: "Without touch it is impossible for an animal to be" (*de Anima* 435b). In *de Anima*, where he lays out the conditions of perception and sensation, Aristotle (1986) identifies touch as occupying a special place in the five senses. Touch alone puts an animal in *direct* sensory contact with the things it appetitively seeks: "Sensation arises immediately on contact" (423a). Unlike the other senses, it is ambiguous since it does not have a defined sense organ connected to it, like the eye or ear. Instead, the "flesh" becomes a "medium" through which we perceive; "we indeed perceive everything through some intermediary, but in the case of the contact senses [taste as well as touch] we fail to notice this" (423b). For Aristotle, despite the fact that touch is placed low on the hierarchy of the senses, and indeed of life itself, coming as it does after the higher order workings of the mind, it is paradoxically also that which opens us to the world most directly and as such is central to our existence. As Pascal Massie (2013) puts it in his reading of Aristotle: "It is 'basic' in the sense that it is *vital*"; an animal can exist without sight, hearing, taste, or smell, "but the loss of tactility is its death" (78). It is this vitality of touch that both sets it apart from and renders it essential to the other senses. To put it in Richard Kearney's (2015) words, for Aristotle, touch is not simply one of the senses but is "the condition sine qua non of *all* the senses" (106) as well as for all animal life.[9]

This relation between touch and being is further amplified when we consider that touch is not only one of the five senses, as Aristotle and commonplace Western frameworks would have it, or one of the six of Buddhist and Brahmanical thought, or one of the eight to twenty-two categorized by psychologists and neuroscientists.[10] As its vitality attests to, it is also the primary way we relate to, in, and with the world through the other senses. By this I mean that the somatic contact we have with things, ideas, and other people through our senses are all variations of touch, at least at the level of epithelial sensitivity. From a biological perspective, epithelial cells are to be found throughout the sense organs, not only the skin, and are part of the gastrointestinal system, respiratory system, vagina, and placenta. They not only largely act at the border with the external environment but can also allow transmission and secretion of fluids. Moreover, sensory receptors, nerve cells, and epidermal cells all derive from embryonic epithelium. Because of these epithelial networks, scientists have found that the skin can perceive light and that tactility can be involved in seeing objects.[11] Thus to claim that our encounters with other elements of the environment are matters of touch is no mere metaphor. As living bodies, we touch and are touched by things continually, floating in a sea of constant sensation.

Touch is also about living paradox: it transgresses borders with the environment through the flow of touching something, whilst also experiencing the flow of being touched. The famous example given by Merleau-Ponty (2012) is of our two hands touching and the chiasmic interface that shifts between subject and object. For phenomenologists, the paradox of touch rests in this shifting of boundaries, further accentuating how consciousness emerges out of these ever-changing moments of perception. As Richard Kearney (2015) notes in his "carnal hermeneutics," unlike the other senses, touch can touch itself touching. "And it is this very sensitivity to differences, opposites, and alterities that makes up our original hermeneutic sensibility: namely, our ability to discern and discriminate . . . through flesh" (105).[12] For Kearney (2021), flesh actively participates in such discernment since "from the beginning it is charged with attraction and retraction" (40).

Such discrimination is important from the point of view of how differences are actually shaped through touch and what we become attached (or not) to. That is, in ways that Ahmed would see as arising through "strange encounters." However, for theorists such as Maxine Sheets-Johnstone (2009, 2011, 2016), understanding encounters through the biological and physiological interaction with the environment offers another approach to reflecting on how difference and events of contact are *corporeally* dynamic, infused as they are with movement across boundaries.[13] The experience of touch is elementary, a literal flowing between inside and outside. Echoing Aristotle, Sheets-Johnstone (2016) claims: "Tactility is immediately and directly experienced in both the felt in-and-out flow of breath and the felt opening and closing of a passageway. It is, of course, immediately and directly experienced in all corporeal~intercoporeal and subject~world relationships in which we touch and are touched by others and by things in our surrounding world. In fact and in truth, we are always in touch with something" (2016, xix).

Sheets-Johnstone understands bodies as organisms that exist with boundaries, surfaces, and coverings—that, in short, have animate *form*. "Membranes are contour-defining; they set off a certain spatial individuality. Indeed in the beginning was not simply a membrane but *form*. The diversity of life is first of all a diversity of *form*" (2009, 136). From the point of view of touch, life forms consist of matter, particularly on the surface, which is in continual contact with elements of the environment, with both things and other animate forms. From the simplest of membranes in the form of bacteria and algae to the epithelial cells of sponges, from the exoskeletal plates and hairs of invertebrates to the skin, scales, and fur of vertebrates, "nature testifies amply both to the import of a boundary—something that in a physical sense separates one organism from another and organisms from the world in which they live—and to the import of surface itself. Exquisitely diverse and complex tactile structures are the fundamental mode by which organisms actively meet the world" (Sheets-Johnstone 2009, 139). This means that our living in the world is shaped by the kinds of surfaces through which we meet elements of it; our very capacity for feeling is conditioned by the corporeal dimensions of our coverings and the sensitivities of their surfaces. This relates to how we can imagine our living with the environment in the time of climate emergency, as chapter 7 explores, since it requires us to think ourselves as intimately relational *of* and *with* the world, instead of merely having a relation "to" it.

This naturalist conception of the living body, replete with borders, allows Sheets-Johnstone (2009) to frame her understanding of the morphological limits of our singular contact with the world. For her, certain experiences are only possible through certain morphologies: "A certain kind of world is congenial to a certain kind of body and a certain kind of body is congenial to a certain kind of world" (2009, 140). As a result, a specific organism will be able to touch and be touched by their environment in mutually informed ways aligned with their morphological specificity.[14] That is, the shape and contours of individual bodies lend themselves to certain forms of contact over others; for humans, as with other animals, experience is literally shaped by our capacities for bodily movement, epithelial sensitivity, and sensory activation. Sheets-Johnstone claims that every creature's attunement to its world is the same as any other because it lies in its "surface sensitivities" which are distinct across species (2009, 140).

Significantly, however, while Sheets-Johnstone claims that all animate organisms have borders and as such are *subject* to the world they live in, she also concedes that their morphologies reflect spatial realities through their relational encounters with the environment—insides and outsides are not so much given as created: "Where there is a world, there is a subject and where there is a subject, there is a world; where there is intercorporeal life, there is corporeal life, and where there is corporeal life, there is intercorporeal life, and this from the beginning in forms of animation inside and out" (2016, ix). Infants, in exploring their environment, move through it, displacing air and coming into physical contact with substances and things. Through this dynamic contact of touching and being touched by, they develop a sense of inside and outside: "Elemental spatial concepts such as near, far, open, close, inside, and outside, are contingent on kinetic/kinesthetic experience; elemental qualitative concepts such as smooth, sudden, intense, attenuated, and soft, are embodied in affective experience" (2009, 365). For Sheets-Johnstone, these represent fundamental *"nonlinguistic corporeal concepts"* (2016, x). Inside and outside are not primarily categories of the intellect but felt concepts. Drawing on Daniel Stern's psychoanalytic work with infants, Sheets-Johnstone notes that for the infant inside is not so much opposed to outside as it is a "felt center of dramas" (2009, 366). That is, it is the sensation generated through contact that actually gives us a *sense* of what we hold to be inner. In this way, inner and outer are *felt* in and through bodies before they are conceptualized linguistically and projected (back) onto our own and other bodies. Echoing the emergence of the subject at the nexus of bodily encounters, our very sense of spatiality—of what is inside—occurs only *as* a relationship with things in our environment.

Thus, on the one hand, Sheets-Johnstone seems to rely on a certain givenness to our morphology in the larger phylogenetic sense that as humans we have skin instead of fur or carapace, as well as epithelial sensitivity across a range of sense organs; the risk is that this can lead too easily, in my view, to an uncritical bioevolutionary account of contact which would miss out on the singularly different ways bodies encounter the world through *specific* and *singular* networks of relation. While not determinant, issues of social identity and memory, as well as instinct and physiology, are nonetheless mobilized through our affective contact with the world. Moreover, there is an insistence at times in her work on boundaries in order to establish that not everything is possible for a given organism and that we are somehow bound to (and not only by) the surfaces of our skin. While skin might indeed be a necessary limit, it is important not to reify or equate the subject or self with the boundaries of the skin—for the primary reason that such reification can also operate as a slippery descent into racist and colonial forms of identification of skin with subjectivity. On the other hand, Sheets-Johnstone at other times pulls back from such reductionism in gesturing toward something far more complex in terms of how the "felt center of dramas" is *experienced*; that is, how inside is not simply a *spatial attribute* of the body developed in relation to touch, or a way of indicating some already given interiority of the subject, but can be seen, rather, as an *affective region or territory of particular intensities*.

As such, the living body is *in-formed* by intensities of touch, to draw once again on Massumi here; by this I mean that as a body relates with things in the environment, it experiences form as felt intensities: brushings, pushings and pullings, caresses, shoves, resistances, and the like. Indeed, these sensations account for the diversity of form itself, across species and all animate life, as they shape and reshape bodies through the kinds of touch each of them encounter. "Contacts create pressures, and pressures, however minimal, create deformations—surface phenomena. Bodies are squeezed by things, bent by things, rustled by things. They are formally deformed in highly varied ways by what they meet. In a very real sense, they *give in* to the world and in giving in, recognize what in the world they are touching. It is thus their very formal deformations that are at the heart of their knowledge" (Sheets-Johnstone 2009, 140). In this view, bodies are susceptible to the world in a way that effects their very formation, the language here suggesting a kind of submission, a release of the body into the world of touch. The economy of touch works something along these lines: to touch something requires a capacity to be touched, and to be touched allows for the opening needed to touch the world. As Kearney (2015) claims: "To touch and be touched simultaneously is to be *connected* with others in a way that opens us up. Flesh is open-hearted; it is where we experience our greatest vulnerability" (105).

Intensities of pressure should not be seen simply in terms of "cutaneous stimulation;" our sensory feelings of touch cannot be captured in stimulus/response models of perception, but are rooted, as Sheets-Johnstone observes, in "animate sensitivity, a sensitivity that by turns may express itself in curiosity, explorations, recoilings, quiverings, affections, hastenings, hesitancies, accelerations, avoidances, persistences, and much more. Surface sensitivities . . . are a tactile-kinaesthetic engagement with the world" (2009, 137). Moreover, neither should intensities of pressure be seen in narrow terms of receptivity. Sensitivity is not only about receiving impressions but about our active, animate movement in the world: a bending of a leg, a reaching out of a hand, a walking through air, an immersing into water. These are living actions, movements that occasion form and create space.[15] Surface sensitivity, as Sheets-Johnstone (2009) remarks, is "not a mere cutaneous event" but "reverberates with the life it touches." It becomes a force itself, an enactment with the world. Living things, because of their surface sensitivities, "are *always potentially at the threshold of the world*, sensitive to its nuances and portents" (138, emphasis added).

Intensities as such are vibratory and, like waves upon the water, they are resonant, rippling out toward the environment, moving between inside and outside with a great deal of fluidity. Thus, while Sheets-Johnstone clearly claims that organisms have borders through their envelopes of membrane and tissue, the paradoxical situation of our skin, laid out in the condition of touching and being touched by, also occasions their porosity, malleability, and potentiality. It is this that lends itself to understanding that the corporeal specificities of touch are a significant aspect of becoming, in Massumi's sense above. "Always potentially at the threshold of the world" means existing in that liminality where bodily transformation is possible: bodies becoming in relation to elements of the environment that are not simply about adaptation or fit but are expressive of their very movement. Thresholds thereby become liminal spaces through which the ambiguity of touch transpires.

Architect Juhani Pallasmaa focuses his attention precisely on this liminality in his most famous work, *The Eyes of the Skin*. Pallasmaa (2012) seeks to trouble the dominant ocularcentric paradigm (both in Western architecture and cultural practices as a whole) not by dismissing vision, but by reformulating it as a relation of touch: "All sensory experiences are modes of touch, and thus related to tactility. Our contact with the world takes place at the boundary line of the self though specialised parts of our enveloping membrane" (12). (This boundary line, he later goes on to state, is really more a condition of liminality than it is a hard-and-fast border.) Moreover, Pallasmaa identifies the importance of "peripheral" sensations in our contact with architecture and draws on Bachelard's understanding of "the polyphony of the senses" in order to highlight the "multi-sensory" nature of our experiences. Thus, when discussing vision, along with other senses, they are rendered as "extensions of the sense of touch" (45).

What makes his work so interesting for considering the dynamic of touching and being touched by is the way the specificities of space are *cocreations* of bodies and their environments. Architectural space is not simply a given but is generated through the tactility of the senses. Pallasmaa (2012) writes, for example, about "acoustic intimacy": "Anyone who has become entranced by the sound of dripping water in the darkness of a ruin can attest to the extraordinary capacity of the ear to carve a volume into the void of darkness. The space traced by the ear in the darkness becomes a cavity sculpted directly in the interior of the mind" (54). While this evocative image seems to rely on a definite distinction between inside and outside, Pallasmaa is also careful to point out the "osmotic" relation between them. Sound creates an experience of space, rather than simply creating a sensation of hearing, which can only be achieved if inside and outside are not so stable. For him, "the most archaic origin of architectural space is in the cavity of the mouth" (63), hence suggesting not simply a projection of morphology onto the world, but a suggestion of the (spatial) continuum along which both architecture and bodies are registered. Speaking of a door pull as a "handshake" of a building (67), Pallasmaa indicates the movement, or action, of architecture. He writes, "Stepping stones set in the grass of a garden are images and imprints of footsteps. As we open a door, the body weight meets the weight of the door; the legs measure the steps as we ascend a stairway, the hand strokes the handrail and the entire body moves diagonally and dramatically through space" (2012, 67). More importantly, there is a promise of function—as Bergson says, objects "reflect its [the body's] possible action upon them" (cited in Pallasmaa 2012, 67). Architectural space in this way is a *living* space; it is not about the formal space of geometry; "it transcends measurability" (68). Importantly, what Pallasmaa is suggesting is that bodies do not only move tactilely through space, but also create space through their very movement and touch as they themselves emerge through that space.

While I will return to this idea of coemergence more thoroughly in chapter 4, at this juncture it is important to highlight that this creation of space allows us to imagine that the liminality between bodies and the environment, the deformations that happen to bodies, and the generative capacities of touch all contribute to a sense of emplacement in the here and now that is always shifting. Moreover, the touch of skin, along with its multisensorial extensions, creates an uncertainty about where my body ends in the relational space that is created.

> We feel pleasure and protection when the body discovers its resonance in space. When experiencing a structure, we unconsciously mimic its configuration with our bones and muscles: the pleasurably animated flow of a piece of music is

subconsciously transformed into bodily sensations, the composition of an abstract painting is experienced as tensions in the muscular system, and the structures of a building are unconsciously imitated and comprehended through the skeletal system. Unknowingly, we perform the task of the column or of the vault with our body. (Pallasmaa 2012, 71–72)

What Pallasmaa's work highlights is that we resonate with things in the world morphologically at the same time as those things resonate with our bodies, generating sensations that alter the felt experiences of insides/outsides. Thus contact with elements of our environment is not so much composed of either anthropomorphic projections or internalizations, which both assume clearly delineated borders of inside and outside; instead the resonance of bodies with the environment confounds them, without total absorption of one into the other.

Membranes, Morphologies, and Touch in Education

To consider educational encounters through living bodies, then, requires foregrounding the dynamics of touching and being touched by and how bodies resonate with elements of the environment. But touch and education make for strange associations. These words, together at least, are rarely part of our explorations into teaching, pedagogy, or curriculum. In fact, the moral panic around touch and physical contact in institutions of education makes such a connection difficult to discuss—and the plague of abuse that continues to haunt schools and other sites of education gives us legitimate cause for discomfort. However, as I hope the foregoing discussion has made clear, simply to ignore the centrality of touch in our educational practices is to ignore a significant dynamic of interaction and exchange upon which education rests. This is not only the case for children or youth in classrooms; how such dynamics play into educational encounters is significant across all ages as well as settings, be these face-to-face or online. If we see education not simply in a cognitive frame but as a project of subjectivity, then we need to take the relational, bodily dynamics of becoming a subject seriously. My plea here is to consider how feeling, sensation, and movement contribute to a much broader sense of education's purpose, as outlined in the previous chapter, and to recognize how central the living body is to the dual aspects of enculturation and becoming. In particular, I outline below some thoughts on the connection between morphology and enculturation, on the one hand, and membranes and becoming a subject, on the other.

First, with respect to the former, I suggested previously that education concerns the ways students and educators translate inherited modes of thought, values, and beliefs through their encounters with ideas, texts, traditions, and rituals; I identified this process as enculturation as distinct from socialization in order to underscore how our encounters are not merely determined by our social positionings or always laced in predictable or determinant ways with colonial, racist, or sexist meanings. Instead, translation as a living meeting with the past in the present entails bodily sensations (or moments of "pure experience") that transform the givenness of culture into unique forms of meaning. These acts of translation, to me, are not only dependent on an intellectual encounter with objects of study, but also on physical and affective encounters of touching and being touched by. Students' encounters with ideas in the form of books, exercises, writing, or art occasion sensations and affects that are indispensable to how they come to embody values, beliefs, and customs. Bodies, and not only minds, are key to understanding the felt responses, the attachments, the sensations of contact that one then identifies as "me" in relation to cultural practices. Moreover, the body's surface sensitivities are—and need to be—mobilized in order for values, beliefs, and customs to repeat and continue, while taking on new *forms*. I am speaking here of the complex bodily dynamics involved in coming to take part in cultural, religious, political, and ethical relations in ways that give rise to emplaced subjectivities. The reaching out to console; the kneeling on the mat; the clasping of hands; the outstretched arm holding a placard—these are all ranges of bodily movement that occasion different kinds of affective contact with the world and through which we come to have a relation to the world that we call *mine* or *ours*. The body is not incidental to the *enactment* of values and customs; it embodies those values through its very movement and touch, through a body's very deformation—without which neither formation nor transformation are possible. As Sheets-Johnstone claims, bodies are continually *de*formed, *re*formed, and *trans*formed through their particular movements. Indeed, many of us easily recognize the discomfort of encountering new ideas, values, and beliefs not only because we feel bodily *expressions* of apprehension, excitement, fear, or anxiety toward them, but also because the bodily *formations* that such ideas require of us are *felt* as strange.

Learning how to pray, to eat, to greet, to interact, to communicate, to dress, to speak a language, all of these involve our bodies taking on specific forms related to cultural practices. We kneel, sit, bow, lean, squeeze, resist—and each of these requires morphological pressures and intensities of sensation that then occasion new formations, new modes of touching and being touched by the world, that become unique to our singular bodies. Even though we might share with others similar patterns of behavior, we nonetheless identify with those sensations in different and sometimes contradictory ways in relation to our memories, instincts, social identities—although, as I have stressed throughout this chapter, without these *determining* in any way those very sensations. What is different from theories of socialization here is that such bodily translations admit the contested nature of cultural inheritance and refuse any simple identification of social positioning with bodily experience. As Ahmed has stressed, while touch might be experienced by some differently than for others due to histories of violence, my focus here is to underline how such histories do not produce those differences directly; rather, differences themselves emerge from the ways bodies interact with the values, beliefs, and artifacts of those histories. In this sense there is a proliferation of difference not tied neatly to social categories. Thus, what I'm suggesting here is that what is *educational* about our contact with elements of the environment lies precisely in how each of us translates such contact and the proliferation of difference this occasions. Enculturation is not a theory about how bodies come to occupy a position on the grid of identity, but about how complex translations arise through our bodily contact with the world.

Secondly, regarding its other dimension, education concerns becoming as a process of transformation through which one emerges as a subject capable of living life well with others. As such it depends on a body which is capable of sensory change. As I argued in the previous chapter, bodies are key to understanding how we *become* singular subjects that can *enact* equality and emancipation. This becoming, as we have seen, is occasioned by our touching and being touched by elements of our environment, the perceptions, sensations, and feelings that are generated through contact, through which a subject becomes distinct and singular. Seeing enactment as crucial for subjectification, for *leading* a life, is dependent upon our capacities for *living* a life, for living it through the very liminality of our contact with things, and through the subtle and varied ways we *feel* the flux of life. Insofar as subjectification rests on becoming, it is also located in the economy of touch, whereby to touch and be touched by signal openings, susceptibilities, and capacities to be surprised. It means thinking about education in ways that acknowledge the movements and sensations that lie in excess of social scripts, that lie in excess of telling students *what* they should become. Instead, an education focused on the living body means allowing for *who* each student is as a potentiality, as a subject capable of enacting their own emancipation, living and leading lives with others. This is not to fall into some individualistic conception of education, replete with its empty phrases of "fulfilling potential" or "pulling oneself up by the bootstraps." Nor is it to condemn context, background, or social identity as irrelevant to education. Instead, the potentiality that opens up by viewing education through the economy of touch is that subjectivity is an unpredictable and surprising emergence arising out of a *network of relations*. This means that it is *relations, not individuals, which carry potential*. The potentiality for a body-subject to emerge lies in the relations we enact; in this sense potential is not a possession or some internal trait to be fulfilled but is an opening in the relational field itself, indicating a possibility of ushering in something new. This relational quality of subjectivity means that education is about individuation and differentiation—not about individuals and fixed categories of social difference. Instead, it concerns a *process* whereby individuation (the becoming of the singular subject) occurs through the differentiation between students and things, ideas, and others. Differentiation is not so much an identifiable given (as in a subject position), as it is something that happens, or transpires, as a relation across membranes. By this I mean that skin is not a covering that isolates us into individuals, but is, by the nature of its composition, a *relational* tissue. It is porous and flexible and as such undergoes change and transformation in its contact with the world. Membranes are fundamentally about relationship: bringing in, expressing, and expelling across cells, blurring the boundary at times of what is inside and outside. Taken literally, membranes are what enable subjectification; they not only able us to take in the world, but also enable us to act on and through the world. I lead my life, enact equality and emancipation, because I affect and am affected by the things I encounter in living that life. I am not saying that reflection, thinking, and consideration are not part of subjectification, but that they are not possible without a body that *enacts* reflection, thinking, and consideration. These are not disembodied faculties or capacities of being but flow out of our bodily engagements with the environment. As James (1912) puts it, they are what grows out of our experience of the flux of life and are always of the time of delay, occurring after the fact or the event of contact itself. Education as it concerns becoming and subjectification necessarily needs to be concerned about the touch of the present and how bodies are actually affected in the everydayness of relations themselves.

Thus taking a sensory view of encounters as essential to both enculturation and becoming means viewing education *as a dynamic of touching and being touched by*. This requires attending to not only the stuff of curriculum—the objects of study, such as particular books, maps, and natural objects—but also the physical and somatic *relation* between students (as well as teachers) and these objects. For instance, as we shall see in chapter 6, how bodies interact with keyboards, monitors, and e-readers matters to education. Moreover, if bodies *literally* take form through the intensities of sensation occasioned by their encounter with elements in their environment, then a student's relation to an object of study is not so easy to bracket off from their relations to other material (including other bodies) in the educational setting—be this a classroom, laboratory, library, museum, or online space.

That is, the *enactment* of studying, discussing, reading, listening, and attending—and of course thinking—means participating in a network of sensory relations that are experienced variously as vital intensities. Bodies sitting on chairs, jostling in groups, leaning on desks, tapping pencils, grasping pens, turning pages, punching keyboards and screens, bending over a display, pointing to objects, raising voices, listening to others' voices, gazing out the window make up a small part of the myriad and banal ways students and teachers are in touch with elements of their environment. Seen through complex networks of sensory relations and intensities, these encounters pulse with the beating of life, the various pressures of the chair against the thighs, buttocks, and lower back, the weight of door as it is pulled by the arm bending toward the body, the brightness of fluorescent lights overhead, the loudness of children running down the hall all work to in-form and impress upon bodies in ways that *make* students (and teachers) out of cells, membranes, nerve endings, and skin. That is, teachers and students are created out of the bodily raw materials which interact with the environment; they are not given. While those pressures largely remain unnoticed until they irritate, please, or obstruct, they act to remind us that bodily contact (through which processes of becoming transpire) involves an array of microperceptions, of touches and touchings, of wave-like intensities of pressure and force that are the raw material for how we come to understand the world, through categories, classifications, and experiences.

Becoming a subject out of this vibratory array of sensation is a generative process, and students become resonant with certain elements in the environment over others. Taking this relational view seriously means seeing that students touch and are touched by the environment *differently*; the educational question is not to assume that the economy of touch is ever predetermined by class, race, sexuality, ability, or ethnicity; neither is it to see students as individuals divorced from such social significations, power relations, backgrounds, and contexts. This means that pedagogical approaches committed to addressing educational challenges such as the climate emergency have to consider these singularities while also attempting to respond to them meaningfully. This requires creating encounters with elements of the environment that enable new paths for becoming beyond what we have imagined thus far. The educational questions to ask are: How does the economy of touch, one's sensory contact with its unique sensations and movements, play a part in new possibilities of subjectivity and new forms of relationality? And how might education embrace the very paradoxicality of the subject as one who both touches and is touched by simultaneously?

Chapter Three

Enculturation, Regimes of Perception, and the Politics of the Senses

> We already know what it means to sense, what seeing, touching, and hearing are. Such assurances and the practices of sense making that enable them are, by definition, political. They relate our bodies to the world, but also determine the conditions through and by which we might sense the world and those who occupy it; in short, such regimes of perception confer what counts as common sense. But, we might ask, what if the relationship between our sensory organs and acts of perception is not as certain as we presume?
>
> —Davide Panagia, *The Political Life of Sensation*

> Attachments matter and the way they matter becomes apparent when you do not take them into account or carry on as if people were free, or should be set free, from them. . . . Attachments are what cause people, including all of us, to feel and think, to be able to become able.
>
> —Isabelle Stengers, "Introductory Notes on an Ecology of Practices"

It is commonplace to assume that schools, like other social institutions such as the family, religion, organized sport, and early childhood settings, all participate to actively encourage youth and children to fit into a given society and to internalize prevalent rules of behavior, structures of social interaction, and forms of civil life. Socialization is indeed about the continuance and functioning of a particular social order in ways that make it appear as "common sense," as Davide Panagia notes above, and contributes to what Russell Jacoby in the 1970s referred to as our "second nature": the gelling of sociohistorical processes into supposedly natural ways of thinking and being.

However, as I have been exploring in previous chapters, education as a *process*—as distinct from an institution, or as distinct from what Carl Anders Säfström (2021) labels as "school*ing*"—does something different. Through enculturation, education is involved in the ways we translate, negotiate, and take on beliefs, values, traditions, and customs, through which we form attachments to the world—attachments, which as Isabelle Stengers remarks in the epigraph above, are central to being able to live our lives. Within multicultural, multiracial, multiethnic, multifaith, and multiabled societies, this specifically *cultural* dimension is important since it also highlights that how we live our lives within a social order is neither uniform nor seamless but plural and contentious; neither does living a life with others always easily map onto *what* we are in terms of our social identities nor does it always simply mirror the structures of inequality and discrimination that underpin those identities within a given social order. By this I mean that, while socialization is always about securing one's place within a given social order, replete with its structural positionings and hierarchies, enculturation allows us to see how one's positionality is not necessarily *lived* in the same way as another's even when we share the same coordinates on the grid of available (and acceptable) positionalities, and even when we belong to shared communities.

Enculturation, while being a mode through which we come to belong and attach to communities, traditions, and faiths, also depicts how we come to be more than the sum of our positions: we come to be more than common sense would dictate. Thus, as I explore below, enculturation offers a more nuanced way of theorizing how we both touch and are touched by the world in ways that move within and beyond the frames of current inequalities and the rigidity of fixed attributes of identity, as well as the social scripts through which we understand them both. To do this, I examine how enculturation is bound up complexly with the senses, perception, and sensation, each of which sometimes supports and sometimes challenges the common sense that governs the social order itself—a social order which is sustained through what Jacques Rancière (and Panagia after him) calls "regimes of perception." Here I explicitly explore enculturation as signaling a process through which we become racialized, engendered, abled, classed, and sexualized subjects through acts of perception. That is, rather than taking the view that we *embody* certain identity positions within a social order which we then carry into our encounters with the world, enculturation occurs in the opposite direction: it allows us to consider instead how our bodily, sensory encounters with elements of the environment act to engender, racialize, and sexualize us as subjects in distinct and varied ways—and not only in the ways demanded by the social order itself. Such verbs mean that these are active, negotiated, and translated subjectivities (in the plural), not fixed structures or singular nodes of signification. Thus, I argue here that our encounters with cultural artifacts, practices, beliefs, and values enable subjectivities and attachments that are at once educational and sensory. Sensory in that they are lived in and through the body; educational in that they assist us in living and leading lives worth living with others through processes of enculturation and becoming. Moreover, I consider here how enculturation can enact a politics of the senses as a way of resisting dominant forms of signification and expressions of inequality through (alternative) sensory experiences.

The Making of "Common Sense": Not the Aim

As I mentioned previously, there is an ofttimes too easy identification of "education" (as institution or social function)[1] with socialization, insofar as the latter aims to inculcate youth into existing structures, social arrangements, and the norms of society at large—in short into "common sense" ways of understanding one's world. By common sense I am referring here to the unquestioned, taken-for-granted meanings of things, events, people in society, not to the ways in which we can build commonality or communities of sense—a point I take up below.[2] This inculcation is what Durkheim referred to as "secondary socialization" (with primary socialization being preserved for the family unit), and his assumptions about the function of "education" as "imprinting" onto children social skills and values have themselves virtually passed into "common sense" within conventional discourses of schooling. Both historically and in our time, this power to instill, imprint, and implant has lent "education" an aura of influence over youth that has been seen to be adaptable to the winds of political change, with each revolutionary movement (as well as more prosaic changes of government) seeking to bend "education" to its political project. In this way, "education" has become an *instrument* for political forces that lie outside its field of practice. More than this, however, education-as-socialization holds the promise of conferring on society a certain stability over time, since it is fundamentally about assuring that the young know their place within the given social order, the social dynamics that define that order, and can take both as "common sense."

As a *social institution*, "education" has thus paradoxically been responsible for socializing the young not only into the positive values of a particular society (such as civility, communalism, respect for elders) but has also been literally instrumental in socializing them into the structures and dispositions compatible with patriarchy, advanced capitalism, and colonialism as well as abled, racial, and ethnic hierarchies. As such, it is no secret that educational institutions have participated profoundly in the continuance of systemic forms of discrimination against the bodies of indigenous populations, the poor, migrants, women, LGBTQ, Travellers, the disabled, neurodivergent people, and "others" who are so differentially identified—and have done so in the name of socialization, establishing certain expressions of language, comportment, attitude, and so on as normative and commonsensical. "Education" has produced these social wrongs through contributing and sustaining cultures of silencing, labeling, and exclusion, as well as through enacting other more egregious acts of violence, all of which have had a powerful normalizing function. These practices are all caught within what Rancière refers to as certain regimes of perception: that is, who is heard, who can speak, who can touch and be touched, who is to receive, who is to act, and who is to be seen are related to *how* we hear, act, touch, listen to and with others, to and with things in the world in general. "Education" in this light has been central in promoting certain regimes of perception that support and instantiate ongoing forms of inequality that rely precisely on these techniques of visibility, touch, and hearing. Hence education as an institution has been seen by both supporters of such inequality (who believe "education" should be about promoting the status quo and keeping people in their place) and by those of us challenging such inequality (who recognize "education's" complicity in systemic oppression) as a *mechanism* for ensuring that one learns to inhabit society in ways that fall into dominant modes of social organization. Thus despite these very different views on the value of the outcome of socialization, the point is that both see it as fundamentally imbricated into the texture of "education" itself.

Indeed, one of the problems in seeing "education" and the school in terms of socialization, as Rancière (1995) has shown, lies in the way it reinforces belief in the current social order:

> School creates inequality precisely because it promotes belief in inequality; in having the children of the poor believe that all who are there are equal, that pupils are marked, classified and selected only on the basis of the talents and intelligence each has, it compels the children of the poor to acknowledge that if they do not succeed it is because they have no talents and are not intelligent, and it would therefore be better if they went somewhere else. . . . [School is a] theatre of a fundamental symbolic violence. (53)

Importantly, however, those concerned with social justice also frequently assume that "education" can be a productive source of alleviating harms wrought by such forms of systemic discrimination. Often, this is to be achieved through more critical forms of interrogation into these systems as well as into our complicity in and vulnerability to them. The aim is to alter not simply one's *understanding* of how discrimination and inequality operate, but to change one's orientation, behavior, and disposition toward and within these systems, and optimally through this work to change the systems themselves. What I want to raise at this point, however, is that how we go about thinking about this change needs to be framed beyond the very mechanistic model of "education" that is often used to analyze the problem in the first place—that is, beyond socialization. We need to be careful not to think of education as "mechanism" or "instrument" that can simply mete out an alternative form of socialization (no matter how equitable, just, and free we think society will be as a result), and this is for two primary reasons.

First, treating education in this way would amount to enacting the same dynamic of "instilling" and "imprinting" which all socialization is based upon, repeating once again the very movement of inequality, disenfranchisement, and alienation toward students that lead to oppression in the first place. Rancière (1995) reminds us that this view simply repeats what one is attempting to extinguish: "The nihilistic vision of school as a form of reproduction of inequality and the progressive vision of school as an instrument for reducing inequalities concur in their effects as they do in their principles: both start with inequality and end up with inequality" (1995, 54). This irony was not lost on Paulo Freire in his insistence that pedagogy start from where students *are*, not from where we would like them to be. The practices of education itself must be *educational*, fully engaging students and teachers in *their* encounters with the world *as veritable equals*, not telling them which ones they ought to have, how they ought to think, how they ought to behave—or how they ought to sense the world. Not, that is, *pretending* they are equals, only to be told that they don't really have the talents or intelligence to be treated as such. Of educational interest here is how students *do* encounter the world in all their richness and actuality; in other words, education is about treating these varied experiences *as equal in worth and value* and not as a means to get somewhere else that is predefined. That is, while there will always be institutional forces at work in society (schools, places of worship, daycares, family homes) that give "common sense" as a justification for why one's life should be lived in a certain way, it cannot be the work of *education* to provide a single option for leading a life, nor for instituting another *regime* of perception no matter how equal or better *we* might believe it to be.

Secondly, seeing education mechanistically does not take into account the complexity of how each one of us encounters the world not only in light of, but in excess of the very scripts we are seeking to change; that is, a mechanistic view assumes "education" to be primarily about putting on offer an alternative form of socialization that one is then supposed to see as another pervasive form of "common sense." It would then embody the tendency to treat issues of inequality and discrimination as solely structural matters instead of also being something that is in the fabric of our bodies, as Frantz Fanon understood very well, and of our senses, as I explore below. Indeed, seeing education as a mechanism (despite the vision of an equitable society we might be seeking to work toward) belies an understanding of subjectivity as that which is socially (re)produced and not at all connected to or even mediated through our actual, living bodily encounters with the world. Instead, as we have seen in chapter 2, subjectivity emerges in myriad ways through bodily networks of relation—that is, through multiple encounters with elements of one's environment. Indeed, this relational, bodily aspect is the very reason why we are both so vulnerable to discrimination, on the one hand, and so entrenched in our habits of discrimination, on the other. Inequality is entwined with our flesh as it were; however, I contend so is equality and the potential for becoming otherwise. Thus, what a mechanistic view of "education" does is elide the way living bodies experience, negotiate, and touch and are touched by their environments in ways that exceed socialization altogether.

Heeding these two points, I want to suggest that if we are serious about the transformational quality of education, then we need to take into account how we perceive and sense the world as mattering to how we live it. Education proper cannot be about fitting people into social orders no matter how well intended we think those orders might be; neither is it about making "common sense" *for* others at all. Indeed, reframing what is educational about education—and more specifically about our encounters—means having to respect and contend with the multiplicity of sense, perception, and sensation beyond deterministic accounts of social identities and positionalities in order to open up alternatives to status quo forms of "common sense." This is not to deny or suspend our backgrounds or attachments, as I discussed in chapter 1, but it is to see how they become relationally entangled with the rich and abundant elements of our environments in ways that do not always pertain to their socialization into the accepted commonsense workings of an unequal society. That is, our encounters with human and more-than-human others, books, trees, maps, ideas, images, movement, paper, screens, pens, and so on cannot simply be seen as being in the service of socialization, but as being open to a range of experiences, imaginings, and acts of translation. Let me be clear, socialization is of course necessary, and we all need to partake in some form of common sense in order to live our lives as social beings. However, my point is that it is neither the purpose nor function of education proper to make this happen. Moreover, part of what has become "common sense" is caught up in violent, degrading, and exclusionary forms of inequality based on specific regimes of perception, and these can never be something education aims toward, even if "education" as an institution contributes to them. Such regimes indeed construe what is appropriate and acceptable modes of sensing the world: how we touch and are touched by the world becomes politically charged and normatively defined. The educational question for me lies not in merely replacing one common sense for another, one regime of perception for another (which is a question of socialization), but to inquire into *how* "common sense" is lived through the body and the senses, on the one hand, and *how* interruptions of "common sense" are also central to ushering in new sensory ways of being in/with/of the world, on the other (which is a question of enculturation). Thus being clear about these differences is necessary if educators wish to take social justice seriously so that we don't yet again impose a set of conditions upon students that end up failing to address their own capacities for becoming, for living and leading lives meaningfully with others at this juncture of both environmental collapse and technodigital existence.

Enculturation: From Discourses to the Senses

In seeking to explore subjectivity (as distinct from social identity) from the point of view of enculturation, my intent here is not to lose sight of the pernicious landscape of inequality, prejudice, and discrimination, but to see how this setting simply doesn't produce subjects or socialize them into its fold, as if subjects thereby occupy or take on predefined positions of race, gender, sexuality, class, and so on. Moreover, my intent is to foreground how specifically sensuous bodies—bodies of sensation, sense, and perception—are involved in complex processes of enculturation. In chapter 1, I discussed how understanding a subject's *relation to* various forms and practices of culture (beliefs, values, traditions, customs, etc.) depends on processes of translation: that one does not simply inhabit or embody culture as a monolithic set of narratives or positionalities, but one *translates* the fragmentary and contested legacies of thought and practice into one's life in the present; one thus embodies not what is given in culture but *embodies a relation to culture*.[3]

An influential way of thinking of subjectivity as both that which is embodied and yet related to discourses and norms of culture has emanated from the work of Judith Butler. Often taken to be a proponent of subject formation and "production," Butler understands all too well the complexity involved in how bodies and subjects are imbricated through discursive conventions in ways that do not simply fulfill socialization's aims. In this her work has something to say about enculturation, while also illustrating, to my mind, some of the limitations inherent to a discursive account of the body itself.

Butler remarks that the idea of the body in the constitution of subjectivity has been rooted in a series of dichotomies:

> Just as philosophy founders time and again on the question of the body, it tends to separate what is called thinking from what

is called sensing, from desire, passion, sexuality, and relations of dependency. It is one of the great contributions of feminist philosophy to call those dichotomies into question and so to ask as well whether in sensing, something called thinking is already at work, whether in acting, we are also acted upon, and whether in coming into the zone of the thinking and speaking I, we are at once radically formed and also bringing something about. (Butler 2015, 15)

What Butler brings to the fore here is the undecidability—and indeed as I see it liminality—of subjectivity; it is both passive and active; constituted and agential; sentient and thoughtful. That is, subjectivity is *of* the body as much as it is of the mind or ego. Disrupting the dichotomies she has listed suggests that the subject is at once a reaching out and a receiving of the world—a touching and being touched by. In this way, we might see that sensory encounters with elements of the environment are sites both of impression and expression: one is not simply "produced" through discourse, as if one "produces" a thing or object; one also bodily *experiences* norms and discursive arrangements (as felt sensations) even as such norms and discourses define that body.

Butler indeed states that "it must be possible to claim that the body is not known or identifiable apart from the linguistic co-ordinates that establish the boundaries of the body—*without* thereby claiming that the body is nothing other than the language by which it is known" (2015, 20). The body, therefore, is "given through language" but it is not "reducible to language" (21). Instead of being purely "inscribed," the body, for Butler, emerges out of ongoing contradictory and complex discursive arrangements.[4] As such, I slough off, break from, and take on different formations, all occurring within specific historical contexts. In this sense, Butler claims that "I am never simply formed, nor am I ever fully self-forming" (6). This interplay between the subject and its discursive, norm-laden environment means that socialization can never be entirely successful in its "production" of subjectivity, largely due to the range of ways the subject negotiates this discursive-normative field: the norms I enact, disregard, or actively work against all set the conditions for my subjectivity. For Butler, subjectivities are constellations and translations of existing discursive norms that do not always follow the predicted path of socialization.

However, while Butler recognizes that we are therefore not condemned to the norms (or common sense) which govern a specific identity position, she insists that the subject (and the body) is nonetheless limited by the available norms on offer. She asks: "Is it not possible to overcome our formation, to break with that matrix that formed any of us as a subject? . . . Of course, it is possible to break with certain norms as they exercise the power to craft us, but that can happen only by the intervention of countervailing norms" (9). Her response indicates that from her discursive position, one normative relation needs to be replaced by another; becoming a subject always demands that we operate within normative horizons. Who we are is always, therefore, a constitutive site of performative iteration of available norms. This is consistent with Butler's Foucauldian leanings, and it suggests that there is no theory of change that lies outside of the subject's engagement with norms that are either prevailing or countervailing. This, however, problematically assumes that the body's interactions and encounters with things, objects, and other animate beings is always already filtered through a normative register as if such encounters are either uncontaminated by sensation and feeling, or that sensation and feeling are always already contaminated by norms themselves. That is, it suggests that the body is only ever in contact with elements of its environment in ways that are normatively framed. As I argued in chapter 2, bodies, however, also emerge through the sheer physicality of deformation and sensation in ways that can defy overarching discursive logics (a point I develop further below). Thus, while Butler calls attention to the need to see the senses, desires, sexuality, and passions as part of the formation of subjectivity, these ultimately are cast in terms of how they behave and operate within the field of circulating norms.

Butler's position is to some extent exacerbated by her use of "the body" in the singular form. To my mind there can be no one universal body that governs subjectivity since bodies themselves are plural singulars and, along with subjectivities, each one different from the next in important ways. Butler is correct in saying that "the body" in the abstract can never "exist" outside of language; however, living, breathing bodies do exist, both within and outside language, and they do so through encounters in/with their surroundings in ways we cannot always fathom through language.[5] Perhaps "the body" can never operate outside of discursive regimes (how we *theorize* "the body," is of course governed by constitutive relations of language), but living bodies, I suggest, can and do operate outside of these norms all the time through their very vitality, affective textures, and physicality—which are untraceable to any specific normative arrangement. Thus, while Butler makes it possible to think about how subjectivity emerges through the bodily translation of norms in ways that resist socialization, bodies themselves are rendered as not acting outside normative frames of reference, and therefore their living "bodiliness," their animation, their touch—their very liveliness and vitality—ultimately become superfluous to such processes.

From an altogether different vantage that aligns the senses more closely with the social body, anthropologist David Howes and cultural historian Constance Classen (2014) explore the bodily dimensions of culture as central to understanding how we are constituted as subjects. In this, they focus on how the senses themselves are both shaped and ordered as well as experienced and felt. "To say that perception is shaped by culture and that society regulates how and what we sense is also to say that there is a politics of the senses. Our ways of sensing affect not only how we experience and engage with our environment, but also how we experience and engage with each other" (Howes and Classen 2014, 5–6). The senses are thus seen to circulate through and be organized by social and cultural practices, while also being corporeal. As they argue, "What makes sensations so forceful is that they are lived experiences, not intellectual abstractions" (7). For them, such sensations[6] are central to understanding how social orders, hierarchies, and prejudices are lived through the body, and in this they, like Butler, see the senses in a normative frame; however, unlike Butler, they also place more emphasis on perception and the senses as buttressing systemic forms of discrimination, understanding that the senses are not merely epiphenomena to the workings of culture and society but indeed *support* these very workings.

For Howes and Classen, we come to inhabit certain ways of being in the world through our senses; we *viscerally* experience inclusion and exclusion, acceptance and rejection, and fair and unjust treatment. Beginning with identifying the hierarchy of vision and hearing within Western societies, Howes and Classen charge that such societies are particularly adept at categorizing certain groups as less visible or indeed invisible. In fact, we can see this clearly through the historical treatment of indigenous people in North America and elsewhere where colonial societies have silenced and muted entire populations by removing them from view. Across time and cultures, this has been accompanied by the mobilization of sensory symbols, models, metaphors, and images. Howes and Classen write: "The use of sensory symbols to characterize groups perceived as potentially threatening to the social order is widespread. The first part of the process involves rendering a social group 'invisible' by keeping it sequestered, by restricting its opportunities, by limiting its representation and by simply ignoring its presence. The 'absent' group is then represented by simple and potent symbols: the beautiful but corrupt seductress; the coarse, malodorous worker; the greasy, slippery foreigner; and so on" (7). Even more importantly, sensory images are not only discursively *used* to ostracize and denigrate, but they work with, on, and through bodies in ways that actually *become* lived experience. That is, it is not simply a matter of "naming" through discourse, as though this weren't bad enough, but it is a matter of *embodying* the very sensations that are associated with specific categories of individuals. The worker actually does become smelly; the woman becomes an object to be touched; the immigrant is experienced as repugnant. Indeed, as Howes and Classen observe, "The social control of perceptibility—who is seen, who is heard, whose pain is recognized—plays an essential role in establishing positions of power within society. Such control is exercised both officially and unofficially, and determines not only *who* is perceived, but also *how* they are perceived" (65–66). Thus different cultures and societies make use of different sensory codes as political instruments; what might be identified in one set of cultural practices as a pleasant or neutral smell can be in another an unpleasant odor. How different societies create "outsiders" takes on specific sensory content and is not generalizable. In this way, our sensations are not entirely "natural" but are part of a complex network of social and communicative strategies that politicize the senses.

Howes and Classen open up the importance of the senses for how we come to "inhabit" our place in the world and in this offer valuable insight into the workings of nationalism, racism, and patriarchy, for example. They demonstrate the thoroughly bodily effects of power in showing how the senses *partake* in already existing hierarchies, systems, and structures of society and therefore contribute to sustaining them. Moreover, they show that our feelings and perceptions themselves, what we take for granted as being mine, or as being "commonsense" ways of the sensing the world, can be socially coded, culturally shaped, and politically defined. In this, they help us to understand how bodies become sites of social signification upon which inequalities are projected and then lived as felt experience.

In this way, their emphasis on the biopolitics of the senses enables us to see how identities of race, class, ethnicity, gender, sexuality, and ability are comprised not simply of structures, but of living bodily sensations.

The physical body, in this view, becomes a social body, indelibly marked by and through particular sense-feelings. As such, we can see how social categories are really *processes of social categorization*. Thus one doesn't occupy some predefined racial category such as blackness or whiteness, one is racial*ized* as black or white through one's bodily encounters with cultural practices of sense-making.

However, their understanding, for instance, of how hierarchies of perception work is largely from the vantage point of the social order itself. That workers become smelly, or women become objects of touch, or immigrants become repugnant, of course say more about class society, patriarchy, and nationalism (and the people who benefit within such systems) than they do about how workers, women, or immigrants *experience themselves* and the world around them. Fanon (1982), for instance, acknowledged that how we are perceived may become part of who we are, but it isn't the entire story. For Fanon, there is always a doubling effect: the black man experiences himself as existing at the border of common sense, embodying a phenomenological splitting: he is at once caught in a racist ontology and an awareness of being otherwise. Thus, even if one internalizes the projected perceptions of a racist, nationalist, and patriarchal society there is something more at stake beyond the social ordering of the senses that Howes and Classen invoke. Surely, how it *feels* to be a worker, woman, or immigrant in a particular culture and society is also part of what creates one's very identity *as* a worker or immigrant *and is not reducible to* how a worker or immigrant *is sensually experienced by others*. This means that although the senses are tied to cultural and social histories of aligning certain sights, smells, sounds, and touch with such positioning, they do not necessarily produce the intended sense experience for everyone all of time, and particularly not for the people who are being categorized in these ways.

Thus, as Butler suggested above in relation to the subject, the senses are never entirely co-opted by the social. That is, they are not determined by discourse, but can also act upon it in ways that call "common sense" into question. Without this capacity of the body to feel otherwise, to experience sensations that are something other than what I have been allowed, told, or enabled to feel, then no change would be possible. Histories of both large-scale social movements and small everyday resistances that minorities, women, and others seeking to affirm their equality engage in are testament to how we are capable of sensing our environment beyond what is given.

By way of concluding this section, what all this means for enculturation are three things: First, educational processes of translating beliefs, values, customs, and traditions into the present, through our bodies, requires not only seeing these as performative iterations, but as sensory modalities through which we make attachments to the world. Enculturation allows us to conceive of these attachments as living sensations, as ways in which our bodies *feel we belong* to communities, physically enact rituals that are part of wider cultural practices of greeting, eating, worshipping, birthing, and dying, and experience the gamut of sensation that connects us to others beyond ourselves (and indeed to things and other animate life beyond the human world).

Secondly, these educational processes of translation transpire through our encounters with specific elements of our environment; even norms and forms of "common sense" make their way to us as images, texts, music, architectural spaces, ideas, smells, objects, animals, and other bodies, enabling our bodies to develop affective connections, associations, and perceptions of the world. Encounters, as I've discussed previously, bring together heterogeneous elements into networks of relation where my senses interrelate with a host of other objects and bodies. And to make things more complex, one's enactment of cultural practices and the sensations we have about them are the stuff of normative contestation and disagreement even from within communities to which (we feel) we belong. Kwame Anthony Appiah (2018) writes of this specifically in relation to social identities, but it is nonetheless apt in reflecting upon cultural affiliations: "But just as there's usually contest or conflict about the boundaries of the group, about who's in and who's out, there's almost always disagreement about what normative significance an identity has" (10). Thus, enculturation is a process that allows for plurality and difference and sees contestation as part of forming attachments in common.

Thirdly, the sensations that emerge through translation must be understood not simply as a form of "common sense" but as something more ambiguous and potentially interruptive than that. That is, they do not simply *mirror* social orders but transverse, interconnect, as well as undermine and defy those orders of common sense. This, to me, is because sensations themselves occur on a different register than the social. They exist as relational affects and felt intensities as bodies touch and are touched by their environment. Sensations are powerful reminders that (a) not everything that transpires through our encounters is about social ordering; (b) subjects and bodies exist beyond social inscription;

and (c) sensations can also fuel our struggles with the social order just as much as (if not more than) they subjugate us to it.

Regimes of Perception, Distribution of the Sensible, and Sensation

I have suggested above, in parallel with my discussion in chapter 2, that sensation and indeed bodies themselves are not reducible to an effect of social ordering, even if social ordering is felt through and sustained by bodily senses. But how exactly is this possible, if Rancière is correct in claiming, as I think he is, and as Howe and Classen's analyses attest to, that each social order functions through certain "regimes of perception"? That is, how can enculturation as a process through which subjectivities become emplaced within, attach themselves to, and are attached by cultural practices, move beyond mirroring this regime? Let us unpack what is at stake in this configuration in order to see how it might actually open up for a different kind of politics.

Such regimes, as both Rancière and Panagia observe, are based on how we align our perception with signification. That is, social orders rely on us to perceive things in particular ways so that there is a shared understanding and meaning about the thing we are perceiving. In this, regimes of perception affect our very ability to see, hear, taste, touch, and smell things, *and* they affect the values we assign to these sense perceptions. This means that the way we understand *in common*—make sense of a social world we share—is always sensed in particular ways, by particular bodies. This is how the field of common sense and ordered social relations become intricately tied to our singular perceptions of the world. For example, schools are often places where children begin to bodily understand what the larger society deems appropriate in contrast to what is appropriate within one's home. This includes a shift from the intimacy of certain smells and practices of touch at home, for instance, to a "common sense" where these very same sensations and practices carry different significations. For the child, this then becomes a site of learning to classify, categorize, and code their and others' bodies according to the extent to which they map on to this "common sense." More than this, a regime will "tell" us that it is "common sense" to understand certain people, actions, and dispositions in very particular ways, labeled and coded according to prevailing rules of what is acceptable; it governs what Rancière calls the "distribution of the sensible" (*partage du sensible*).⁷

> I call the distribution of the sensible the system of self-evident facts of sense perception that simultaneously discloses the existence of something in common and the limitations that define the respective parts and positions within it. A distribution of the sensible therefore establishes at one and the same time something common that is shared and exclusive parts. This apportionment of parts and positions is based on a distribution of spaces, times and forms of activity that determines the very manner in which something in common lends itself to participation and in what way various individuals have a part in this distribution. (2006, 7)

But how, you might be wondering, is this different from the discursive view of Butler or the anthropological view of Howes and Classen discussed above? On the one hand, Rancière is indeed, like them, suggesting that each social order (or in his terminology, the *police*) "polices" how one is placed within the *sensory logic* of a given society, each one of us assigned a position (or positions) according to one's attributes and characteristics (which are bodily sensed). These are then granted meaning (given sense) as being someone who counts or not, someone who is included or excluded, as part of the whole. Rancière claims that those who have "no part" in society are in fact "parts" who are defined through a negation of their participation in society—in other words, their exclusion is in fact "distributed" by what is permitted through the regime of perception (e.g., the poor, the homeless, and refugees). They occupy a position of a "part who has no part": they are "included *as* excluded." As he claims, "Having a particular 'occupation' thereby determines the ability or inability to take charge of what is common to the community; it defines what is visible or not in a common space, endowed with a common language, etc." (2006, 8). In this, we can see that senses distribute, and are distributed by, the very borders of "common sense," with effects on who and/or what belongs (by inclusion or negation) within the bounds of political communities.

On the other hand, however, Rancière sees that the distribution of the sensible is never fixed in stone. The inequality that results is not inherent to anyone (as those who embrace eugenics and other forms of racist, classist, and sexist reductionisms would have one believe) but is purely based on this distribution. Inequality is (merely) a form of social organization. Nothing more, nothing less. The very people who are deemed excluded are equal in the sense of their capacity for intelligence—in the sense, that is, that they are quite able to live and lead lives with others and can understand the system of inequality they are in. For Rancière, the phrase "*politics* of the senses" does not refer to the fact that our senses are ordered into society, but to the fact that we can enact an interruption of the given, through claiming (verifying) our *equality*. He writes of the difference: "The *police*, to begin with, is defined as an organizational system of coordinates that establishes a distribution of the sensible or a law that divides the community into groups, social positions, and functions . . . The essence of *politics* consists in interrupting the distribution of the sensible by supplementing it with those who have no part in the perceptual coordinates of the community, thereby modifying the very aesthetic-political field of possibility" (Rancière 2006, xiv). For Rancière, politics is therefore about creating a shift in whose voices are heard, who is seen, who can speak and participate, who can touch the world—it is about changing the horizons of perception for all and creating new "communities of sense." It is here, in this moment of transformation, in this moment of redistributing the sensible, that sensation comes to play a central role. And it is this which sets Rancière's thinking off from the normative framings of the social order as a given, beyond what Butler, and Howes and Classen claim. For him, "Politics is not primarily a matter of laws and constitutions. Rather, it is a matter of configuring the sensible texture of the community for which those laws and constitutions make sense. What objects are common? What subjects are included in the community? Which subjects are able to see and voice what is common?" (Rancière 2014, 453).

For Rancière, politics happens when it challenges the social order of commonsense-making, redistributing the sensible in ways that make possible new modes of being in the world and new modes of envisioning the "common" in "common sense." But it can only do that, not by appealing to the rationality of the subject, or forming consensus around issues pertaining to inequality but by creating a "sensible or perceptual shock caused . . . by that which resists signification" (2006, 59)—by, in other words, engaging the senses on a different register than "common sense." This is what Rancière identifies as belonging to aesthetics. Through encounters with art the very texture of sensibility alters; or to put it more appropriately, the altering of sensibility is the condition of art itself. Aesthetic in this understanding is about the engagement with forms that exist outside of regimes of sense. There is thus a "*dissensus*" with what is given, what is signified, through the shock of experiencing, feeling, sensing something that otherwise escapes logics of common sense. For Rancière, this is the purview of an aesthetic politics insofar as what is sensible (i.e., meaningful) is challenged by what is now sensed as bodily *sensation*.

Indeed, sensation is key to this redistribution, to this repartitioning of the sensible. As Panagia writes in the *Political Life of Sensation*, sensation offers us "an experience of unrepresentability" that "interrupt[s] our conventional ways of perceiving the world and giving it value" (2009, 2). In this way sensation challenges the hermeneutic assumption that things must be meaningful (have sense) in order to count as valuable in the first place. This seemingly counterintuitive position suggests that things and people achieve their value not by the part they already occupy within a given regime of perception, but by asserting their equality when it does not "make sense," when people have become invisible, or when voices have been silenced. The mobilization of Black Lives Matter, for instance, in the face of violence that has become all too commonplace, is one such assertion. It challenges the very limitations of perception within a society that does not "see" black lives *as* mattering and inserts its claim to equality within a social order that is based on a racist regime of visibility (e.g., the racist profiling and stereotypical depictions of black Americans that lead to physical as well as symbolic violence).

Drawing on Rancière, what Panagia brings to the fore is that sensation is precisely that which disrupts our common sense, breaking the chain of "correspondence between perception and signification" (2009, 5). Sensation is not merely a feeling we acquire through a particular sense organ, but akin to Massumi's affect, it is that which we experience beyond the social inscription of feeling. Sensations are precisely those experiences that are unable to be scripted since they are not of the police, but of living bodies. While we might wish to claim that sensations can be "read" through social categories, this is to once again co-opt them in ways that deny their very livingness, their very vitality—in short their unrepresentability.[8] It is precisely because they *are* unrepresentable, and lie outside regimes of perception, that they can enable us to see, hear, and feel the world differently—outside of the totalization of social orders.

Bringing this back to my discussion about educational encounters of enculturation means having to think of how I become "enculturated" in ways that are both *of* and *outside of* regimes of perception, *of* and *outside of* specific distributions of the sensible. What is important to note at this juncture are two things: (1) That inequality does not simply operate on the level of will or intellect, on the one hand, or at the level of language and discourse, on the other. It operates at the very level of bodily perception. As such, any challenge to inequality needs to contend with the sensory level of experience; and (2) that social orders, discursive practices, and norms can never wholly determine how we perceive something. As such, regimes of perception are never absolute; there is always room for the singularity of sensation, always the possibility of an experience that can shock and surprise us. Thus, how does enculturation and our everyday translations of cultural values, beliefs, and traditions into present bodily practices participate in such regimes and how can they, through sensation, redistribute the sensible?

Enculturation, Aesthetic Interruptions, or Remaking Sense as Common

Given both of these dimensions, enculturation shows that how we perceive and sense our environment can be regulated, on the one hand, and that our sensations can also be the source of interrupting such regulation, on the other hand. This, to me, is central to understanding how educational encounters are always involved in an *aesthetic* as well as a *political* relation to culture. Or rather, that the interruptive force of politics requires an aesthetic reworking of sense, as mentioned above.

Education as enculturation enables students and teachers to *translate* their encounters with cultural customs, traditions, and inheritances into ways of living and leading a life with others. This necessarily means that habits, ideals, principles, convictions, civilities, and social behaviors are living, bodily engagements with the world, not intellectual abstractions. Such translations do not simply occur through *critical conversations* with place, thought, belief, and value, as though our relationship to culture were solely (or even primarily) an exercise of rationality and critical judgment. Of course, we do make critical judgments all the time about what views we hold or practices we value; my point is merely that this is not the primary way we come to belong to communities or cultural groups, particularly as children and youth. Instead, we develop attachments and feel belongingness, through complex relational networks that invoke, evoke, and provoke sensations in and of the body—and these networks do so in ways that are frequently not part of our field of awareness, never mind subject to rational scrutiny. As I discussed in the previous chapter in relation to microperceptions, our body responds to elements of our environment as intensities that only subsequently either become the stuff of signification or present us with an obstacle that finds no immediate home in common sense. That is, such intensities can be subsumed into an ongoing cultural narrative or story, or they can actually catalyze another framing of our life and our place within the world as we know it. Thus when students encounter the words of the Bible or Qur'an, the histories of slavery or the Holocaust, the novels of Atwood or the plays of Shakespeare, natural objects such as plants or insects, the bodies of classmates or teachers, or the injunctions or rules of the school, they do so in ways that link their bodily experiences of culture to existing frames of understanding and/or in ways that can create a disjuncture with those very frames. This does not mean that all existing cultural significations are negative and all disjunctures are positive. But what I want to suggest is that it is precisely when disjunctures occur that an interruption into common sense is possible. And this is important since it means that sensations can act to undermine those regimes of perception that currently support inequalities based on colonial, racist, classist, sexist, and ableist practices. From an educational point of view, this allows us to see that enculturation can be about change in ways that do not simply replace one society for another, but actually can engage in the aesthetic, sensory aspects of them through our encounters. Attending to the aesthetic dimensions of our encounters, then, offers us a way of connecting our bodily experiences of culture to a politics of the senses.

One way of conceiving of this connection has been discussed by Shusterman (2012) in his advocacy of somaesthetics as an intervention into regimes of perception at the level of the individual:

> Most ethnic and racial hostility is the product not of rational thought but of deep prejudices that are somatically marked in terms of vague uncomfortable feelings aroused by alien bodies, feelings that are experienced implicitly and thus engrained beneath the level of explicit consciousness. Such prejudices and feelings therefore resist correction by mere discursive

arguments for tolerance, which can be accepted on the rational level without changing the visceral grip of the prejudice. We often deny we even have such prejudices because we do not realize that we feel them, and the first step to controlling them or eventually expunging them is to develop the somatic awareness to recognize them in ourselves. (2012, 29)

What Shusterman makes clear here is that any attempt to deal with overcoming inequality needs both to understand that the "visceral grip" of prejudice is a real, embodied response to a perceived difference, and to see that an interruption of such responses requires a commensurate shift in bodily sensibilities. Shusterman advocates "somatic awareness" as a mode of overcoming our individual and personal attitudes and dispositions.

This idea of "somaesthetic awareness" is developed in his book *Body Consciousness* (2008) to include a way of seeing patterns of reaction and their physical manifestations, and becoming observant of how our bodies hold, express, produce, and constitute certain emotions. It demands focusing on such things as breathing, movement, pulsations, muscle contractions, and the like. Bodily awareness practices such as yoga or Feldenkrais Method are seen by Shusterman as "disciplines of somatic education" through which we can "learn to read one's own somaesthetic signs" and develop skills of self-observation (2008, 121). For Shusterman, these practices are central to further developing somaesthetic control, such as learning to regulate breathing to relax fear. "Once emotions are thematized in consciousness, we can take a critical distance and thus both understand and manage them with greater mastery (which does not mean with greater repression)" (2008, 121). This form of distancing is basic to many forms of Buddhist meditation practice, such as vipassana and mindfulness, as it is with other traditions including sport psychology, kinesthetics, and musical training. For Shusterman, addressing the "visceral grip" of prejudice means recognizing and paying attention to how our bodies are entangled with ongoing cultural practices at a very basic level of sensation. And it offers a model for not only coming to some form of understanding about our responses to and participation in cultures of inequality, but also seeks to give us a practice through which we can interrupt, interrogate, and begin to redress the habits of what we have bodily taken for granted.[9]

As a meditator and yoga practitioner myself, I value Shusterman's suggestions for how we can begin to "see" our bodies anew—as incarnations of habits, customs, and indeed prejudices which are often invisible to us. In this, it can indeed shift what is perceptible and act as a bulwark against, or a fuel for challenging, specific regimes of perception. That is, this new way of seeing simultaneously recognizes the body as something that both participates in and yet cannot be reduced to discursive norms. The socially normative ways our bodies are encoded are not insurmountable. Somaesthetics, like other practices such as yoga and meditation (along indeed with some forms of psychoanalysis and therapy), presents one way of becoming mindful of those practices and attuning to their patterns of arising in order to gain some skill and insight which moves us away from the reactivity that can be deleterious to ourselves and others. That is, in my attending aesthetically to my body, the idea is not necessarily to break with all habitual ways of thinking and feeling (this would be impossible), but to bring a sense of awareness to them so they do not rule over us. We thus come to our encounters with an expanded sense of ourselves and our place within them.

While I do not want to question what this can offer to developing a sense of one's own awareness and attention, and the ways in which one's individual actions do indeed matter in the world, I do think there is a risk of seeing somaesthetics as an individual exercise that is not equipped to deal fully with the complexity of enculturation, nor with the political aspects of perceptibility. Thus, although somaesthetics can nudge us out of normative constraints of the body (Butler) and socially coded framings of sense (Howes and Classon), it requires moving beyond its focus on the individual as the key source of transformation if it is to be effective. While the argument could be made that if each of us was indeed more aware and attentive to interrupting the "visceral grip" of prejudice then all of society would be rid of it, I think such an argument elides the very relationalities that constitute sense as common and cultural in the first place.

Another way of connecting our bodily experiences to a politics of the senses is to draw on Rancière's understanding of the distribution of the sensible discussed above. This means not taking the *individual* as the starting point, but the *relational aspects of our encounters themselves*. In line with the relational ontology this book espouses, this means that while the singular subject of sensation plays a crucial role in the politics of the senses, the politics of the senses does not begin with the individual. In fact, even within certain meditation traditions, such as Zen, it is the nondual and interdependent relation with the world that is at the heart of practice. So, this does not mean that somaesthetic practices cannot inform political activity, merely that we need to align them with a more relational, nonindividual approach.[10]

Interrupting regimes of common sense in order to create new communities of sense means not that there is an individual body that "acts" to transform the world, but that there are relations between us, between bodies and elements of their environment, that shift the frame of sense-making itself. That is, to return to my discussion of Sheets-Johnstone in the previous chapter, bodies are formed and deformed through their interrelationships with the physical environment. As such, these thoroughly corporeal relations form a significant basis for an interruptive politics of the senses. To reiterate, our very bodies *take form* in relation to what (and who) it is we are encountering and we create nonlinguistic concepts through our movement in space. As such they are open and susceptible to elements of the environment in ways that can easily lend themselves to theories of socialization (a given environment will socially code the body so that it feels like second nature, or common sense). But this is only one side of the story. Because our bodies are living and sensing entities, there is also a built-in unpredictability to their formations and the kinds of nonlinguistic thinking they can engage in. Being exposed to something that is not part of one's usual way of sensing, our bodies can feel differently and think differently, move differently and act differently. Encounters can jolt us into new modes of being in the world.

This is the "perceptual shock" that Rancière names as part of an interruptive politics of the senses. In conceiving of interruption on aesthetic terms, through practices that cannot be contained within normative modes of intelligibility, Rancière draws our attention not only to the function of art per se, but to the art-full ways that challenges to common sense are posed, since they cannot rely on our regular logics of representation and perceptual sense. Aesthetic practices are sensory encounters that work at the level of viscera. They challenge us to feel otherwise. And like all shocks, we are left wondering what it is about, seeking languages, frames of reference, connections to others, to make sense of the sensory relationship.

For educational encounters to be interruptive, to enable enculturation as that which necessarily exists beyond socialization, they need to embed a different grammar, a different style, a different mode of communication that shakes up their intelligibility. They need to queer the encounter with objects of study, making them strange and skewing the regular relationship to them ever so slightly. For instance, the art collective Sisters Hope, whom I introduced in the Introduction, create installations in upper secondary schools where regular classes of math, geography, biology, and history are taught through encounters involving touch and movement, including dance and tactile experiences with different surfaces. This is not in order to make a concept or idea more fun but to offer an alternative framework of sense that can challenge accepted modalities of knowledge generation and the language we use to express it. This is the aesthetic dimension of educational encounters: to be able to fashion opportunities for new modes of sense in creative ways. This of course goes against the grain of normative demands to "just make sense," which can be seen as a call to maintain the social order which depends on a given regime of sense to exist. The opposite of this is not to become obtuse or elitist. Quite the contrary, since being socialized into the social order itself is always about the regulation of senses in practices of exclusion. Instead, the point of interruption is to invite students to "make sense" as an activity of renewal and possibility. As an educator, this requires having faith in what sense students can make together when they are given the chance to do so.

Creating new communities of sense means challenging the very forms of relationality (not simply our individual attitudes or awareness) upon which the social order of inequality relies as "common sense." This is done through staging, designing, and curating encounters that engage the senses in unexpected ways, drawing students into new relations with elements of the environment through their bodily experiences. For if the inequality of "education" is to be challenged, then we need to invest in educational practices that interrupt the established ways we sense the world. The next chapter is about looking more closely at these new forms of encounters and the relations they make possible.

Chapter Four

Forms and Formations of Encounters

> In observing contemporary art practices, we ought to talk of "formations" rather than "forms." Unlike an object that is closed in on itself by the intervention of a style and a signature, present-day art shows that form only exists in the encounter and in the dynamic relationship enjoyed by an artistic proposition with other formations, artistic or otherwise.
>
> —Nicolas Bourriaud, *Relational Aesthetics*

On the face of it, contemporary art practices to which Nicolas Bourriaud refers above (such as those grouped under participatory, socially engaged, community-based, or "new genre public" art)[1] do not offer an immediate parallel with educational ones. After all, the work of the artist is quite distinct from the work of the educator, as is the purpose of art compared to that of education. Nonetheless, when it comes to their respective practices, both are involved in staging and even curating encounters, and in this they rely on creating the conditions for certain forms of relationality to take place.[2] Thus, contemporary art practices—and more particularly, the language we use to understand those practices—offer, to my mind, a useful entry point for considering educational encounters as aesthetic and relational forms.

When we think about form from an educational point of view, it seems obvious perhaps to frame it primarily in terms of how a classroom, lecture hall, or museum space is organized physically, spatially, and visually: the layout of furniture; the seating arrangement; the location of the windows; the color of the walls; and the placement of books, pictures, maps, and other artifacts around a room. On this account, the form education takes involves designing, planning, and curating space. Understood in this way, the form acts like a container which physically holds or encloses educational encounters; it is a space that is styled in such a way so as to produce an aesthetic/educational effect. Teaching a subject or educating in an early childhood setting, for example, does not occur without some attention being paid to form, from the actual objects of study to environmental materials. Indeed, in the introduction to this book, I mentioned a particular art project I was a participant in: *The Boarding School* by Danish art collective Sisters Hope. As an immersive installation, Sisters Hope created a curated space by lining the walls of the museum with red velvet drapery, infusing the rooms with soundscape, and mobilizing specific materials in the environment in the teaching of certain "classes." Nonetheless, the form of education on offer here was more than the sum of these spatial designs.

While the physical organization and appearance of space is important to encounters—we see this all the time in how the physicality of classroom space can be experienced as more or less inclusive for minorities and the differently abled, more or less welcoming of certain activities over others, and more or less respectful of traditions and histories—and while educators can indeed exert some influence over physical space at least insofar as they are able to design it consciously within given physical structures (about which more will be said below), my emphasis here moves away from the view that educational encounters simply transpire *within* already defined forms, such as buildings, rooms, or activity centers. Instead, I propose that educational encounters are *dynamically constitutive* of those forms, including what we usually think of as a classroom, a pedagogical activity, or style of teaching. Indeed, the form of *The Boarding School* did not lie simply in the space that was designed in/as the museum/school, but in what we were doing as participants together and in the relational intensity of our encounters. More importantly, it was these encounters that gave form to the space we were in. In this there was no artwork called *The Boarding School* without the participants who created it through their aesthetic, sensory relations with elements of their environment.[3] Whereas in the previous chapter I examined the aesthetics of sensation as a potentially political challenge to current regimes of perception, this chapter explores how sensation is an aesthetic relation that participates in creating new forms—or more precisely formations—of education, new formations, that is, of enculturation and becoming. This approach, as I explore in more detail in chapter 6, allows us to think about online education as potentially creating precisely such formations; that is, by uncoupling form from the "givenness" of a room or lecture hall, we can see how relationships actually matter to generating educational spaces even through digital encounters.

As indicated in the epigraph, Bourriaud's understanding of art practices as form*ations*, rather than forms, turns toward the idea that it is *through relationships* that something comes into being as substance, object, or thing. This returns us to a key point echoed throughout this book: that entities do not simply make relationships, rather it is relationships that make entities. So while one usually speaks of form as shape, contour, and matter, formation unveils the sense of relational dynamism and process that lies at the heart of what we usually think of as thing or substance. In line with the relational perspective I am taking here, Bourriaud's understanding of artworks as formations further opens up questions of importance for education, since it directly deals with how form *emerges* from a field of encounters, from, that is, our aesthetic, sensual relations with each other, things, and other animate beings. As discussed previously in chapter 2, touching and being touched by the elements of our environment indeed form, deform, and transform the very physicality of our corporeal selves. Our bodies are thus *of* the environment and not merely *in* it. In light of the political and aesthetic dimensions of sensation outlined in chapter 3, we have seen how those environments are framed by regimes of perception, which set the initial conditions for how bodies are not only "seen," but also how they are felt, experienced, and take shape. More importantly, I discussed how sensation itself can contribute to altering those regimes in order to create new communities of sense. What this chapter aims to do is to argue more extensively for understanding how our everyday educational forms of encounter embody particular *relations of sensation* that enable precisely such opportunities to arise. Specifically, I do so through exploring the pedagogical act of teaching itself.

This perspective of viewing the relational element of form (that is, viewing forms *as* formations) enables those of us in education to make two interrelated moves: First, it allows us to analyze forms in terms of the relations they support. In this move, we can examine existing forms of practice to see how they favor certain educational and aesthetic relations over others—that is, we can analyze teaching practices and classroom configurations in order to deduce, for example, patterns of dominance, cooperation, openness, or constriction. The second move operates inductively and enables us to consider how relations give rise to a particular educational form. For example, how the relations that inform the positioning of students' and teachers' bodies in the classroom or the sensory encounters with objects, gestures, and rituals that make up schooling life create pedagogical places and spaces. That is, it allows us to see how relations can generate—however provisionally—a certain form of educational practice. Engaging in both of these analytic moves, I focus on offering an aesthetic reading of a common educational form that sees the teacher as the one who embodies a gesture and posture of pointing. In this vein, I explore how the relatively simple (and popular) form of the teacher as one who directs students' attention by pointing at something is suggestive of a particular network of relations. The next part of the chapter develops some alternative ways of thinking about formations of encounter, exploring Erin Manning's ideas of touch, and how teachers might begin to see their work as curatorial of such formations. Before turning to these discussions, I first outline Bourriaud's relational aesthetics as a framework for approaching educational encounters and discuss some examples to illustrate key points from contemporary art practice. As chapter 7 explores in more detail in terms of a specific climate art project, *Ice Watch* by Olafur Eliasson, such relational art practices also demonstrate how aesthetic encounters generate possibilities for becoming.

Relational Aesthetics: A Language for Educational Encounters

The art critic and theorist Nicolas Bourriaud seeks to refashion an aesthetic language to complement what he sees as a relational turn in art practices since the 1990s. This turn is evident in a wide range of projects that have at their center engaging participants in new encounters and situations, often (although not exclusively) through collaborative, dialogical, and participant-led means. Such projects frequently involve individuals in some type of community-based intervention that disrupts one's sense of the given. And many projects, especially those falling under the category of socially engaged art practice, have as their aim to challenge relations of power that factor into patterns of social inequality. Thus art along these lines does not primarily fit modernist expectations aimed at producing a recognizable artform such as painting, sculpture, or architecture, but instead has at its heart the active transformation of social relationships through aesthetic experience. Lars Bang Larsen (2006), a well-known art historian and curator, refers to such projects in terms of "social aesthetics" in which the "artwork involves a utilitarian or practical aspect that gives a sense of purpose and direct involvement" (172). These art projects are marked by their experimental and evolving character and offer emergent ways of working with communities, individuals, institutions, and organizations. For Bourriaud, they particularly explore alternative ways of being in the world by highlighting relation as a central issue for art and are consequently more focused on their collaborative function than they are on their objective form.[4] In this sense, many scholars have made the link between contemporary art practices and "educational" or "pedagogical" practices of experimentation.[5]

For Bourriaud, as a result of this relational shift, art is "unreadable" (2002, 7) through conventional twentieth-century aesthetics since it disrupts the meaning of those issues that are normally located within the purview of modernity: issues such as form, encounter, and private symbolic space. His purpose, therefore, is to develop a new aesthetic language for reading these new art practices and introduces terms and vocabulary that highlight their specifically *relational* nature. For Bourriaud, artworks are not solely about objective formal properties but invite us into an alternative set of social relations: "Each particular artwork is a proposal to live in a shared world, and the work of every artist is a bundle of relations with the world, giving rise to other relations, and so on and so forth, ad infinitum" (22). Thus for Bourriaud, art is a practice that resists foundational claims to essence: "Artistic activity is a game, whose forms, patterns and functions develop and evolve according to periods and social contexts; it is not an immutable essence" (11).

The modern political era, in contrast to the one since the 1990s, linked aesthetics to ideas of emancipation and freedom of individuals and peoples. Growing out of the Enlightenment, modern aesthetics is therefore not unlike modern education in this regard. Both were thought to open up possibilities for living in the world in a better way; and even if modern education was focused on progress and art on promoting new sensibilities, new ways of engaging the world, each was nonetheless charged with the creation of new intellectual and imaginary horizons, respectively. Nonetheless, as scholars across numerous disciplines have shown, such modernist assumptions also operated from an exclusionary vantage point: emancipation and freedom were shaped within white, Eurocentric, patriarchal, and ableist notions of subjectivity.

Although not writing explicitly of the underbelly of modernity, Bourriaud does mention that the very task of art has shifted in recent times: "Art was intended to prepare and announce a future world: today it is modelling possible universes. . . . Otherwise put, the role of artworks is no longer to form imaginary and utopian realities, but to actually be ways of living and models of action within the existing real, whatever the scale chosen by the artist" (13). Continuing with this theme of contemporary art's breaking with modernist presuppositions, Bourriaud identifies that "the possibility of a *relational* art (an art taking as its theoretical horizon the realm of human interactions and its social context, rather than the assertion of an independent and *private* symbolic space), points to a radical upheaval of the aesthetic, cultural and political goals introduced by modern art" (14).

What Bourriaud stresses here is that it is not simply that relational art challenges work which has come before it—indeed, the canonical trajectory of art history is full of refusals, rebellions, and recuperations of tradition; artworks have always enacted their own translations of legacies. Rather it is that these contemporary artworks challenge the very conditions by which art is made and becomes readable within the modernist project. In fact Bourriaud defines art as "an activity consisting in producing relationships with the world with the help of signs, forms, actions and objects" (107). Relational art is thereby not marked by its purely aesthetic principles (aesthetic here meaning theoretical or philosophical principles of art), but by its social practices—and as I see it, aesthetic (read: sensory) encounters—which give rise to a politics of aesthetics as one centered on new possibilities for coexistence. Indeed, for Bourriaud, coexistence is a key criterion for understanding relational art: "All works of art produce a model of sociability, which transposes reality or might be conveyed in it. So there is a question we are entitled to ask in front of any aesthetic production: 'Does this work permit me to enter into dialogue? Could I exist, and how, in the space it defines?' A form is more or less democratic" (109).[6] The art practice Bourriaud writes of puts relation at the center of its concern; its political challenge derives not only from mobilizing relationships that counter particular structures or norms but also from interrogating the relationships through which structures and norms are themselves enabled and maintained. "Contemporary art is definitely developing a political project when it endeavors to move into the relational realm by turning it into an issue" (17). Thus the transformative character of art, for Bourriaud, is located in turning relationality itself into an aesthetic and political concern in order to create new forms of (primarily human) relations. Hence Bourriaud can conceive of form in relation to democracy, in relation to what relationality the artwork invites or makes possible. In this sense, art becomes "a state of encounter" (18). That is, art engages its participants in a situation that names its field of operation as such: the situation *is* the art form.[7]

As a state of encounter, art *enacts* form through its very relationality, and it is worth mentioning some examples to get a sense of how diverse such enactments can be. For instance, art projects such as Lisa Gross's *League of Kitchens* in New York, which brings together people from minority communities around cooking; Stephanie Springgay's *Artists' Soup Kitchen* in Toronto, which became a lunch time gathering place for artists; and Rirkrit Tiravanija's *pad thai* in which the artist cooked food for gallery visitors create states of encounter that take their form through the relations of preparing, sharing, and eating food. Each artwork involves people, from the museum-going public to members of minority communities and artists, participating in new forms of relationality. While these projects stage these relations in different ways (the artist is the chef in an exhibition setting, recent immigrants prepare meals together in their own homes, and artists create conversational experiences in a restaurant environment), the point is that these artworks instantiate forms that challenge our preconceptions of conventional hierarchies and the social relations that sustain them.

Other examples aside from kitchens and food are plentiful. Mammalian Diving Reflex is a Toronto art collective led by Darren O'Donnell that has worked with youth in communities and schools to create alternative and often playful ways of being together. In *Nightwalks with Teenagers*, teens lead other teens whom they do not know on street tours that displace their regular sense of being and embodiment. The art practice allows for a more radical play with sociality; they inhabit an alternative place together, at once forming new modes of relationality and new ways of being in the world that position them as authorities while interrogating dominant perceptions and cultural representations of "youth on streets at night."

The 2015 winner of the Turner Prize, Assemble is an art cooperative that worked with residents in an inner-city neighborhood of Liverpool that was undergoing a ruthless gentrification process with the demolition of houses and along with it a sense of community. The cooperative led a project whereby residents learned the arts of restoration and various skilled crafts to recapture and redeploy the use of different places in the neighborhood. In so doing they changed the policies affecting community planning, altered the landscape of their day-to-day lives, and came to inhabit an entirely different relation to each other.

Silver Action (2013) is a work by American artist Suzanne Lacy who is known for working with different communities to shape emergent collaborative projects. In this piece, she brings older women together to coconstruct events centered on their remembered and lived participation in political protest. One of the final public events (after a long process involving the sharing of their experiences in more intimate settings) entailed individuals sitting at tables and narrating their stories to another person who types them into a computer, the text of which is simultaneously projected on the walls on a large scale. Their collective stories form a digital tapestry, turning the walls into testimonies, compelling those who witness them also to witness the transformative moment of calling these women activists into being. The project itself is an enactment of relations that challenge normative constructions of older women and their work in shaping a political landscape.

To return to Bourriaud, while art practices such as these may challenge existing relations, they do so because they are *generating* new forms through the relational encounters that they stage. Indeed, the artworks mentioned above do not necessarily share very much between them: each works with different communities, participants, settings, and types of engagement. Yet, they each create alternative relational formations: that is, the work is not about showing others (viewers, spectators) an alternative point of view, but about offering an opportunity to embody alternative social relationships for the participants themselves. Relational art is no mere spectator event but is an attempt at offering a "perceptual shock," to revisit Rancière's phrase. Its alternative universes not only interrupt current regimes of perception, but optimally enable new forms of sensory encounter, new modalities of subjectivity. This is why relational art, as Bourriaud puts it, is more about formations rather than forms: "form only exists in the encounter and in the dynamic relationship enjoyed by an artistic proposition with other formations, artistic or otherwise" (2002, 21).

Importantly, then, form seen *as* formation opens up questions not only for art practices but for educational practices as well. It allows for a rethinking of educational encounters as embodying relationships that carry the potential to transform our ways of thinking about teaching, learning, and curriculum. In calling attention to "states of encounter," Bourriaud also invites us to consider how we, as educators, *curate* educational encounters along the lines of setting in motion a series of relations, not unlike what socially engaged artists do, that engage bodies in a variety of sensory moments. Without collapsing the differences between curation, art making, and teaching, as Claudia Ruitenberg (2015) rightly warns against, it is worth considering how forms of teaching can both be shaped by educators and enact relationships beyond their intentionality. As relational art practices reveal, one does not know what the artwork will be without the participants who do in fact make it. Similarly, teaching embodies forms of encounters that can enable, privilege, shut down, and question certain sensory relationships with elements in the environment not through what one is purporting to do, but through the very bodily enactment of the form of teaching itself.

From Form to Formation of Teaching

There is something profoundly banal about portrayals of teaching. From famous works of art to Google searches, normalized figurations of the teacher draw a surprisingly similar picture: the teacher is recognizable as one who stands and points, with hand and finger gesturing toward something beyond the frame of the student. There is an iconographic stability in this image of the teacher, from Raphael's *The School of Athens* of 1511, to Jan Steen's school paintings in the seventeenth century, to the numerous contemporary photographs of Western classrooms found on the web. In pointing, the teacher not only seems to know (about) something outside the students' repertoire of experience, but the pointing itself becomes the gestural form that defines the activity *as* teaching and that allows us to identify who the teacher is in a given image.[8] Pointing also carries significant power, both in light of the teacher's relation to students and in light of its iconographic symbolism in systems of oppression: pointing often acts to tell others who they are or who they should be, displaying at times a thoroughly modernist and colonialist impulse. The "form" of the teacher who points is one example of what Lovisa Bergdahl and Elisabet Langmann (2018b) refer to as "geometries of educational relations": that is, the postures, positionalities, and gestures that make up our physical encounters are reflective of and promote certain relations between teachers, students, and subject matter.

Whilst one might be tempted to dismiss this form of teaching as reflecting a traditional transmission model of instruction, it has nonetheless emerged quite strongly in recent scholarship focused on reclaiming teaching beyond the notion of instruction that so often permeates current instrumentalist accounts of education (Biesta 2017; Säfström 2021). Some scholars within this renewed attention to teaching write specifically of the importance of the teacher as someone who directs students' attention to "stimulate interest" (Masschelein and Simons 2013, 86; see also Rytzler 2021; Vlieghe and Zamojski 2019). For these authors, the teacher is one who points out to students what is to be attended to and plays a pivotal role in enabling them to make a relationship to whatever object of study is at hand. "Pedagogical responsibility lies not in aiming directly for the (the needs of) the child or student, but in things and one's relation to those things, that is, the relation that the teacher as pedagogue has to these things" (Masschelein and Simons 2013, 86). However, a few questions arise if we think of this practice of attention-making not just in figurative terms but as literal and embodied, seen not only through the *form* of the teacher who points but also as a *formation* that embodies a particular set of sensory relations: What is such a form of teaching presuming about educational relations? What kinds of bodily, sensory encounters does it make (or not) possible?

It is important to contextualize this form of teaching within the broader perspective of education being argued for in these authors' work. Although they do not collectively speak of the form of teaching, as I do here, they do write of the school as a form that emerges out of specific "scholastic practices." For instance, Masschelein and Simons (whose work is central in the area) write that practices of study and attention are what create the form of school.[9] As a form, the school can thereby be found in a multitude of spaces and places and not just within the four walls of a building we call a school through social convention. Thus, wherever those scholastic practices arise, the form of school likewise arises. This understanding of form draws on, as I do here, Isabelle Stengers's (2005) notion of "ecology of practices." The school can only take the form of a school if the practices making it a school are present—otherwise it becomes an empty idea. However, when viewed from the perspective of formations, the emphasis necessarily shifts away from *practices* of study and attention to the *relations that subtend or inform those practices*. What is central to my mind is not just *that* study and attention are practiced, but *how* they do so actually matters to the creation of the form itself. As Bourriaud (2002) points out, what is central to formation is understanding how it participates in creating states of encounter—that is, the relational contact certain practices limit, make possible, or challenge. In this sense, the formation of the school is continually emergent and dependent upon the relations students have to things, ideas, and others *as* they study and attend. While this seems to echo Masschelein and Simons's own view of teaching as a set of relations (see the quote above), my point is that because teaching is a bodily (indeed sensory) formation, it *sets into motion* relationships that are not fully accounted for within their conceptualization of school or teaching. Most importantly for my discussion is that it is not only the relationships between students and objects of study that matter, but also the relationships that are afforded by the form of teaching being enacted. The formation of the school, it seems to me, must also therefore be deeply dependent on which relations teaching makes possible or not.

For Masschelein and Simons teachers are engaged in putting objects "on the table" in an act of suspension, disentangling these objects from their "worldly meaning" to allow them to circulate anew in a common space of study and inquiry. As they rightfully acknowledge, teaching involves expanding students' horizons beyond their everyday concerns, stimulating new areas of interest. It involves teachers pointing out to students something that students can explore, examine, and inquire into that is neither dependent on the object's "ordinary" use in society nor determined by the student's social background, identity, or context. As discussed in chapter 1, for Masschelein and Simons the act of suspension means that students are able to encounter objects of study freed from the predetermination (and resultant prejudices) of ability and interest that is so often linked to their social positioning. In this, the idea of suspension helps us move away from deficit models that frequently plague students coming from minority or "disadvantaged" communities. While the act of suspension they advocate allows us to think about educating students on terms beyond their social contexts, it nonetheless poses some difficulties for thinking about the complexity of encounters between students and objects of study, which necessarily involve living bodies that are already part of a network of relations and that translate across borders between home and school, between thought and feeling, between past and future. By this I mean that bodies are emplaced and entangled with their environments; they cannot entirely be freed from these contexts even while they should be freed from the prejudice and discrimination that accompany those contexts. My concern, as I discussed in chapter 1, is that suspension does not deviate sufficiently away from traditional models of teaching in recognizing the complexity of students' relational lives. Masschelein and Simons's view seems to conjure a figure of the teacher as a body who indicates and gestures toward the object of study which they have placed on the proverbial table. Similarly, Vlieghe, and Zamojski (2019) speak of teachers as literally pointing to the materiality of subject matter in their idea of a "thing-centred pedagogy": for them, teaching as pointing is a gesture of love for the world that is opened up to students. In these accounts, the attention of students is directed toward the subject matter and its object of study (e.g., a map, a poem, or an equation), and pointing it out ostensibly acts in a manner that detaches the object from its use and meaning outside of the school, wrested from the social lives of teachers and students themselves. While I wholeheartedly agree that students should be able to generate exploratory relations—and perhaps even develop passions!—about those objects of study that teachers make available to them, my query is that if teachers indeed are to offer an exploratory space for students to make knowledges that are new to them, then I wonder if pointing, showing, and indicating are the gestural forms most helpful to such tasks.

Indeed, as queer theorist Eve Kosofsky Sedgwick (2003) recounts in a playful anecdote about her cat, pointing as a form of teaching actually displays an ambiguity that lies at the heart of teaching itself. Located within a chapter entitled the "Pedagogy of Buddhism," Sedgwick (2003) writes: "Whenever I want my cat to look at something instructive—a full moon, say, or a photograph of herself—a predictable choreography ensues. I point at the thing I want her to look at, and she, roused to curiosity, fixes her attention on the tip of my extended index finger and begins to explore it with delicate sniffs" (168). This "scene of failed pedagogy," for Sedgwick, not only means that she is "no better at learning not to point than her cat is at learning not to sniff" (168), it also signals a long-standing pedagogical paradox within the heart of Buddhist teachings—and I would suggest within the form of teaching as pointing more generally.

Within the Mahayana tradition, as Sedgwick outlines it, lies an understanding that while we might learn from the words of Buddha's sutras, they themselves should be considered merely as "the finger that points to the moon." This well-known metaphor suggests that the words of the sutras are not to be taken literally but are to be seen as directing our attention to something beyond what is being said. The words are not ends-in-themselves, even if students of Buddhism sometimes confuse the finger for the moon, as does Sedgwick's cat, in adhering to literal doctrinal readings of those teachings. So far, this would seem to be in line with the formulation of teaching as that which directs attention to something beyond itself. However, complications arise when we consider that the "gesture of indication" is not simply a benign *form* but a *performative act* of teaching. As Sedgwick notes, "To put the issue another way, the overattached learner—my cat, say—is mistaking the kind of speech act, or can we just say the kind of act, that pointing is: for me the relevant illocution is 'to indicate,' while for her, it is 'to proffer'" (170). Pointing is not simply a form, for Sedgwick, but an action that signals a *movement* of relations between teacher, student/cat, and object; the teacher points to an object, and if the student understands this as a performative signal she then discovers the object that lies at the end of the gestural trajectory. Pointing is thus an action that both displays something beyond one's own finger and yet in so doing displays something more concrete than this: the gesture itself. One can say along with Sedgwick that it would be a mistake to view pointing as a form of proffering, as though cats (or students) merely have misunderstood the intentionality of the gesture that is made for their benefit (e.g., the ubiquitous phrase, "students don't get it" is often referring to this supposed misunderstanding). However, I think what Sedgwick opens up for consideration is a more complex understanding of the form of pointing, which to my mind actually relies on this misunderstanding for its own authority, its own directionality. The gesture calls attention to itself in a way that paradoxically locates "indicating" and "proffering" along the same bodily register. That is, with this form of teaching, students need to attend to the pointing *in order to* attend to the object; they need to pay attention to the physicality of the gesture and to the teacher's body who is making it. The relation between teacher, student, and object presents us with a "choreography," as Sedgwick puts it, a moving formation that is not simply about whether a student "traces" the teacher's finger to its destination point, like a rainbow to its pot of gold, but also involves the relational, bodily conditions under which such "tracing" can even begin.

In other words, it presumes a certain bodily encounter between teacher and student (and an awareness of that encounter) so that, in turn, an encounter with the object of study can be initiated (so perhaps it is not so much that the "students don't get it" but that they either have not attended to the authority of the finger at all, or understand all too well that they need to pay attention to the finger very carefully *as* a symbol of authority; for in terms of some teacher-student dynamics it's often not the pot of gold that matters, but the rainbow itself).

Another aspect of this form of teaching as pointing is important to bear in mind from the vantage of the body, and this concerns the "uprightness" from which the teacher points: the literal erectness of teaching. The teacher who points is both literally and figuratively the one who, in directing students' attention, does so from a position of height, echoing a strong European humanist tradition, which finds its ultimate expression, perhaps, in Pestalozzi's "object lesson." Critiquing the "rectitude" of the teacher, as put forth primarily by Masschelein and Simons (2013), Bergdahl and Langmann (2018b) draw particular attention to posture as key to understanding different modes of subjectivity in education. Following Adriana Cavarero (2016), they see rectitude as mapping onto a history of particularly masculine figurations of teaching. Rectitude signals for Cavarero (2016) an "egocentric verticality" (11) that has masqueraded as the epitome of the subject throughout philosophy as well as the humanities and the arts more generally. It relies on a form—what Cavarero calls a "postural geometry" (11)—of standing upright and independent; a form which denies the relational aspect of subjectivity. Drawing on her line of thought, Bergdahl and Langmann (2018b) consider a posture of inclination as an alternative to rectitude and what that can mean for teaching and for reimagining scholastic practices. Here they excavate inclination as a maternal posture from its subjugation under "homo erectus": "The maternal posture we are suggesting is the posture of someone who is aware of an *originary indebtedness* to what and who is 'other,' 'after' or 'before.' Here, the most truthful response to a complex content matter or question might be this: 'I lean towards x,' 'I support my argument on y' or 'I am inclined to think x'" (Bergdahl and Langmann 2018b, 322).

Inclination calls for a different kind of understanding of the educational relation than rectitude does. Inclination here works against a presumption of uprightness in its movement toward someone or something and sees attention as less about visual focus, or mental concentration, and more about a "reaching out"—from the Latin *a-tendere*—with the "tenderness" of touch. Indeed inclination is more about a horizontal plane of teaching that is supportive of students than it is a vertical one whose task is to initiate students into the world "so that they can begin forming themselves" (Masschelein and Simons 2013, 144). For Bergdahl and Langmann (2018b), this suggests a lack of acknowledgment of the relational (and I would say entangled) aspects of teaching. This does not mean that postures of rectitude do not promote their own educational relations *in actuality*, based as they are on particular dynamics of authority, but unlike postures of inclination, they do not acknowledge relations themselves as central to their concept of teaching.

Taking a look at Rembrandt's (c. 1635) drawing of a child learning to walk, one can see inclination in action. In this educational encounter, two women lean toward a young child between them in a gesture that is both supportive and potentially open. The arm of the one on the left extending outward, directing not the child's attention to an object but opening toward something indefinite, while her other hand, along with that of the second woman, holds the child and offers stability in these early steps. While we could say that the outward-seeking gesture of the woman's arm is either merely an aesthetic decision on the part of Rembrandt to balance the composition or that it is yet again trying to direct the child's attention, this would be to reduce the gesture itself to a static one of pointing. In fact, the whole drawing is about balance in movement, about tending to the wobbly infant, about the relationality that constitutes walking. It requires each woman to touch and be touched by the child, just as the child is part of the similar dynamic of touching and being touched by two women. Teaching a child to walk is not about pointing something out from a position of uprightness that the child is then to pay attention to, but a bending, tending, and attending gesture that balances between the present and the future, between stillness and movement. It is powerfully suggestive of the relation of attunement to the child's movement that is required to keep the child from falling (see figure 4.1).

A posture of pointing and rectitude is also deeply paradoxical. It is a form of teaching that is never merely about the target object to which it is pointing, but also an expression of movement: an arm raising, a finger lifting. A teacher's body can only assume the form of

Figure 4.1. Rembrandt, *Two Women Teaching a Child to Walk*, drawing, c. 1635.

pointing through enacting certain movements—and relationships. As stated above, the teacher's pointing does not simply indicate the object statically as a street sign, say, would; rather it is a directional, purposive movement. Unlike inclination, however, pointing is a movement that does not recognize itself as such, since the student is to pay attention to the object being pointed at and not to the movement of the finger doing the pointing. Pointing in this sense erases its own movement and seemingly functions symbolically as opposed to corporeally—the arm or finger of the teacher's body acting as a cipher for the object to which students are to pay attention. It is a movement commanding interest as opposed to a movement of support; a movement away from the person-student toward the object-thing. And although it poses as a bridge between students and the object of study, it does so by promoting a form of teaching that ignores its own relationality, its own formation, and also thereby risks ignoring its own responsibility in the conditions it is creating for students' becoming and transformation through education. By this I mean that whether or not teaching takes the form of rectitude or inclination, what it cannot escape is its own movement and the possibilities and limitations it opens up physically and aesthetically for students to experience themselves differently.

As I discuss in the next section, this reticence to conceive of movement as part of teaching is in part based on a myth of stillness in educational encounters, taking their form as static; even the most rectitudinous of teachers who point with little animation are always performing and enacting animate relations that say more than what they are pointing to. Moreover, as Sedgwick (2003) notes, there is a "choreography" inherent to pedagogy and, as any dancer knows, choreographies involve bodies that move, relate, sense, and touch.

Moving from Stillness

Stillness is often associated with paying attention in education, and thus it is no surprise that the form of teaching as pointing cannot conceive of its own movement as central to what and how students encounter the world as educational. As Erin Manning (2016), whose work focuses on the processual role that movement plays in creating new formations of being and becoming, writes: "Most of our education systems are based on starting from stillness. We learn in chairs. We associate concentration with being quiet. We discourage the movement of thought we call daydreaming, particularly in the context of 'learning.' We consider the immanent movements of doodling to be a distraction. We are told not to fidget. Reason is aligned with keeping the body still" (Manning 2016, 122). Recognizing stillness as a myth opens up possibilities for reconsidering the processual force of teaching. As a Buddhist meditator, I know all too well that stillness is more a state of mind than it is a total absence of movement; in its awareness of the breath, for example, the mind knows the body is never completely still. Such stillness only comes with death and even then the physical body is consumed by bacteria, insects, and other life forms; it is never static. In everyday life, even postures we think of as still are physically complex activities. Take standing, the exemplary posture of rectitude, for example: "Standing still requires constant correction. These are not conscious corrections. They are virtual micromovements that move through the feeling of standing still. When these micromovements are felt as such, they take over the event of standing, and you experience co-contraction: you lose your balance" (Manning 2012, 43).

Instead of seeing stillness as opposed to movement, Manning rephrases stillness as itself an action: a "movement that is stilling" (2012, 43). Stillness takes on a form that is never, ironically, still. This shift means understanding that "stillness is always on its way to movement" (2012, 43); it is not a complete absence of movement, but instead involves a host of smaller movements that are barely perceptible. Worst of it is that when we try to deny the movement behind the veil of stillness, as we sometimes do in yoga postures, it can no longer sustain itself: "Asking you to stand still is like asking you to become aware of your special characteristic. Why does it feel so punitive? Perhaps because we think we should not move. Because we believe we should have the capacity to stop. But we can't. And so we move, and we try to hide that moving by ignoring the movement moving. But the more we ignore the movement within stillness, the more we lose our balance. To be balanced is in fact to move with micromovements moving" (Manning 2012, 44). Moving with these micromovements is a productive way to think of the balance required in teaching. For Manning (2012), both stillness and posture are forms of incipient action. We might understand it this way: they appear as pauses in action, but they are merely tendencies of momentariness. They are qualities of movement that tend toward slowing it down, de-intensifying its velocity. Movement can "move," "speed up," "slow down," or "still," but it does not stop.

To return to the teacher's posture from this perspective, both inclination and rectitude can be read through their movements. The inclining posture, like the posture of rectitude, is a movement that is in the process of stilling, and to shift postures is to do so as a movement that is moving (Manning 2012, 44). Changing posture requires you to move; the different modes of subjectivity and relationality that teaching postures give rise to are based on different kinds of incipient action, even when that action does not look like an action at all. The form of teaching as pointing therefore invites an interpretation that recognizes its movement and what this movement means for teacher-student-object relations. Manning comments that since posture is a transient movement "there is no ideal posture: if the tendency of your intensive movement is a fidget or a squirm, the quality of your posture will itself be a squirm in the making" (Manning, 2012, 45).

Thus, the pointing body of the teacher, we could argue, embodies a kind of movement-in-the-making. However, what this movement-in-the-making can be remains caught within the singularity of the action, like all postures, including inclination. That is, we cannot know that the gesture of pointing is about an incipient squirm, a contraction, a relaxation, or an extension. Yet, the posture encourages a certain relationship with its physical, material environment. "When we move, we move around the posture's quasi-chaotic center" (2012, 45). By this Manning means that a given posture contains incipient tendencies: certain postures "lend themselves" to certain movements. From this point of view, a posture of rectitude will necessarily lend itself to the potentiality of different movements than one of inclination. The pointing teacher has a range of tendencies, which physically span from a stiffness and rigidity in the arm to a more sweeping gesture, from a quick movement of a finger, to a slow, languorous stretching out of the hand. While the body does surprise and movements can never be fully predicted, there are nonetheless certain suggestions of movement that are more or less possible from within a given posture. The body simply cannot go from prone to standing in one fell swoop. And here, I think, is where responding to the environment through our senses, and being affected and susceptible to one's surroundings, lead teachers to move in ways that are educationally significant. The importance of pointing, then, comes not from its supposed intention to direct attention but from the relations it affords (or not) and the kinds of encounters it makes possible for students and teachers alike through its movements. Pointing can act as a gesture of mastery or a gesture of invitation. But as long as it is conceived as being divorced from the very movement it is generating and as possessing a singular aim of directing attention, the pointing remains blind to what it is doing at a relational level.

Relational Encounters of Touch

Thus far I have been critical of views of teaching that rely on the traditional form of pointing and gesturing toward some*thing* for the way they fail to recognize pointing's own relational formation. While Bergdahl and Langmann (2018b) rightfully call for balance in teaching, I read that balance not in terms of complementing moments of rectitude with moments of inclination, as they do, but more in terms of how teachers are always in movement and as such need to develop a sense of the micromovements of teaching. The trick is to do so, perhaps, without entirely becoming conscious of them, otherwise, as Manning (2012) reminds us, we fall over. Moreover, the trick is also to do so while in relation with students and objects of study, as part, that is, of a larger pedagogical choreography, or state of encounter as Bourriaud would put it. In this view, teaching becomes something other than indicating that a student focus one's thought or vision on a particular object of study; instead, it suggests that, returning to the Latin roots of attention once again, *a-tendere* is about "reaching out" to have contact with another. This reaching out involves nothing less than a complicated dance of touch. Touch becomes a sensory modality of attention and experience whereby bodily constellations and "borders" become made and unmade, porous and redefined in the creation of educational spaces (Todd, 2016b).

Reading this with respect to movement, and inspired by Manning and Bourriaud's thinking, touch "creates space" as relation. As a reaching out, it is a movement that is not easily fixed or intelligible within given systems of meaning, since it is itself the very movement of signification. "When I touch you, what I cannot know is what infra(sensual)language our reciprocal touch will create. Nor can I predict how my touching you will provide spaced times and timed spaces" (Manning 2007, 57). This focus on the relationality of touch, the touching and being touched by something or someone, is at the heart of how we become bodily subjects of the world—through, that is, the relationality of all the senses. Thus it is not just the *physicality* of touch that matters here, but how it engages in *processes* of individuation and togetherness: movement is space-making through the touch that it generates. Touch draws us together as it separates us, blurring borders between our bodies and between my body and the environment. Taking water as an example: Is my body the water I drink? The rain that soaks my skin? The water I feel as warm or cool? The tears I weep? Similarly, in classroom life, clear boundaries from the elements of the environment we are in relation with are not so easy to detect. Is the desk supporting my elbow as I rest my head on my hand, or is my elbow pressing on the desk while my hand seeks out my face? Is the bump on my right hand's middle finger merely the result of my holding a pen or does the pen itself exert its own pressures on me, which then, in turn, recalibrate as my bump hardens or softens over time. Sensation is the meeting place of these forces and movements.

In this view, and echoing my discussion in chapter 2, there is no body experience without either movement or touch. As Manning observes, there is no "givenness" to the body; it is a "dynamic constellation in co-composition with the environment . . . an ecology of practices" (2016, 115). In a fundamental way, the body *is* touch; the body is sensory encounter—touch creates space between (at least) two. To touch and be touched by challenges the cultural intelligibility of the body. As Manning writes, touch draws "to our attention the limit-space between your skin, my skin, and the world. . . . When I reach to touch you, I touch not the you who is fixed in space as pre-orchestrated matter/form. I touch the you that you will become in response to my reaching toward" (2007, 87). This reaching toward marks the way teachers are both becoming themselves and implicit in relations of becoming for others. Understanding touch in this way can also be interruptive of the conventional ways we think about becoming, since the body is never only just fixed within a social script. As our bodies touch, they have the potential to exceed the kinds of normative relations that work to keep certain bodies in their place: for example, the disabled body, the transgendered body, the racialized body. In reaching toward you, I do not touch—in a sheerly physical way—the social significations of a body or the labels attached to bodies. Because of this, as Manning suggests, there is also the resistant politics of touch inherent in bodies reaching out toward one another. "What touch achieves . . . is the potentiality to apprehend bodies not as containers of preordained individual significations, but as orbs continually readjusting themselves to the infralanguages and movements of desire through which they interact" (2007, 57).

Touch as a form of movement and reaching out therefore is not only aesthetic in light of its sensory dimensions but is also political. It not only resists dominant vocabularies of what bodies signify, but also creates a "relationscape" (Manning 2012) that enables new formations of becoming. Bodies are engendered through their encounters with things, objects, and other matter as well as with other bodies. Our capacity to touch and be touched creates an environment of entanglement and interrelationality; an environment that enables new movements and actions to emerge, and through them new bodies and new experiences. And this is the case too for online educational spaces, as we shall see in a later chapter, albeit on different terms than face-to-face classrooms.

Teaching as a formation, whether through forms of pointing and rectitude or ones of inclination, cogenerates spaces with students as well as with the material objects of study. It also means that teaching, through its relationality and its bodily enactment, is both aesthetic and political—particularly with respect to the degree to which it enables counternormative experiences of racialization, sexualization, and nationalization to emerge. Teaching is therefore a sensory engagement with the environment that brings into being the teacher herself while opening up new worlds through which their own—and students'—becoming is never complete.

Staging Formations of Encounter

As a state of encounter that brings into form certain educational relations, teaching enacts its own universes, to echo a phrase from Bourriaud. It sets up conditions of sensation, of touching and being touched by, that enact our entanglement with each other as well as with things and other animate beings. It does so in ways that can, at times, sustain and, at other times, interrogate those relationships that prop up normative structures. Through its movement it is therefore generative of certain limits as well as possibilities, creating relationscapes that are neither easy to predict nor to control. This means that the bodily enactment of teaching affords opportunities of touching and being touched in ways that exceed even the best of intentions. So this raises a few questions: How can we think about *planning* for teaching in such a way that minimizes harmful relations even if we cannot entirely predict the relational impact of our teaching? What qualities of encounter is it possible to stage? Or, to borrow from Bourriaud again, how might teaching make educational relations themselves, as opposed to objects of study, a point of concern?

By posing these questions, I am not trying to suggest that subject matter is unimportant or that objects of study should not be attended to—quite the contrary. It is rather to see that the transformative core of educational encounters with those objects (and with each other) are themselves relational. Even attention, for instance, can be understood as not merely a mental or cognitive state or disposition, but a sensory relation of touch that one makes and remakes with various elements of the environment. Robin Wall Kimmerer (2013), an indigenous botanist, puts it this way: "Paying attention acknowledges that we have something to learn from intelligences other than our own. Listening, standing witness, creates an openness to the world in which the boundaries between us can dissolve in a raindrop" (300).

Thus because of its relationality, its formation of encounters, teaching is more akin to certain practices involved in art making than what we perhaps first imagined at the beginning of this chapter. And as such, it allows us to frame planning differently from conventional ways of understanding pedagogical and curricular development. Claudia Ruitenberg suggests that while teachers are not "just like" a curator, they nonetheless set and participate in the "the scene of learning" (2015, 231).

> The main difference between a curator and a teacher (at least in the popular image of those roles) seems to be that a curator's focus is on setting the scene for the encounter between a work of art and a viewer or, in the case of a web curator, between online information and a reader. A teacher's focus is on inhabiting that scene, of being present, either physically or virtually, in the encounter, of accompanying the student in that encounter, and forming a bridge between the work and the student—sometimes very prominently, by telling he student about the work, explaining the work, and so forth, sometimes more subtly by being available in the background as guide and resource in the student's own grappling with the work. (Ruitenberg 2015, 230–231)

What is noteworthy here is how the very form that teaching takes is marked by the teacher's presence, which is rooted in the relations she is creating between students and objects of study through the encounters she stages. This is different from pointing out the object to indicate to students that *they* need to pay attention. As Ruitenberg underlines, the form is bridge-like and "accompanying," more akin to a supportive role of inclination than a distanced one of rectitude. The teacher through her presence in the scene itself is indeed distinct from a curator and perhaps more like a relational artist.

That is, following Bourriaud once again, teachers in their design of educational encounters are part of the relational world they are constructing. Even when they may seem to be engaging in curricular choices about which objects of study to put on the table (and thus come closest to traditional curatorial practices), teachers by their very movement of reaching out generate encounters that seek to challenge the students' current relationship to subject matter—and indeed to themselves and others; they thus cannot be divorced from the educational stage themselves. The presence of the teacher (even in a digital space) in the formation of encounters, which marks the difference between the curator and the teacher as Ruitenberg points out, is indeed akin to the presence of relational art practitioners who involve themselves in the artwork along with the participants. The curatorial element is thus not divorced from the artist's creative production of the work because the encounter *is* the work. Likewise with education, teachers are both planners and collaborators in the choreography of the classroom, and thus encounters, both planned and serendipitous, *are* the work of education.

To think about the qualities of our encounters which seek to create alternatives to debilitating and discriminatory social relations means thinking about to what degree various encounters allow others to enter into dialogue, in Bourriaud's sense mentioned above. Planning and enacting formations of encounter means putting the pedagogical relation as a question to be explored, talked about, and experienced as opposed to assuming it has an already premade relational structure—or, as in the case of pointing, which ignores this structure altogether. That is, part of designing and staging encounters requires being able to hold the diverse ways students touch and are touched by the things (and other bodies) that teachers place in front of them both in face-to-face and online settings. It is an aesthetic approach to interrogating our being together which understands the balance between what is common and what is unique. Thus my staging of encounters involves paying particular attention to how the form of my teaching both opens up and shuts down certain avenues of experience for students, which are singularly felt but shared in the common space created by the encounter itself. To paraphrase Bourriaud's earlier question, how can students become in the space created by the encounter? This is perhaps *the* guiding question of teaching around which all decisions about form take place. And it is to this time of becoming which I now turn.

Chapter Five

Becoming as a Time of Unfolding

> Being-time has the quality of flowing. It flows into tomorrow, today flows into yesterday and yesterday flows into today. And today flows into today, tomorrow flows into tomorrow. Because flowing is a quality of time, moments of past and present do not overlap or line up side by side.
>
> —Eihei Dōgen, "Uji," *Shōbōgenzō*

> Times are legion: a different one for every point in space. There is not one single time; there is a vast multitude of them.
>
> —Carlo Rovelli, *The Order of Time*

Time can be so intimate it almost pains one to think of its passing. All that is lost in the past, all that we cannot know for certain will come tomorrow. And yet, we live on, breathing, moving, planning, and educating—in the present, or more accurately, in a seeming series of presents. But somewhere we also feel the elasticity of time, a time that strokes us, invites us, tempts us, compels us even to stretch backward and forward, to reach near and far from where we are now. Time does not only pass; it also flows in many directions. More like currents in water than a definite line in the sand. Living itself is *of* this time, but it is a present that is complex and (perhaps counterintuitively) multitemporal, comprised of moments where past-present-future merge together. This view of time is educationally significant when we consider the process of becoming that educational encounters make possible. When we think about the idea of education as transformation, we are necessarily speaking of a change in *who* one is at a given moment, which involves not only a change in shape or substance but also a temporal shift. Becoming is an event of coalescence, the coming together of myriad elements into a now that is our being, which then morphs into another now, and another—another time, another being. Change and process thereby involve a temporal dimension: a movement from one state to another, an emergence that continually transpires and unfolds.

In previous chapters we have looked at educational encounters in physical and spatial terms; this chapter explores the specifically temporal dimension of these physical encounters in terms of this movement of transformation. Here I seek to lay out the conditions of becoming through education as a *time of unfolding*. This unfolding is not something that transpires *within* the present but is in fact what instantiates it. In this view, the present is the time of education par excellence. Not because it acts as rupture or gap between past and future, as Hannah Arendt stresses,[1] nor because it in some way either reflects the past or prepares for the future. Instead, the time of unfolding suggests the fluidity of the present, a break not with past and future per se, but with linear time itself. The present has an ability simultaneously to take on shades of historical legacies (such as colonialism), to open up to potential futures (such as decolonization) while dwelling in the nowness of experience. Thus, the time of education occurs at a convergence of temporalities, a flow of moments, through which one's becoming unfolds. Unfolding acts metaphorically here to indicate a process of opening and of movement, just as a flower bud uniquely unfolds in all directions through its relations to sun, earth, water, and other plants. The flower becomes a time event that flows outward and inward, connected to things that enable it to bloom (or not) in myriad ways. Each bud not only encounters its environment differently, allowing for variation even within the same species, but does so as a flow through time, each moment a movement of touch (with the particles of earth, the sun's rays, the molecules of water). To explore this idea of becoming as a time of unfolding more fully requires reflecting not only on how bodily space and form is created out of the relationships of our encounters, as I have done in previous chapters, but also on the temporal dimensions of those encounters as moments of living, as moments of touching and being touched by. More importantly, this chapter outlines a view of the present as a temporality that is not simply part of linear time or *chronos*, but that is a complex moment of living time, or *kairos*.[2] Through this I move away from the dominance of chronological time within educational thinking and practice to a present where becoming is part of a different temporal dimension, characterized by relationship, fluidity, and infinity. In chapter 7, I discuss how this shapes our pedagogical responses to the climate emergency, focusing on nonchronological time as a central element to what we can offer as teachers. In this chapter, I outline different modalities of chronological time and what they seem to miss with respect to educational becoming. I then turn to a discussion of the fluidity of the present primarily drawing on Buddhist sources and explore this reframing of the present through past and future. To this end, I draw out the idea of the past as being presenced in the here and now, following discussions about traumatic time and drawing on the work of D. W. Winnicott and Mark Epstein. This is followed by a discussion of the not-yet, invoking what Erin Manning links to the tense of the future anterior. In particular, I focus here on the body that both touches and is touched by and how this sensory dimension can be understood as central to the time of becoming.

The Limits of Chronology in Educational Becoming

Outlining a few distinctions about how I am *not* mobilizing the present here might be useful since education is rife with temporal commitments: from aiming to produce future workers and good citizens to goals concerned with transmitting values from the past. But these linear conceptions of time are not all of a kind, and while what follows is not an exhaustive list, these distinctions are useful for mapping out the course I am charting by highlighting a need for reconceiving the present as something other than a moment of transition between past and future.

First, my focus on the present is not to be equated with what I call an *insomniac* view of the present as present*ism*. This I see as an agitated focus on here and now that aligns itself all too well with societies of acquisition and consumerism. Such societies depend on a view of present time both as acceleration and repetition, a time that is paradoxically both fleeting and recycles in sameness. According to this temporal logic, desires for consumption are to be acted on without thought about either their legacies or their implications, as though the present exists in a vacuum. With respect to education, it can take the form of constant entertainment, of finding new modes of instruction through which material is to be consumed by learners; teachers and students are thereby reduced to the mechanics of pedagogical innovation. Moreover, once such desires are satiated—equally fleetingly—the cycle repeats, creating a flow of time punctuated by moment to moment impulses. Like the experience of insomnia it is restless—and relentless.

Secondly, I seek to avoid an oversimplified understanding of how the past is causally related to the present. There is within the logics of reproduction, stereotypical thinking, and some forms of identity politics a close alignment between the past and the present; an overdetermination and condensation of what one or a group of people has been (and perceived to be) into what *is* and what one therefore *will be* in the future. This is a *neurotic* view of the present, both fixated on and reductive of its relation to the past. Indeed, it marks the present both as a mirroring of the past and as a fulfilment of preordained expectations or prophecies. The present operates in the time of simple cause and effect, being reduced to a predictable moment of an imagined synchronicity from which it cannot escape. We see this regularly with respect to how children and youth from "disadvantaged" backgrounds are viewed as mere reflections of their (stereotyped) pasts (however brief those pasts may in fact be!). A neurotic sense of time is unable to open itself to the possibilities of change, negotiation, and translation that the present can offer.

Thirdly, closely related to this is a *developmental* sense of the present. Often perceived through stages or hierarchies, time moves along a specific sequence of development. The child is perceived as progressing through specified points along a continuum, and the task of the teacher—and indeed the whole education system—is to determine age- or grade-appropriate material and experiences. To do this requires that the child be "captured" within a particular stage. The present is thereby reduced to a nodal point along the developmental trajectory. This is not to say that children do not develop in the sense of gaining adeptness, growth, and maturation, but that they all do so consistently and irrevocably through universal stages corresponding to specific ages is to reduce the richness of children's experiences of the present to predetermined, transcendental ideas of humanhood (Biswas 2021). It is one thing for patterns of behavior to be observed from within (Eurocentric) theories of cognition and moral development, and it is entirely another to overlay these onto a linear temporal order which *qualifies* becoming for all children everywhere and ignores the complexity of children's and youth's lives and the singular nature of their experiences.

Fourthly, there is the present that is conceived from a position of *nostalgia*, so often propagated by nationalist and populist political agendas in education. The present, in this view, is put into the service of an imagined past: students are to encounter the world through originary narratives that (ironically) deny their own historicity. That is, the present is to be experienced as though it can return to the past, even though that past—defined through its ostensibly fixed ahistorical values, traditions, and so on—is but a projection of what one would have liked the world to be. That is, it projects onto the past an illusory sense of unity from which it seeks to define the present. In this, it is closely related to the next, fifth framing.

This is the *anachronistic* sense of the present which is especially common within instrumental accounts of education. The present, in this view, is seen from the perspective of a desired future. It is conceived backward from an imaginary point of the anticipated outcome. Its trajectory is somewhat akin to the nostalgic view of time, but the arc moves in the opposite direction. For instance, if we desire a democratic society, global citizenry, or flexible work force, we treat the present as something to be measured against this imagined future. Instead of the present serving the desire for the past, as one finds in nostalgic accounts, it serves the desire for a specific future; and no matter how well intentioned or socially desirable this image of the future might be, it nonetheless operates in such a way that sees the present as merely the handmaiden to its aspirations.

The sixth and final framing can be considered as an *amnesiac* sense of time which can only see the present as an opening to the future, and thereby risks conceiving it as something entirely decontextualized, ahistorical, and transparent. This is a time of forgetting, where the present takes on a monumentalism that contributes to the erasure of one's embeddedness and emplacement through processes of enculturation. While avoiding the overdetermination of the past (neurotic), the restless repetition of the moment (insomniac), the staged progression of the child through past-present-future (developmental), the fantastical return to the past (nostalgic), and the retroactive projection of an imagined future (anachronistic), the amnesiac sense of time forecloses on the complexity of the present by seeing it solely as a progressive movement where anything can happen, a movement untainted by the messiness of different trajectories of subjectivity and the trace of different historical legacies. In education, this denial takes on various forms in "color- or gender-blind" discourses, in adages such as, "you can be anything you want to be," and in appeals to "suspension," as I discussed in chapter 1.

All these variants of how chronological time intersects with education indicate that it can never easily be mapped onto the encounters and relations that constitute the form education takes. My point here is not that we can simply do away with chronological time, particularly as it structures—and *needs* to structure—our social lives, but rather to question the assumption that chronological time can get to the heart of what makes encounters educational in the first place. That is, the linear sense of past-present-future does not really capture what is transformational about our encounters in terms of the processes that enable new forms of becoming *as* education. Thus, while I also speak of the present in terms of its potentiality and its generative capacity, as do those suffering from amnesia, I seek to do so in ways that resist the naiveté that so often accompanies the collapse of the present into continual newness, as though relationships subtending our encounters are also not part of wider formations of racism, sexism, and ableism—without, of course, allowing these contexts to determine in any direct way the very possibilities of becoming.

In moving beyond these six different chronological views of the present, I sketch out an idea of the present as an unfolding of time that refuses linearity and investigates the present from different vantage points. That is, rather than see education through the lens of chronological time, where the present is always serving some specific, desired end (past, present, or future), I seek to explore the time of the present through the lens of living, bodily educational encounters. This shift enables a reworking of the temporal dimensions of becoming in ways that do not see the present as a moment we simply pass by on the way to or from somewhere else. Instead, it enables a complex, manifold, and relational conception of the present where past and future are deeply intertwined.

Fluidity of the Present

The Buddhist theory of codependent arising (*paticca-samuppada*, which is sometimes translated as dependent origination, dependent arising, or conditioned arising) offers a way of thinking of the present that invites complexity and lends a certain textured layering to our experience of time. It is concerned with a conceptualization of the present that highlights the relationality that lies at the heart of all forms of existence. Codependent arising offers the idea of existence as a *living emergence*, one that transpires through our relations to various elements of the environment. In many ways, it presages both relational ontology's current commitments and the confounding notion of time promoted by quantum physicists, such as Carlo Rovelli articulates it.[3] These relations are what comprise *things* in the world; matter (including human matter) does not hold some essence but is transient and dependent on the encounters that have constituted its makeup.

In Buddhist theory, the cycle of codependent arising traditionally consists of twelve factors, each of which acts as a condition for the others: ignorance, volitional actions, consciousness, mental and physical phenomena, the six senses (the usual five plus mind), contact, sensation, desire, attachment, becoming, birth, death.[4] Although the original Pali suttas in which this theory appears often list these in sequence, which can lend itself to a reading of them as strict relations of cause and effect along a chronological time line, Buddhist scholarship has consistently pointed to their interdependence, as well as seeing the movement of "arising" as in no way deterministic. In this, it emphasizes the relative, conditioned nature of existence as arising from multiple conditions simultaneously. This understanding is also supported by other facets of Buddhist philosophy and doctrine and has given rise to the idea of the present moment as something that is other than a fixed point on a temporal continuum. In *living* our lives (which always occurs in the present, from one breath to the next), there can never be a simple sequencing of causes, as if one thing automatically leads to another through some chronological ordering of discrete events. Rather the theory of codependent arising is about the conditions that enable a particular moment in time to be experienced in a particular way by a particular body. Thus, while the present is conditioned, it is relatively so, with each element of the arising allowing for countless rippling effects that incite other elements into being. A moment in the present is thus not only the "effect" of a single "cause," such as we find in stereotypical accounts of why children from certain "disadvantaged" backgrounds (cause) "perform poorly" academically (effect). Instead, a moment in time—*this* moment in time—occurs against an infinite array of possibility. Moreover, it is upon our ability to glimpse this time (most often through meditation) that the whole Buddhist wheel turns. However, you'll be relieved to know that my intent is not to suggest that readers need to meditate to experience this time; rather, casting the present in terms of this codependent arising offers a heuristic that allows us to ask some crucial questions concerning our everyday encounters in education.

For instance, let us take a simple example of the lead up to a child's response to a teacher's question about trees in science class as conditioned in this way. Mapping onto some of the conditions listed above, their response will depend on a host of factors that come together in a particular moment:

1. Ignorance: what they cannot see or understand about trees yet;
2. Volition: their active attentiveness to what is happening, indicating an interest in the topic of trees;
3. Consciousness: their becoming aware of a real tree outside the window they happen to be gazing through while the lesson is going on;
4. Mental and physical phenomena: an image of getting out of the chair and climbing out of the window onto a branch of the tree outside;
5. Six senses: hearing the teacher repeat her question;
6. Contact: the physical contact they have with their chair at this moment in the lesson;
7. Sensation: the heat and hardness of the chair they feel beneath their buttocks and backs of their legs;
8. Desire: their wanting both to move to see the tree outside better and to give the right answer to the teacher's question about the tree in the lesson;
9. Attachment: identifying the heat and hardness of the chair as extremely uncomfortable;
10. Becoming: begins to act, both squirming and fidgeting;
11. Birth: their decision to stay quiet and continue gazing out the window;
12. Death: the passing away of the opportunity to respond aloud.

To make matters even more complex, at each of these points, a number of other things are also happening to the student and they are equally transient even if they might not become equally significant. For instance their attachment to their discomfort can make them even more fidgety, fueling a desire to escape out the window; or their desire to give the right answer might occasion the sensation of butterflies in the stomach.

We can see how easy it is for teachers (and researchers) to short-circuit this network of relations when we attribute causal effects in presuming to know the reason why this child acted a certain way in a given moment. And this is particularly the case when we ascribe gendered, cultural, and racial categories (and stereotypes) as supposed reasons for the silence we observe: for example, that the child didn't know the answer because they didn't understand (the language, the question), or because they were being their usual disruptive self, or because they didn't have the "appropriate" background knowledge to respond. A problem arises when we attempt to attribute a single "cause" to their silence, since there is never simply one that directly determines any particular moment. What the idea of dependent arising allows us to see is how coming into existence through our actions is a temporal and bodily event that is compounded by a range of fleeting and necessary factors. Each moment is multiply conditioned and unfolds singularly.

Taking this idea to a more radical level, the thirteenth-century Zen master, Dōgen, expresses this moment of arising as "being-time." In his famous essay entitled "Uji," Dōgen understands that whatever exists is not *in* time but *is* time itself: for him, all beings *are* time because they exist in the present—are *of* the present—including streams, mountains, and flowers.[5] Each has been created through an arising that is infinite in nature in any given moment since it involves multiple conditioning that is open to endless variation. In this *uji* can be thought of as a "dynamic presencing."[6] Thus while our conditioned arising takes shape, it does so through the momentary nature of existence. If something exists it does so not only spatially (it is *there* materially), but also temporally (it *emerges* as a flow of time).

For Dōgen the self is an "array" connected to all other things that are similarly arrayed: "The way the self arrays itself is the form of the entire world. See each thing in this entire world as a moment of time" (Dōgen, Tanahashi translation 2013, 92). It is not as if there is a self or plant or animal that exists *in* time and which is then subject to impermanence and change; rather beings *are* time—they are ever-changing moments in the very act of living. It is thus that we are connected to all time and to all beings, through the very movement that inheres in the present. To be clear, for Dōgen a "moment of time" is not something to be seen as a fixed point along a line of chronological time, but as fluidity and flux—not unlike William James's notion of pure experience I discussed in chapter 2. The present is best understood as an action of unfolding, of presencing. As Buddhist scholar Stephen Batchelor claims, to speak of it as "*the* present moment" is problematic. It is worth quoting him at length:

> I would argue that there is really no present moment. The present moment is one of these things that Buddhists have become terribly attached to. If you think about it, to try to find the present moment, you will never find anything. The present moment is actually just a concept; it can be a very useful strategic concept . . . I will often say when instructing in meditation, "Stay in the present moment." But I don't mean by that, try to find this elusive thing called the present moment and stay in it. It's basically a way of saying, Don't get caught up in the unknown future. Don't get caught up in reminiscing about the past. But confront the situation at hand. And the situation at hand is always unfolding. It's fluid. It's like water, it's like a stream. Things are constantly impacting your senses, constantly bubbling up in your thoughts, constantly emerging as emotions and feelings; it's always in motion, it's moving. And it's such a mobile experience that the notion of "the present moment" really has no place there. There's no point really. So, every situation that occurs, and you could call it "at the present moment" if you wish, but it's basically an unfolding of events that is calling forth an appropriate response. And in this sense, it's always in time. (Batchelor 2014, n.p.)

The present as an "unfolding of events" opens it up to a different kind of connection with past and future. According to Ronald Purser, the present does not have "a linear from–to structure; time does not really flow from the past to the present. Rather, we could say that all time flows from the present" (2015, 685). That is, it flows from where we *are* as being-time; from what we are experiencing *now*, not from some absolute position on a clock that measures out a sequential order, but from a position of particularity that arises through coconditioned events or encounters. As Batchelor puts it above, our bodies, minds, and feelings are always "bubbling up" in interaction with things and others of the environment, from moment to moment, resisting a totalitarian view of the present as some fixed point in time which we can observe, as if we could (or should) remove ourselves from the flow of experiencing. To do so requires seeing the present as something stripped of its relationality along with its conditioning. The present is not, therefore, a mere convention that indicates a unit of time which is separate from the flow of which I am a part, something that I can stand outside of. Instead, as Dōgen would put it, being-time indicates a relational present. It is, we might say, a time of interconnection. Dōgen writes: "Do not think that time merely flies away. Do not see flying away as the only function of time. If time merely flies away, you would be separated from time. The reason you do not clearly understand the time-being is that you think of time only as passing. In essence, all things in the entire world are linked with one another as moments. Because all moments are the time-being, they are your time-being" (Dōgen, Tanahashi translation 2013, 92). What these notions of time and codependent arising lend to this educational discussion is a deep understanding of the present as a nexus of temporalities and felt experiences that are always unfolding in relation to something else. Present time itself is relational and not discrete. Existence, in this view, is a process of emergent becoming, with each moment a flow that connects us to others in our environment. It is this time of interdependency and interrelationality that suggests that the present moves through—or more accurately *is*—encounters as they are punctuated by various conditions that then move us into new formations of becoming.

Educationally speaking, encounters staged through teaching, for instance, act as potential conditioning events. The sensory contacts occasioned by these encounters are part of a flow of experience that each student participates in in relation to specific objects and people, which are also part of this fluid present. To be clear, the flow of the present is not a flow from past to present to future. Rather the flow is present time itself, just as the wind is air and the stream is water. The time of unfolding allows us to apprehend that our teaching is a movement that conditions possibilities for students' (and teachers') existence, for their being-time.

To return specifically to the realm of the senses, that is to how one touches and is touched by elements of the environment, means reframing the temporal dimension of education itself. Rather than see education in terms of the chronological framings mentioned above, where education transpires in the "now" as either a transition or a gap between past and future, there is something about the density of time as it is lived and felt by bodies that offers other tenses for understanding what is happening through our educational encounters and who we are becoming. The idea of the present as presencing, as activity, unfolding, and flow, troubles conventional ways we have of understanding our encounters, both in relation to the past on the one hand, since what has passed can only ever be encountered and experienced in the present, either as it is remembered or more directly in terms of (re)experiencing it, and in relation to the future, on the other hand, since it poses as an experiential horizon of possibility that our encounters are always reinstalling. It is to reframing the past and future in light of "presencing" that I now turn.

The "Traumatic" Time of Education: The Past That Is

Most of us have experienced that strange state when the past becomes fused with the present. Sometimes an encounter can act as a reminder of events long ago, carrying us back into a time through revery and nostalgic reconstruction. Like Proust's madeleines, sensory encounters can launch epic journeys through the landscapes of our earlier experiences. The smell of a particular fruit, the touch of a piece of fabric, the sound of a birdcall can send us suddenly to a time and place that seems alive in the here and now. We are *there* in the field, by the stream, in the classroom, on the street, with our family, a friend, strangers, or alone sensing the feeling of "being there." But these memorial moments, despite their evocative force, are also still resonant with chronological time; we know that we are in the midst of remembering a time that is no longer, even as we feel its textures, scents, and resonances.

At other times, however, this fusion becomes more acute—more part of the flow of experiencing than part of a field of remembering as sensory retrieval; at these times, we respond to our current environment *as though* there were no distinction at all between present and past. It is often phrased as a "reliving" of the past in the present, as opposed to the "revisiting" of the past that occurs through memory. That is, the past becomes actualized and unfolds in the now of experiencing it. It is perhaps more accurate to say that it is not so much a *re*-living of a past experience, but more of a living of a current experience that embodies the past: the past continues to live in and through our bodies in the present, and we respond to our environment without making distinctions between now and then.[7] Conditions of dementia, hallucinatory states, and psychosis are often distinguished in this way from the revisiting of the past that occurs through memory, daydreaming, and nostalgic recollection. However, it is not only in such states that the power of the body to actualize the past is evident. The acknowledgment of this fusion has also been addressed in the field of trauma studies, which attempts to grasp the complexities of trauma, particularly in terms of trauma's relation to the body as a site of activation. What is significant for my purposes here about this area of scholarship is how the body bypasses our conventional understanding of the past through conscious memory, in ways that do not signal, for example, dementia or psychosis.

Theories of the bodily aspects of trauma such as those proposed by Bessel van der Kolk (2015) and Peter Levine (2015) open up questions about how the past is lived in the present through our bodies. Their work highlights how while our bodies live in the moment, they also hold on to sensations in such a way that past and present become indistinguishable. Bodily responses to one's environment in the here and now do not happen in an isolated fashion but are also interconnected with the way the body has previously responded, creating certain ways of being physically that do not necessarily map onto one's conscious experience, memory, or thought. This means that the body, as a relational entity that emerges out of complex processes of sensation and feeling with the environment (see chapter 2), does not necessarily operate according to the same logic of chronological time that structures our thinking and conscious awareness. What van der Kolk (2015) stresses, for instance, is that under traumatic conditions (such as rape; sexual, emotional, and physical abuse; severe neglect; car accidents; or witnessing scenes of violence) the body stores responses to the event and plays these responses out even when the present environment is no longer objectively traumatic. It is not so much that the present environment triggers the body to return to the past, but that the body is living in the past while also living in the present—time coalesces. But lest we think that living in time that is fused in this way is only for those of us who have suffered extreme forms of trauma, Mark Epstein, a Buddhist psychiatrist, writes of the "trauma of everyday life"—that is, those forms of suffering, tragic events, unexpected harms, and painful surprises which make up living from day to day.

In these forms of trauma, too, there is not so much a disconnect between reality as it is lived now and reality as it was lived then, as there is a deep interconnection between the two. Epstein sees our capacity to live with this interconnection, to live with the flow of time, to put it in Dōgen's terms, as neither pathological nor something to eschew. Rather, the flow of living simultaneously in past and present can also have therapeutic and liberatory effects. Epstein draws on a paper by D. W. Winnicott that brilliantly illustrates how this temporal dimension works psychoanalytically.

For Winnicott (1974), and for others (see Caruth 1996), trauma, or what he refers to as "primitive agonies" (104), is by its very nature something we have not fully "experienced" in the sense that we have not thoroughly felt, processed, and symbolized our responses to an event that has objectively happened but which lies outside our normal channels of recall and consciousness. Yet, it is precisely because it continues to lie outside these channels that it can exert a distorting power over our lives which we have difficulty accessing. As a consequence, to be able to integrate this event fully into our lives, to be able to *presence* it, is to be able to heal. This leads to a confounding circular question, however: How to integrate something that has already happened but which we cannot remember because we have not yet integrated it?

There are two moves that Winnicott makes in response. First he points out that even though we have not integrated the event, which is often the case in the early years of life when we are most vulnerable and dependent, the event lives on (for him, as an unconscious psychic dynamic, and for body theorists such as van der Kolk through the body's sensations). It fuels, he suggests, our worry of it happening in the future—not happening *again* since we are unaware that it has already transpired. For example, an infant who has been abandoned can be fearful of abandonment later in life even when the actual abandonment cannot be cognitively retrieved (but can be bodily felt). For Winnicott, while the patient is fearful that the pain and agony will overcome them, thus living in fear of its anticipated arrival in the future, they are unaware that it *"has already been"* (1974, 104, emphasis in original). More importantly still, they are unaware that what is happening to them in the present—the fear or worry for the future—has also been conditioned by a past event.

Second, Winnicott's response to this situation illustrates the ways a relational encounter with another, in this case the analyst, can act to promote a different relation to the temporality of living experience:

> The purpose of this paper is to draw attention to the possibility that the breakdown has already happened, near the beginning of the individual's life. The patient needs to "remember" this but it is not possible to remember something that has not yet happened [from the patient's vantage point, that is], and this thing of the past has not happened yet because the patient was not there for it to happen to. The only way to "remember" in this case is for the patient to experience this past thing for the first time in the present, that is to say, in the transference. This past and future thing then becomes a matter of the here and now, and becomes experienced by the patient for the first time. (105)

What does Winnicott mean that "patient was not yet there for it to happen to"? Understanding this is key to unlocking the paradoxical question I posed above. On the one hand, the traumatic event, say of being abandoned, cannot, from a psychoanalytic perspective, be experienced since there is no consolidated ego from which to do so; the infant is simply too young and undeveloped to "take in" in any meaningful way what has happened. On the other hand, the event cannot be experienced because, and this a more radical reading—one that is not concerned necessarily with infants, but with all life stages—the event is what makes the experiencer; that is, there is no one to experience the event prior to that event happening (Nagarjuna's poem in chapter 2 comes to mind here). On this latter view, the conditions of trauma create "someone" who is simply not amenable to experiencing. The shock, distress, and sadness of the event is too overwhelming for the psyche to process and make any sense of. Relationally speaking, the environment itself generates limited possibilities for experiencing. This means that traumatic events are relational formations that give rise to bodily sensations that are not fully integrated into experience. Thus, an act of abandonment (for example, a caregiver who stops showing up for the infant) creates the conditions through which a child comes into being as one who *feels* anxious and fearful, or more accurately—and forensically—feels stomach cramping, palpitations, shortness of breath. It is not that the child feels anxious and then feels these sensations; rather it is the bodily feeling of these sensations in response to a lack of care that then becomes the anxious child. This reversal is important, as we discussed in chapter 2, because it highlights that past events have not simply "happened" *to* someone, but that our existential horizons are fashioned out of the bodily qualities of contact and sensation that our encounters make possible.

What Winnicott draws our attention to here is that the past (and its anticipated "return") requires presencing for it to be named, felt, understood, and experienced. This is not only the case for the traumatized patient, but for each of us who lives as a being-time. The past need not be some long ago, infant tragedy but can be that which we experienced yesterday, this morning, or a moment ago: the confusions, anxieties, hurts, and sorrows that punctuate daily existence. This is the everyday "trauma" of which Epstein writes. What Epstein and Winnicott, as well as body theorists such as van der Kolk, make clear is that the dynamic of time reveals a larger temporal truth about how the past can coalesce with the present, bringing about a profound learning while creating new conditions of becoming. It is this dynamic of time that is so crucial to understanding what is happening temporally in and through our educational encounters.

To illustrate this more clearly in an everyday educational context, let us return to the example of the student from Daniel Pennac's *School Blues* that I discussed in chapter 1. You might recall that Jocelyne is upset about her parents' fighting and is agitated and distraught. She is unable to focus, is in tears, troubled, and inattentive. Pennac gives her Henry James's novel *What Maisie Knew*, through which she sees what is happening to her parents via the main characters in the novel: "They are arguing just like the Faranges, sir!" Jocelyne declares (1038). While I argued earlier that her encounter with the novel enabled Jocelyne to *translate* her "background" issues into the setting of the novel thereby setting off potentially new relations for her becoming, there is also a temporal dimension to take into consideration here. Through the encounter both with the words on the page and with Pennac himself who inquires after her, Jocelyne is able to bring the event/s that give rise to her pain and distress into the present. More accurately, she is able to *presence* them, in this case through her articulation of the situation through the novel's protagonists. There is thus a temporal enactment to the encounter that enables the past to come into being, to be experienced in the now of the moment, as opposed to merely being the source that is propelling her inattention and distraction. Jocelyne's living present is thus neither cut off from nor determined by the past but is that flow of experiencing through which transforming relations to past events are made possible. The present is the time when the past *comes into being as the past* and also thereby shifts the directionality of the future from one that is bound to repeat the past (which would mean Jocelyne would continue to be distracted and inattentive) to one that is open to other possibilities from the position of the present; that is, the presencing of the past thus also releases the future from the chains of history.

To be clear, this is not to say that educational encounters are or should be therapeutic; rather it is they have the potential to enable a presencing that allows us to make new relations to our pasts and the bodily, affective ways we relate to those pasts. Seeing our educational encounters in this way does not so much suspend one's past or background as it does make it visible, tactile, and palpable. This also speaks to how those encounters can and do condition what arises in the next moment. In other words, it allows us to change from one moment to the next, to see the world differently in ways that exceed our past frames of reference. This is why seeing the past either as something that determines us, or as something we need to hold at bay, fails to understand how its presencing actually creates opportunities for transformation.

Unfolding as the Future Anterior of Becoming

We often think about the future as giving the present a meaning or purpose. Working toward sustainability, decoloniality, social justice, and equity often fuels the ways we practice education in the present. We pose utopian visions, infuse what we do with hope for the future, work toward a not yet attained goal, and allow our imagination of what the world can be to become the horizon of our now. Those seeking to transform society through education frequently base what it is we *do* in the present upon such formations, seeing our educational relations as ideally leading to the future we have proposed. As discussed earlier in terms of anachronistic time, this risks, however, instrumentalizing education and can risk creating a standard against which we measure our students and colleagues who might not fully fall in line with our vision.

And yet, understanding the connection between education and social change does not need to condemn us to such an instrumentalist fate. The future is not something that needs to be tethered so tightly to our present in any chronological sense; we do not need to set the present up as a time of transition to a better "then" in the future. Being-time, following Dōgen here, suggests that the flow of time is far more vast than what we can imagine or indeed hope for. The future is not simply a desired horizon or goal. Our own experience reminds of this every day, both in our personal lives as well as in our professional lives as teachers; futures—that time of "not yet"—open up in ways that consistently exceed our intentions and desires, and we are therefore continually surprised, disturbed, challenged, disappointed, and astonished by our encounters because what is happening now is not what we expected it to be. And this is as it should be. There is a need to see how our visions of the future operate in a cycle, creating formations of expectations which in turn create relations in the present that then loop back and are filtered through the screen of our wishes. The student or colleague who surprises or disappoints us by their opinions or actions does so at times because of our own projection onto *now* of what we think the future ought to look like. The now becomes intolerable when it cannot uphold the futurity embedded in our expectations. In these moments the present and future do not align the way we thought they should. It is this neat alignment between what we are doing now and what is yet to happen that needs to be rethought if we are to appreciate how living time works to contribute to future becomings. What I am proposing here is that there is still a way of practicing education beyond the instrumental dynamics such alignment inevitably produces, without abandoning the idea of social change altogether. It requires opening the future up to something beyond our hopes, dreams, and convictions and seeing change itself as part of this beyond; it means, as I discuss below, loosening the future's link with our individual will and moving toward a relational process of unfolding and presencing.

The coalescing of the present with the future can be seen, first and foremost, in terms of the codependent arising discussed earlier: the present is a process of changing conditions whereby multiple encounters are giving rise to other, incipient conditions—and since they are incipient, conditions are always *on their way to* emerging. In other words, presencing brings us to an understanding of the future that is always unfolding and interdependent with a host of emerging conditions. Drawing on her understanding of Alfred North Whitehead's work, which echoes this activity of codependent arising, Erin Manning writes: "A subject is in-time, coming into itself just this way in this set of conditions only to change again with the force of a different set of conditions. A subject can therefore never be reduced to a single occasion as though that iteration of experience could map onto every past and future instance of what it might have meant to have come into oneself. Such an account would leave no room for the liveliness of difference in the world" (Manning 2020, 33). For Manning, there is a shifting and impermanent aspect of the present to consider that is not unlike the Buddhist notion of time outlined above. The subject can never be solid or stable since it is continually emerging in a field of impermanence, a landscape of change. Moreover, seeing the subject in this way invites us into a plurality that is essential to time itself—that change is experienced differently by different subjects who come into being through varying conditions. Not seeing that our experience in the present solidifies into a particularity (an identity) that is then transposed across our life chronologically, across past and future, as Manning suggests, means that the present is far more about the event of contact itself: it is a "force of pastnesses future-presenting, a fold rather than a line" (Manning 2020, 34). By this Manning is intimating the manifold nature of contact that temporally reaches outward and inward and sideways all at once. Unlike linear, chronological time, living time folds in multiple directions from the presencing activity that occurs in the now. As folds, our encounters with elements of our environment allow for a perpetual movement of unfolding, a continual unfurling and opening out that is not so much chronologically sequential as it is a mingling of living temporalities as they are presenced. This is life itself—a vitalist movement of continual alteration occasioned through conditions that are themselves coming and going, emergent, convergent, and divergent.

Manning sees the body itself, and particularly touch, as key to this process of unfolding. The future for Manning is conceived not so much in terms of a fixed site of futurity—an *after* to the present—but as liminal and porous, profoundly connected to the present as a relational movement between entities. Touch reverberates with a relationality that radically exceeds our usual boundaries and identities. Thinking with Gilbert Simondon's philosophy of individuation, she writes, "I reach out to touch you in order to invent a relation that will, in turn, invent me. To touch is to engage in the potential of an individuation" (2007, 15). For Manning, "individuation is understood . . . as the capacity to become *beyond* identity" (2007, xv). Individuation is not simply about separation from an assembly and retraction into a defined category (such as a social identity), but about becoming itself as something fluid that remains connected and yet is singular. There is thus a state of anticipation without predictability ("a *potential* of an individuation") engendered in touch and in the very movement of "reaching out" to touch. Encounters of touch are those within which bodies both relate and individuate, they are encounters both of togetherness and singularity. I do not feel the same thing as you do in an encounter; each is a one-of-a-kind event. Yet, I can only feel because you have touched me. In the previous chapter, I discussed how this touching and being touched by generates spaces, but as Manning points out there is also a temporal element insofar as our encounters generate "spaced times and timed spaces" (2007, 67).

Presencing the future, bringing it into the present in a way that allows it to *exist*, is very much about a bodily becoming that is never achievable as a solo project but is only possible through a network of relations of reciprocal touchings. As we have seen in earlier chapters, as animate beings, we are not simply receivers of cultural imprint, or solely subject to impingement from our environment, but also create ourselves through our sensitivity to and with that environment. We *become*, in other words, through our relations to our surroundings, through the movement of presencing. In this way, presencing is also copresencing; it is an emergent interpenetration of being-times.

Manning suggests that such generative capacity is not only about the surface of the body touching something in its environment but is about how the body is explorative in its very *reaching out* to touch—and it is this explorative dimension that calls into being a future temporality in our encounters. As she puts it, "To touch is always to attempt to touch the incorporeality of a body, to touch what *is* not yet. I do not touch the you that I think you are, I reach toward the one you will become" (Manning 2007, xix). Manning discusses this gesture of reaching out as occurring in the time of the future anterior (the "will have become"). This strange tense allows us to imagine the openness of the not-yet as part of what we are doing *now*. I am always reaching for what you are not yet, but when I touch you, you/I will be. It is thus both conditional and anticipatory in the sense that the future anterior is constructed from a will have + a past participle. "I will have become" implies that something will be accomplished when a passing condition has arisen (e.g., I will have written this text by the time you read these words; you will have touched me by the time I feel your touch; I will have become in the moment of your contact). Thinking about this in relation to becoming a subject means that what I will become cannot be categorized beforehand; it is not an identity position that is waiting for me to jump into it like firefighter boots at the bottom of the pole. Your touch does not simply push me into this given position. Rather, what Manning focuses on is the *flow* of the touch. Touch is not an isolated point of contact but a gesture and movement through time. There is a reaching out, an incipient movement, that conditions any contact. Rather than see this budding gesture solely sequentially (I first lift my arm, then raise my hand, then reach out, then place my finger on the surface of your shoulder), framing it as a future anterior more aptly captures how the movement gestures toward something that is not yet—and it always and irrevocably does so. For if we only touched what was already there, we would be living a spool of time played backward. The shoulder that I reached out for moments ago is not the same one I will land my finger on. It has shifted because like all elements of the environment it is in flux, shifting with the rise and fall of your breath, moving with your mood, charged with affective energy at my anticipated touch. Reaching out is not a gesture that *moves toward* the present (since it is always occurring in the flux of the present) but *toward that which is yet to happen*. This creates a time of virtuality, potentiality, and possibility. In this way, my becoming is a process of presencing that traverses temporalities, not a taking up of a pre-given identity fixed in a future time defined chronologically. This temporal conditionality, it seems to me, is something to welcome from an educational point of view, since it enables us to think about the contextuality of the practices that inform our encounters in the present without assuming context "determines" becoming in any prescribed way; context instead is the practical environment out of which the futurity of becoming emerges.

Let's look for a moment at a concrete example of touch and think of an everyday gesture of a teacher touching a student on the shoulder. The touch is a reaching out, but it is also received; and it is received by the student who is also in motion. Receiving is never without its own movement. A student can be hesitant, leaning toward or away, or stiff with fear. The touch is encountered by both teacher and student differently as a sensation in the present, but its effects are not "known" until the touch has been presenced. It is not just that the present "sets the condition for" or "prepares for" or "causes" becoming based on any value preassigned to the touch (it was welcomed, repudiated, violent, soothing, etc. and *therefore* a certain becoming transpires), but its very momentariness (its instantiation, its presencing) enables something to occur (or nothing much to occur, as the case may be). That is, one does not decide prior to the touch on the shoulder happening that it is inappropriate, dangerous, caring, compassionate; those affects can only come about when it has arisen as a condition. It is a happening or event that is contained within the future anterior itself.

Importantly, this moves us away from seeing our "intentions" as markers of what is possible; a gesture is experienced as caring or abusive in its presencing and is not firmly tied to what the teacher meant by it. Binding our intentionality to specific effects or outcomes reflects a chronological ordering of time that is imposed on the living time of the present: a past intention is supposed to align neatly with the effects it is creating now. Instead, seen through the future anterior, a gesture is moving toward something which has not yet come into being. As such, signification can only arise in the relational encounter, not in the intention that one forms in one's head prior to the touch itself.

This means that in your reaching out to touch a me that does not yet exist you cannot be certain what we will cogenerate together. Your intended caring tap on the shoulder can become a shameful reprimand; my body responds in relation to other conditions as well as your touch. Your touch, too, arises out of myriad conditionings, and together our responses both bind us to together and separate us. In this way, processes of individuation are possible through our relation. The touch on the shoulder draws you and me into a new relation that has never taken place before (even if it might *feel* similar to previous ones), and we become new yous, new mes. Like the breath, each touch is unique, each sensation it produces is a potentiality. These singular sensations together create a relational matrix of emergence that is ongoing, part of the flow of life itself.

But is this not to romanticize touch? After all, *actual* touches can be experienced as unwanted, violent, and abusive, as well as supportive and compassionate. The point I wish to make, however, is that the time of the future anterior is a *relational* time and because of this the very quality of touch is determined by how it affects another and not by one's will or intent. In this sense no one can justify violence for a given end or hide behind a narrative of one's good intentions. Moreover, touch, like all forms of sensory contact, is transitive, and in this it opens up to the not-yet of another's being-time. This is what makes touching and being touched by so powerful—that each of us becomes a bodily subject in and through a relational network full of potentiality. This dynamic allows us to see more clearly the very *ethical* dimensions of what we are creating together and to inquire into the quality of interrelationships our educational encounters are enabling. Do they invite, for instance, a way of becoming in the now that enables us to live with elements in the environment in nonviolent and life-enhancing ways? Do they recognize our implication in another's being-time? Such questions are ways of framing our responsibility as teachers, seeing our implication in the lives of others as mattering to the educational work we do.

Presencing as the Time of Education

Focusing here in this chapter on the living time of the present has meant exploring educational encounters as *acts* of presencing. Turning *the* present from a noun—a substantive point along the line of chronological time—to a verb allows us to consider how becoming transpires in neither a linear nor straightforward direction. Moreover, it is not something I do or that is done to me; becoming is what emerges out of a field of living. Through our acts of presencing, through the event of encounter, what is past makes itself available for new relationships, insights, and articulations and what is future is that continual element of the not-yet through which all transformation flows. There are a number of implications to this sense of unfolding that I think speak directly to our formations of educational practice and the relations that subtend them.

The first is that there is no fixed and unitary "self," no determinant being, just "vectors of intensity that emerge through contact," as Manning (2007, 136) puts it. Echoing Buddhist philosophy more generally, this understanding of emergence suggests that the nature of encounter and the "I" that emerges within it are transient. Decoupling fixed ideas of the self from the living time of education opens up our views of what it is we actually do in its name. It means that our work as educators with both children and adults recognizes that it is not geared toward a specific end point, at least in terms of who we think students should become: a particular self, a specific identity. To treat our educational practices in this way means that we are more concerned with the socialization dimension of teaching and learning and less concerned with how our own educating can have a profound impact on the changing lives of students. That is, we risk undermining our very practices as educators when we insist that what we are doing is "trying to get students to become who we think they should be." This is the path of chronology, which, as discussed at the beginning of this chapter, can take on a number of trajectories and characteristics; it is a path we cannot always entirely avoid, since we do operate within systems of measured time, and moving students from one place to the next (the next grade level, the next test, the next level of skill, the next layer of analysis, the next job) is part of what schools and universities do. However, if we are not simply going to fall into seeing "education" as socialization or qualification (Biesta 2010), the question we need to ask ourselves is: how do the relational practices we engage in together make certain unfoldings possible? This, to me, invites another attitude toward the temporality of education, since we are not supposing that what we do will automatically (or *ought* to automatically) lead to something definite in the future. In other words, it resists the language of outcomes, achievements, and results. This does not mean that education operates without purpose or plans, merely that these cannot be rendered in terms of cognition or skills or dispositions that are measurable, standardizable, or generalizable. Instead, our very purposes can be formulated more open-endedly to include qualities of becoming that contribute to leading and living lives well with others. In this our educational practices may be purposeful, but they do not have to be prescriptive.

Relatedly, the second issue to face is that this decoupling of education from normative ideas of the self or subject raises the question of what becoming means in the context of specifically educational encounters. That is, is all becoming educational? Is becoming a thief, for example, educational, to paraphrase a question posed by Dewey himself one hundred years ago? To be clear, becoming as unfolding is not about moving toward a fixed identity position—thief, citizen, scholar, or otherwise—in some linear ordering of time. That is, becoming a "what" as a *kind* of becoming has not been my focus. The very temporality of unfolding works against casting our emergent being in categorical terms, which fix us into specific positions. Rather, what I am discussing here is that what makes our becoming through our encounters specifically educational is that it is about the "who" that can emerge out of the coalescence of varying conditions, a transient and impermanent "who" that is interrelated and interconnected with past and future. Shutting down this "who" is the work of systems and ways of thinking that seek to envelope one's becoming within oppressive categories and limited modes of being. It is the work of both physical and symbolic violence. While this might happen in schools and universities quite regularly, and while this might happen through the sheer force of socialization, the time of education itself lies in *living* time, not chronological time. Seeing the present as an act of presencing through which both past and future coalesce is to rethink education itself as that which occurs in this temporal space of continual emergence. There is thus no becoming that is not educational on these terms.

Thirdly, the time of presencing allows us to see the plurality of student's lives as mattering to who they will have become as they arise out of multiple conditions. The time of unfolding resists any easy alignment between *what* students are—in terms of the categories of class, race, ethnicity, sexuality, gender, and disability—and who students become. It is a resistance that does not deny, however, the significant ways such backgrounds and past experiences are presenced. That is, while I argued above that *who* someone becomes is not derived from the *what*, that does not mean that past experience does not matter at all. Rather, seeing time as a flow of presencing means that students are living their backgrounds in the present in ways that cannot simply be captured through the temporal movement of cause and effect, neither can they be predetermined and attributed to their particular identity positions. They are *living* their pasts and creating futures through the network of relations that form life in and through educational encounters. To see the presencing of the past as significant to becoming challenges the stereotyped and deterministic frameworks through which the past is said to define the present for students. Such frameworks either see students as exceptions to the rule or as fulfilling dangerous prophesies that adhere to notions of disadvantage. Instead, the time of unfolding breaks through the rigidity of our frameworks of thought that continue to fuel harmful modes of perception and affect.

Finally, what the relational time of unfolding reveals is how much we are implicated in one another's becoming. Educational encounters are times of coemergence. Our contact with each other as well as with other elements of our environment are in a continual, mutual dance of transformation. And although that dance is performed together, it unfolds differently for each one of us, uniquely arising within a host of conditions as a singular event of presencing.

PART TWO

Encounters in/of Education

Chapter Six

Digital Encounters

Online Education and the Space-Time of the Virtual

> Nothing is more destructive for the thinking and imaging of the virtual than equating it with the digital.
>
> —Brian Massumi, *Parables for the Virtual*

Over the course of the past two years, my computer has taken on an importance I never thought it would—a lifeline to friends and family, colleagues, and students. People whom I should see regularly in life-size form, now appear to me only as small heads on my screen, with clarity at the mercy of our respective internet connections. Distant in body, proximate in image, fragile in constancy. It was not as if communicating online were totally a new phenomenon for those of us who have had the advantage of relatively stable forms of connectivity prior to the pandemic—which of course remains not the case for the majority of people on this planet—but the quantity of these encounters has shifted over into *qualitatively* different experiences of social and educational life. This makes it more urgent to ask what kind of spaces and times are generated out of these online presences, specifically in the context of education. And given this is globally by no means a universal phenomenon, how do online educational practices speak to our specific contexts/environments as well as the qualitatively different modes of becoming these practices seem to afford? Moreover, how are sensory encounters, which I have been arguing are so central to educational processes of enculturation and becoming, possible within digital settings?

Part of the difficulty in responding to these issues, particularly from the point of view of the senses and the body more generally, is that the very naming of these practices seems to encourage a disembodied, dislocated, and detached sense of education. The naming of a set of online practices as distance education, remote learning, and e-learning, reflects the nature of the problem, to some degree, since what is being distanced, made remote, or electronically mediated is not people, namely educators and students, but education or learning itself. The designations reveal, therefore, a double form of distancing in failing to capture the rather obvious fact that it is our bodies that are distanced rather than our education, teaching, or learning. Perhaps it is telling that most standard nomenclature does not refer to teaching per se. Distance teaching and e-teaching are seldom used as generic terms by platforms and educational technology companies, although remote teaching has been a phrase adopted at least by my university during the pandemic, and colleagues both in universities and schools regularly refer colloquially to the work they do as online teaching. This omission of teaching in digital educational discourse echoes what Biesta (2010) calls the "learnification" of education, and society more broadly speaking, in which the activities of teaching and educating are seen to be meaningful only insofar as they are *effective*—that is, that they lead to a demonstrably measurable learning outcomes. Thus distance education can be caught up with the erasure of teaching as an activity that exists in its own right (requiring the curating of encounters as discussed in chapter 4, and the host of decisions that go into planning, designing, and executing such encounters). Furthermore, to contemplate the opposite of distance, remote, or electronically mediated education requires bringing to mind specifically spatial designations such as close, near, direct, proximate, and perhaps even intimate—designations which we do not often attribute to face-to-face forms of education. My point being is that in thinking the opposite, we can more accurately see how accepted terminology problematically sets up an alignment of spatial categories with educational practices and the people who participate in them (and a temporal alignment as well when reflecting on synchronous and asynchronous forms of online education).

In thinking through what place the senses and the body have in relation to digital educational encounters, I see it as crucial therefore to give consideration to the kind of terminology we are using and why, and what this means for a broader understanding of our educational practices and the people who physically engage in them. For this reason, I have chosen to use the adjective *online* to designate a quasi-site *through which* our encounters are happening and *education* as the noun to denote the processes of becoming and enculturation which mark those encounters, as I have discussed throughout this book. Referencing online as a quasi-site means seeing that it signals a space of engagement that is not necessarily experienced as distant at all, involving as it does actual encounters with screens, mouses, texts, images, and sounds, while also allowing for virtual encounters of potentiality. Indeed, this chapter sets out to make distinctions between the actual and the virtual, and the virtual and the digital, by drawing on Brian Massumi's and Pierre Lévy's understanding of the virtual as involved in processes of becoming. I do this in order to argue that online education involves practices of teaching and student engagement that are very much about an actual-virtual dynamic. This dynamic might play out differently in online education than it does in a physical educational setting, but it nonetheless creates its own educational spaces and times. Specifically, I address the relational and sensory dimensions of this dynamic and what it means for the formation of teaching online.

Relational, Bodily, and Virtual Contexts of Online Education

Advocates for online education see mainly the benefits it affords in terms of accessibility, flexibility, interactivity, nonsynchronous opportunities, and self-pacing (Adedoyin and Soykan 2020, 6). Such positive accounts are frequently embedded in a view of education as learning, with instructional technologies taking on an ever-increasing importance as modes of information delivery. Critics of online education, however, have often focused precisely on giving the opposite reasons for why it is problematic: that its accessibility is profoundly dependent on one's geo-socio-economic context; that the emphasis is on information delivery and training as opposed to human connection and knowledge creation; and that there is a rigidity inherent to its screen-focused pedagogy. Many have written on the impoverishment of teaching online, particularly with respect to how it seems to reinforce disembodied discourses of education, which focus on the delivery and acquisition of knowledge as discrete cognitive nuggets divorced from the messy realities of living bodies that are continually interacting with and responding to their environments. When bodies are acknowledged in online spaces, as Lander (2005) suggests, they often become "consuming bodies" (157) ingesting knowledge and information, whose materiality paradoxically disappears within the purported nonmateriality of digital communication.

Linking the wider context of online education to the more micro levels of pedagogical experience, Williamson et al. (2020) write of the "political economy of pandemic pedagogy" (108), which they argue is changing our understanding of educational practices. In fact a number of scholars cite the invidious ways the new emphasis on online education is socially divisive, making evident the clear split between access to and the unavailability of devices and internet connection, creating "new forms of digital in/exclusion" (Selwyn et al. 2020, 2). Crucially such divisions have not only to do with accessing computers, but also with a host of other conditions upon which online education depends. As Schwartzman (2020) observes in his article "Performing Pandemic Pedagogy," for university students these include: "no space suitably adaptable for uninterrupted work, escalating or irregular work schedules to compensate for reduced family income amid pandemic economic disruptions, additional family care responsibilities since younger children no longer attended school outside the home, and much more" (505). Critical of the digital inequalities that plague the move toward BYOD, or bring your own device, schools (see Alirezabeigi et al. 2020 for an analysis of such schools), Williamson et al. (2020) see that new relations of inequality are also emerging from the opposite direction, in terms of BYOSH, or bring your own school home. What can be extrapolated from their analysis is that online education is not just about what appears on the screen but is about how "physical spaces of the home are colonized and co-opted" (111). This does not concern simply working at the kitchen table while a family member is trying to prepare dinner for a host of hungry children—as if that weren't difficult enough. But it also concerns what online education is essentially relying on in order to function *as* online education. "Those grappling with the delicate ecosystem of parenting in the digital age realize that this is anything but *remote* learning. It is up close and personal and with the customary territorial trade-offs of colonization" (Williamson et al. 2020, 111). This means that digital encounters in effect lean on and are conditioned by the very physical spaces—and places—that teachers and students need to teach and study. "Home" thereby becomes a necessary condition for online engagement (or some other place, such as cafés, buses, trains, and parks). The conditions that give rise to and enable our digital encounters are therefore multifaceted and complex, and rarely have to do with any educationally designed space. To decolonize such conditional spaces requires thinking creatively and relationally about online educational practices in ways that understand how bodies and spaces are generated differentially across times and locations—and not just for the teachers and students who are directly engaged in digital encounters. The political economy of such colonizing practices is not simply about how middle-class homes are co-opted by the demands of online work; rather it is also profoundly related to the unequal distribution of global wealth, to the mining of minerals needed for digital devices as both a source of environmental degradation and human misery, and to the toxic waste dumps far from our homes in the Global North that devices are sent to once they are unwanted. Too often, online education is seen as a "freeing up" from both the regular rhythms of our daily lives (we don't need to work within a 9-to-5 time slot, but can work anytime anywhere, from bed, bench, or breakfast table), and from the larger economic, social, and political conditions which allow us to study and teach in this way. Indeed, we frequently imagine digital encounters as occurring between an individual student's mind (disconnected from place and body) and the material on a screen (which is seen to be neutral). Instead, decolonizing online education, like similar efforts in face-to-face contexts, requires understanding it as thoroughly intertwined with physical, bodily, and material relations that are also linked to a wider network of relations ranging from the intimate ones of home life to the distant ones of global capital, human suffering, and environmental degradation.

Somewhat paradoxically, online education can also provide opportunities for challenging business-as-usual forms of pedagogy, as Schwartzman (2020), Selwyn et al. (2020), and Williamson et al. (2020) also make clear. Bayne et al.'s (2020) *The Manifesto for Teaching Online* draws attention to what they refer to as the "recoding" of education, opening up opportunities for educators to modify what they *do* as educators. This bears out anecdotally as well. In speaking with colleagues across numerous contexts, I have heard them repeatedly say that what digital encounters potentially also afford is a rethinking of conventional pedagogical practices. Practices developed for site-specific teaching are necessarily challenged, since the encounters usually staged by educators in classrooms, museums, lecture halls, and the outdoors are simply not possible in digital environments. One can approximate certain pedagogical activities, but the formation of online educational encounters inevitably invokes different modes of relationality. Encounters with objects, images, and other people cannot simply be transferred willy-nilly into digital encounters without undergoing some form of translation and transformation. It means taking something from one context and qualitatively changing it into another one; while it still may be recognizable as pedagogical activity, its shape has shifted, creating new spaces and temporal orderings through which potentialities for becoming emerge, what Pierre Lévy (1998) refers to as "virtualizations." In this sense, transforming our place-based pedagogies to online ones sets into motion a qualitatively different set of relationships that enable different modes of becoming.

Before turning to discuss this more thoroughly, I think it is important to reflect on why this type of inquiry into online education is necessary from the point of view of the senses and the body more generally. After all, online education seems disembodied in the extreme, reduced as it is to a field of images on a two-dimensional surface. It seems to regulate our encounters to the purely visual at the expense of other sensory modalities; a visuality that is profoundly mediated through the types of devices we are interacting with—along, of course, with the strength of our connectivity. Phones, tablets, and computers all produce different types of images, privileging certain ways of seeing over others. Yet, bodies are not only *subject* to various digital devices, they are also intra-active with their digital environments; that is bodies do not simply *inter*act with the images and texts that appear on the screen, but they are part of the digital field itself and thus are *intra*-active with digital material. In their study of sensor technologies in educational architectural space, de Freitas, Rousell, and Jäger (2019) point out that the relational quality of our bodies means that we are never entirely separate from the technologies used to create such environments. Bodies are porous in mediating "the molecular, biochemical, and semiotic 'trafficking' of data . . . WiFi signals, for instance, pass through the walls of buildings and human tissue alike, respecting no fixed boundary between body and environment" (2019, 18). Just as holobionts are comprised of multiple life forms, bodies are not inert receptors in digital encounters; tablets, phones, and computers are not just static objects we use or that use us, mining us for data, but can be relationally understood as giving rise to certain modes of corporeal being and becoming.

Discussions abound about the porosity between our bodies and our devices, and what it signifies in terms of memory, neural plasticity, and our ability to experience and process information, from ideas of distributed cognition to AI models of intelligence. While much of this scholarship does not deal directly with education, H. Katherine Hayles, for one, writes eloquently of "embodied cognition" in the context of student engagement with digital media. As an English professor and digital humanities scholar, Hayles (2012) is all too aware of the shift that has taken place between reading print text and reading digital materials. For Hayles, there is not only a shift in the practice of reading but a shift in cognitive modes, "from deep attention characteristic of humanistic inquiry to the hyper attention characteristic of someone scanning web pages" (2012, 69). Careful not simply to dismiss the latter in favor of the former, Hayles is concerned with the role they both play in education: "Deep attention is essential for coping with complex phenomena such as mathematical theorems, challenging literary works, and complex musical compositions; hyper attention is useful for its flexibility in switching between different information streams, its quick grasp of the gist of material, and its ability to move rapidly among and between different kinds of texts" (69). What Hayles's work suggests is that the ways in which bodies touch and are touched by both the physical and graphic forms of text make a significant difference to how we think. The kind of visual contact made possible through different forms of media gives rise to very different sets of relationships with the content of those texts. As I discuss below, the rapid eye movements across a screen, the furrowed brow, the coordination of the eye with the hand, which might be poised at the edge of a page or hovering over a trackpad, are bodily activities that turn thinking itself into a relational formation. In their study of "reading qualities" across a range of media, including e-books, physical books, e-book readers, and audiobooks, Fuchsberger and Meneweger (2019) discuss key aspects of "materialized reading" practices, one of which is how individuals reading digital material do not have the same "solid external crutches that are formed by different sensory processes" (19) as they do when they read physical books. As an avid e-book reader myself, I have nonetheless lamented the disappearance of those crutches: not being able to see where I am physically in the text; or not finding the location of a certain passage on a particular page that I normally would have memorized as a gestalt image with a printed book; or not being greeted by the title and author's name on the cover each time I return to the text (although most recent editions of Kindle software has attempted to address this—clearly I was not the only one missing this). Furthermore, accessibility in the sense of both differently abled (sight impairments, fine-motor issues) and situational context (driving a car, sitting in a cafe, lying in bed) have a profound effect on the qualities of experience of reading. For Fuchsberger and Meneweger, this all points to the differential ways the body, mind, material, and environmental complex creates conditions for reading practices and what we get out of them.

These approaches underline how important it is to reflect not only on the material conditions of online education but also on the diverse ways bodies are thoroughly engaged in digital encounters. Hayles, and Fuchsberger and Meneweger make evident the changing and shifting nature of our encounters that in turn open up potentially different modes of being and becoming, as readers, as thinkers, as students and as educators. That is, while it is through our actual tangible contacts with digital media, the space and time of becoming gestures toward a realm of what is nontangible, what I have discussed earlier in terms of "reaching out" toward what is not yet (Manning 2007). There is thus something beyond the actual material in these encounters, what Elizabeth Grosz (2017) defines as the "incorporeal" element of our corporeal encounters or what Luce Irigaray (1993) refers to as the "sensible transcendental"— that is, the ways we have of exceeding ourselves through sensory contact with the world around us, including I would suggest contact with digital devices and the images they display. This opening up to the beyond of the *actual* is what Brian Massumi (2002) names the "virtual." Digital encounters can thus be seen both as bodily, sensory formations of contact that are *of* online environments and as virtual formations insofar as they invite us to spaces and times of becoming.

Virtual-Actual, Analog-Digital

We often informally equate the virtual with the digital and speak of online space as virtual space. Through nonimmersive, semi-immersive, and fully immersive simulations, the virtual is also thought to be its own reality through which we can have augmented perceptual experiences. In this sense the virtual is seen to be the epitome of Baudrillard's infamous simulacra—an image that is no longer representational of some reality but becomes reality itself. In common parlance, the virtual also denotes something that is almost but not quite there; it is an approximation of reality, something less than what is given. All of these understandings of the virtual have reality as their touchstone: the virtual is either real, hyperreal, or unreal, depending on the context.

Yet, there is another story to the virtual, one that is more closely connected to the body itself in terms of its movements and affects, its propulsions and impetuses, and one that I have gestured to above. The virtual signifies, according to Massumi (2002), that "pressing crowd of incipiencies and tendencies [as] a realm of *potential*" (30). Here, the virtual signals a dimension of our actions, expressions, and modes of becoming that are not (yet) *actual*. The virtual, therefore, has affinity not with reality, but with actuality. Significantly, the virtual also plays a role in the establishment of what *becomes* actual, without having any power of determination. For instance, as discussed in previous chapters, the *movement of reaching out* is very much part of touching something or someone. As such, this incipient action contains a virtual element since the touch has *not yet* actualized. In this, the virtual is a complex amalgam of tendencies. However, not all of those tendencies come to fruition or find expression in the corporeal, physical, *actual* realm of encounters. That is the movement of reaching out might not end in the actual placing of my hand on your shoulder; there are a host of other tendencies present that might give rise to a different outcome. The virtual in this sense is open-ended.

There is an obvious tension to consider here. While the virtual is *embodied* in its movement since it is a fundamental aspect of bodily and sensory encounters with elements of the environment, it is nonetheless *not actual*; it is not physical in the way we usually think of the body in terms of its materiality and substance. For Massumi (2002), "to think the body in movement means accepting the paradox that there is an incorporeal dimension *of the body*. Of it, but not it" (5). This incorporeality is always connected to actual living and breathing bodies as they transform out of a crowded field of potentialities. According to Massumi, a good way of thinking about this is through topology, where the same figure can take on numerous shapes through various deformations without its geometrical properties being broken: the square's edges can be stretched out into a circle; the coffee mug can be folded into itself so the empty space of the handle becomes the hole of what is now effectively a donut; the rubber toy puppy can be expanded from within to become a round sphere. There is multiplicity within the form itself that is not determinable from its original starting point in coordinate space.

The virtual, along these lines, contains these incipient modes of becoming. Pierre Lévy (1998) refers to this topological shape-shifting as virtualizations, which he sees as transformations that proceed from the actual to the virtual (and sometimes back to the actual again), rather than the other way around. Actualization, he writes, is dependent on the virtual as the "knot of tensions, constraints and projects that animate" a given entity (Lévy 1998, 25). He takes the everyday instance of the trajectory from seed to tree: "The seed's problem, for example, is the growth of the tree. The seed *is* this problem, even if it is also something more than that. This does not signify that the seed *knows* exactly what the shape of the tree will be, which will one day burst into bloom and spread its leaves above it. Based on its internal limitations, the seed will have to invent the tree, coproduce it together with the circumstances it encounters" (24). What both Lévy and Massumi call attention to is the movement of potentiality that exists in the actualization of all life. Potentiality here is not to be confused with possibility; for both authors, possibility is something that is already constituted, it merely "exists in a state of limbo" (Lévy 1998, 24). That is, possibilities are an array of happenings that are already predetermined, presuggested; which one is chosen or transpires is a contained state of affairs. Just like answers to multiple-choice questions, the possible exists as limited offerings. Potentialities, on the other hand, exist on a qualitatively different register. They are actualized in the here and now as a stable (and temporary) solution to a virtual problem—that knot of incipient tendencies.

But what Lévy is most concerned with is not how potentialities become transformed into stable positions or entities, but with virtualization, which is "the movement of actualization in reverse" (Lévy 1998, 26). It is worth quoting him at length:

> We now have a better idea of the difference between realization (the occurrence of a predetermined possible) and actualization (the invention of a solution required by a problematic complex). But what is virtualization? No longer the virtual as a way of being but virtualization as a dynamic. Virtualization can be defined as the movement of actualization in reverse. It consists in the transition from the actual to the virtual, and *exponentiation* of the entity under consideration. Virtualization is not a derealization (the transformation of a reality into a collection of possibles) but a change of identity, a displacement of the center of ontological gravity of the object considered. Rather than being defined principally through its actuality (a solution), the entity now finds its essential consistency within

a problematic field. The virtualization of a given entity consists in determining the general question to which it responds, in mutating the entity in the direction of this question and redefining the initial actuality as the response to a specific question. (Lévy 1998, 26)

While Lévy gives the example of a company that *virtualizes* its practices to illustrate this movement, one can imagine a university or school here. Through virtualization, the "center of ontological gravity" is displaced from buildings, offices, classrooms, defined schedules, and face-to-face meetings to an IT communications network where the spatial and temporal ordering of teaching and studying is continually problematized; it is not a stable solution since it sets into motion a series of issues that have no stable point of reference and "reinvents a nomadic culture" (29). The university is "not there" in the conventional sense but can be understood as creating multiple times and spaces where the "limits of interaction are no longer self-evident" (34). People and communities become detached from "conventional physical or geographical space and the temporality of the clock or calendar" (29). This is particularly true of social media spaces as well as some forms of online education, where the asynchronous time of connection is seen as its particular strength: our ability to communicate across times and spaces that do not need to share a specific *here* or *now*.

While Lévy's example seems to reproduce a view of virtualization that feels all too familiar from the point of view of life in the 2020s—and of the neoliberal and colonial impulses of organizing time and space that have been going on for the past three decades across a range of public and private institutions—it is important to keep in mind that he views the fossilization of these movements (which have been galvanized into market-driven markers of success) as reification, "a reduction of the thing to the 'real'" (34). Thus the virtualization of the university is not necessarily a negative move, so long as it can keep open its sense of ontological transformation. This transformative promise is something that Massumi identifies as being more closely aligned with the analog than the digital.

On Massumi's terms, the analog is a "continuously variable impulse or momentum that can cross from a qualitatively different medium into another. Like electricity into sound waves. Or heat into pain. Or light waves into vision. Or vision into imagination. Or noise in the ear into music in the heart. Or *outside coming in*" (2002, 135). For Massumi, the analog—as opposed to the digital—is the primary modality for the virtual, since it allows for qualitative transformation of the "crowd of pressing tendencies" into action, thought, sensation; it transduces. In addition, the analog, to my mind, also indicates a process of translation, as well as transduction; a form that is analogous to whatever is being referenced or measured: the sweep of the hands of the clock measure chronological time; electrical impulses reference my beating heart; the dial on the scale measures my weight. The analog is also a metaphoric process that changes categorically the thing being referenced: for instance, my heartbeat *becomes* the electrical impulse. To me, this metaphorical, transformative aspect of the analog is creative insofar as it relies on coming up with new modalities for thinking and feeling through different technologies. ECGs, or the translation of electricity into "my heartbeat," are not the only way to take account of my heart's throbs; the stethoscope also references my beating heart but does so in channeling its sound waves. There is something of the aesthetic gesture in such analog technologies, poetic, metaphorical, and metonymical. The digital, on the other hand, is no such translator or transducer, but acts through numerical reduction. It does not re-present information from one source to another in different form but converts information into numerical "language" or "currency." Quantification into ones and zeros means that information is not *transformed* but coded. Codification is not the same thing as transformation. For this reason, Massumi understands the digital to be firmly located within the realm of possibility, not of potentiality and certainly not of virtuality (2002, 137).

Importantly, for my purposes here, the body plays a significant role in analogic transformation of the virtual. "In sensation the thinking-feeling body is operating as transducer. If sensation is the analog processing by body-matter of ongoing transformative forces, then foremost among them are forces of appearing as such: of coming into being, registering as becoming. The body, sensor of change, is a transducer of the virtual" (Massumi 2002, 135). Bodies appear and materialize out of the transduction of the virtual through analogic means. This means that the digital per se has little to do with such appearances and becomings, since they are not about qualitative change but simulation and systemization. As Massumi points out, digital technologies, unlike the arts and other technologies, do not "envelop the virtual" (137). Digital technologies have connection to the virtual "only through the analog" (138).

Giving the example of word-processing, Massumi notes that the digital "always circuits into the analog"; the digital text needs to be read to be actualized. Language might be coded digitally but "words *appear* on screen, in being read. Reading is the qualitative transformation of alphabetical figures into figures of speech and thought" (138). More importantly, is how digital text is reliant upon the virtuality of the body in order for this transformation to occur. That is, there is a bodily translation of ASCII code into analog reading practices:

> Reading, however cerebral it may be, does not entirely think out sensation. It is not purified of it. A knitting of the brows or pursing of the lips is a self-referential action. . . . The acts of attention performed during reading are forms of incipient action. . . . Enfolded in the muscular, tactile, and visceral sensations of attention are incipient perceptions. When we read, we do not see the individual letters and words. That is what learning to read is all about: learning to stop seeing the letters so you can see *through* them. Through the letters, we directly experience fleeting visionlike sensations, inklings of sound, faint brushes of movement. . . . In the experience of reading, conscious thought, sensation, and all the modalities of perception fold into and out of each other. Attention most twisted. (Massumi 2002, 139)

What Massumi does here is to show how through analogical transformation of the virtual through our sensation, movement, and perception, our bodies play a significant role in the formation of digital encounters, participating in what Mark Hansen (2006) calls "mixed realities" simultaneously: the digital world of the screen with its ASCII-coded letters and the virtual world of incipient becoming that transduces the digital into altered modes of being. For Massumi, the interaction between the digital form (including television, movies, text messages, hypertext) and the formation of attention echoes Hayles's ideas above, but an important caveat is that while Hayles equates "deep" or "hyper" forms of attention to specific types of reading, Massumi suggests that these forms of attention can vary within a type itself—even within the rhythms of internet surfing, vacillating as they often do between attention and distraction (Massumi 2002, 139).

So if the analog is associated with the virtual, and the virtual is a source of potential becoming, then how might our digital encounters be understood more analogically? This to me is a key question since it is the qualitatively transformative process of becoming that surely marks out digital encounters as educational ones. This requires framing our teaching practices as being *more rather than less virtual* in online spaces.

Connecting Digital Encounters with Virtual Teaching

Following on from the previous discussion, we can see how online education is involved not only in digital environments, but in actual and virtual ones as well. That is, our *actual* bodies are involved in touching and being touched by our devices and home setups, as well as by images and texts on the screen, while the *virtual* dimension is a source for *how* we interact (intra-act) with all these elements in our environment—a source of potentialities for thinking, moving, sensing, and feeling. To return to the example above, although reading is often thought to be primarily a visual activity, it is also deeply tied to sensations and bodily affects that condition new modes of thinking. The eyes do not translate the ASCII code into letters and then into words and then into sentences only for its meaning to then suddenly appear; there is a synesthetic dimension to the virtual that allows us to engage with digital text as being something other than it is, through our myriad sensations, feelings, and thought processes. This element of translation and transduction, properties of the analog, speaks deeply I think to the specifically educational elements of our digital encounters.

Focusing on the virtual allows for a reframing of online education in ways that highlight the relational quality of digital encounters. The sensory modalities through which teachers and students touch and are touched by the world are not so much mediated by the digital as they are by the analogical ways we are interconnected. That is, our capacity to qualitatively transform digital media into practices of reading, attention, and study, for example, is quintessentially an analogical move. While the digital makes it *possible* to come together across distance in space and time, it is the analog that *transforms potentialities* to create communities out of these disparate times and places. Rather than seeing our online teaching practices as having to replicate digitally what we do in physical spaces such as seminar rooms and lecture halls—I'm thinking here of the ubiquitous turning of face-to-face lectures into digital recordings—the question becomes how do we create digital environments in ways that amplify their analogic-virtual connections, in ways that enable the transformation of digital material into practices that move beyond the consumption of information, practices that bring students and teachers together with educational purpose? This requires a different view of the body than the "consuming" one that is only there to ingest what it is given, as well as a different view of digital encounters themselves.

For instance, the digital recording of a lecture might transmit content knowledge, and might help in providing information, but it falls flat as a pedagogical practice if the aim is to *educate*, that is to allow for the transformation of new thinking and new ways of being in the world. Like with physical teaching, this can only come from students' encounters with the material, which as both Hayles and Massumi discuss, are tied to bodily, sensory, and affective relations to the material at hand. Eyes scan, heads lean on hands, eyebrows raise, breathing slows, backs begin to ache—all of this speaks to the body's incipient action, not to the specifically digital content. My point here is not to say that recorded lectures are themselves uneducational, but that they are noneducational until opportunities for student engagement become interwoven into the pedagogical activity that surrounds them. The task of teaching is therefore to curate these digital encounters in ways that enhance their virtuality, that augment the experiential dimensions of those encounters and that provide opportunities for potentialities to become actual.

As discussed in chapter 4, curating educational encounters as relational formations requires an aesthetic approach which allows for the nonpredictable (and nonprobable) to emerge. Online teaching is by its nature problem-posing since it is not clear where the center of ontological gravity lies in any given configuration. It requires transforming what are multiply diverse physical sites (students and teachers at home or elsewhere) into a shared, communal space. Bringing people together around a common theme, topic, object of study requires an analogical-virtual solution, one that involves the senses, that makes the sensory encounters with digital material part of the pedagogical design itself. Designing digital encounters analogically is, of course, not perhaps straightforward in online contexts, since what is made common within a group (a class, a seminar, a lecture) faces specific spatial and temporal challenges—not that face-to-face groups do not experience challenges, merely that online ones are *different* in kind and quality. The "relationscape" (Manning 2012) of online education is complicated by the heightened individuality of circumstances that in part condition the coming together over the internet. Both physical and online encounters are cocreated spaces, and both also depend on a host of hidden conditions for students and teachers to be present. For instance, traveling long distances to the university class, working long hours to pay for tuition and transport, and juggling family commitments with attendance are all complications familiar to face-to-face classes. However, the difference with online education is that it relies on certain conditions being met *in order to* enact its pedagogical practices. That is, it is not enough to show up or even enough to be eager to engage; with face-to-face classes, once one has made it to class there is a shared opportunity (possibility) for engagement through the pedagogical activities that are on offer. This is not the case with online education. Engagement has not only to do with the activities and encounters that are being curated, but with the myriad places in which each participant is studying or teaching; the types of devices one is using; the camera, microphone, and software functionality; the stability of the connection; the synchronous or asynchronous nature of the encounters; and the sequencing, availability, and archiving of digital material. All of this makes it more, not less, difficult to hold the space as a communal one, raising questions as well about how one is present in such space. How are students and teachers present with each other? How do teachers and students encounter both the curricular material and the digital media through which that material is made available? That is, insofar as educational encounters enact a form of presencing in creating a living contact between students, teachers, and objects of study, we need to be aware of how online contexts constitute multiple presents for those who are participating in class, since one student can log on one evening to write a comment on a Mural board, and another the next morning. Again, it is not that physical teaching does not also have to account for the differential ways in which students encounter material and the asynchronicity of it all (they always read and write at different times and in different places), but during a shared, collective synchronous online class it is much less obvious how this engagement is happening for students, since we rely as teachers on a host of perceptual cues (not just facial ones) to make such judgments. In online settings, teachers cannot move around and overhear multiple group discussions simultaneously, nor is it easy to detect changes in attention. More importantly, absent are those microperceptions of classroom interaction: the quick glances, the shift in mood, the subtle change of tone, the alteration of bodily positions, the navigation of shared space. What is palpable in a physical classroom is barely registered online, even with cameras, microphones, connectivity, and software working smoothly—without, that is, strategies for addressing this virtual dimension.

Moving toward the virtual in digital spaces also means opening up our teaching practices, just as we would do in physical spaces, to self-examination and scrutiny. But not simply from the point of view of types of digital material we are offering students (the films, the readings, the games, the evaluation tools, the recordings, the podcasts, the educational software we are using). Indeed, while this is the stuff from which we can create curriculum experiences with students, it is the *quality of encounters* that we are setting up in relation to them that matter and that speak directly to the virtual as a process of becoming. It is precisely because the digital cannot transduce from one form to another that curating digital encounters analogically becomes so necessary if our classes are not to become mere simulations of social media platforms. That is, to find the educational in the digital means ensuring that the virtual is part of what it is we are curating. Designing educational encounters in this way further means that we, as teachers, enact a form of analogical transformation for ourselves. Decisions about content and process can be understood as openings for our own becoming—from classroom teachers to virtual educators.

As virtual (and not merely online) educators there is an opportunity for presencing potentiality as part of the project of decolonizing online education mentioned earlier. It means staging digital encounters that through their performative effect—their formation of relations—actually bring our profound interconnection with others near and far, remembered and forgotten, accepted and dismissed into the living time of study. Online education is *not* the great equalizer; what is required, to return to Rancière here, is a "perceptual shock" that can reconfigure the political basis from which we teach. Online education can either contribute to regimes of perception that continue to make invisible the lives of others and the material conditions upon which our digital connections depend, or it can aim at inciting new modes of visibility, new synesthetic approaches to digital material in order to create new communities of sense. We do not necessarily need to be in the same physical room at the same time for this to happen. While the fact that bodies are distanced in online contexts is a source of lament for some, it can also serve as a potential source for exploring more deliberately how spaces and times can be generated out of the "not there" and "not yet," which are always implicit in digital spaces. To make visible does not simply mean choosing specific digital *content* (read: information) that shows how colonization operates in education, but more to do with making evident the interrelationships we have to others: other people, the earth's materials, and the things without which online education itself would not be possible. Curating digital encounters analogically means seeing our online spaces not as self-contained worlds, but as aesthetic happenings, relational formations, that challenge the sensory conditions that keep them within this myth of containment. Decolonizing online education means rupturing the given sensory conditions that rhetorically function to keep it disembodied, distanced, remote. Instead, attending to the virtual puts the transformative potential back into digital encounters to be something other than what they often purport to be.

Chapter Seven

Encounters with Climate Change
Teaching in the Presence of Climate Sorrow

> Humans are tuned for relationship. The eyes, the skin, the tongue, ears, and nostrils—all are gates where our body receives the nourishment of otherness.
>
> —David Abram, *The Spell of the Sensuous*

> The expression "relation to the world" itself demonstrates the extent to which we are, so to speak, *alienated*.
>
> —Bruno Latour, *Facing Gaia*

In December 2018 Danish-Icelandic artist Olafur Eliasson deposited thirty chunks of glacial ice into central London as part of an interactive artwork entitled *Ice Watch*. The transported ice had broken off from Greenland glaciers and twenty-four blocks were laid in front of the Tate Modern for the public to interact with. From the documentation, it is evident that the relation to this relatively small slice of the world was a deeply sensual one, involving people touching, rubbing, licking, listening, smelling, and observing the ice. It was a complex relation that moved between the concreteness of the pieces of ice, their liquid melting, and their eventual evaporation into air. It was a relation, in other words, that spoke of transformation, transition, loss, and to the passing of time as well as to the present immediacy of the ice as it was experienced through the senses.

Eliasson's work reminds us that the enormity of the current climate emergency can be felt through singular moments of encounter. Indeed one might say it is the very task of an artist to stage encounters that can provoke and offer a "perceptual shock" (to echo once again Rancière's phrase) that reorder our relation to the world.[1] While the work of the educator, as we have seen, carries with it different responsibilities than the artist, it also echoes the installation artist's considerations as it too stages encounters between students and elements in the environment (through contact with plants, insects, water, soil, stones, animals, etc.). As discussed in chapter 4, teaching, like art production, is very much about a certain form of "curation" (Ruitenberg 2015) that takes place both within and outside formal schooling contexts and offers opportunities for students to have new and life-enhancing experiences; in this educators devise the form their pedagogies will take by designing activities, planning their duration, setting up the physical space, creating conditions for interaction, and choosing the content, objects, and material that students will interact with; as such it is not dissimilar to the aesthetic decisions that artists and curators have to make. But it is also very different, since there is another kind of educational responsibility built into our practices as teachers, particularly acute when working with children and youth: to help them live and lead lives with others in a context that is sensitive, attuned, and responsive to their concerns and experiences. Such an overt educational and ethical sensibility is not a formal obligation for the artist. Educators create opportunities for students to explore their relations to the world through encounters that are not only aesthetic but must also be educationally responsive. As such, it is important to see how the encounters we stage can reflect life-enhancing experiences as well as possibly prompting anxiety, dread, and fear for students in contemplating the possible end of life as we know it within their lifetimes. Indeed we are compelled to ask ourselves as teachers: What relation can we have to the world in the present when the climate emergency puts into question the futurability (Berardi 2017) of life itself? Do we side-step the horror of our collective predicament and proceed with business as usual, pushing it into a place of denial, or do we face up to its magnitude and begin the work of dealing with what feminist psychoanalyst Susie Orbach refers to as "climate sorrow"?

As Orbach (2019) writes, climate sorrow "opens up into wretched states of mind and heart. We can find it unbearable. Without even meaning to repress or split off our feelings, we do so. I am doing so now as I write. Staying with such feelings can be bruising and can make us feel helpless and despairing. It is hard, very hard, to stay with, and yet there is value in this if we can create contexts for doing so" (68).² Orbach's passage raises the question: Can our educational encounters, particularly for youth, become such a context? For as she suggests, if we are going to change the course of the current path of destruction, then we need to face up to those difficult feelings that prevent us from acting for change in the first place. And, insofar as environmental education seeks to encourage such transformation, then we need not only to take our own feelings into account as adults but to offer an educational space and time for youth to confront and begin to deal with their own existential worries and concerns. Thus if education is to become a context for facing climate sorrow, what "relations to the world" are we imagining might help youth—and indeed ourselves—to stay with difficult feelings about the future by enabling them to develop a living relationship to the more-than-human world in the present?

After first situating the importance of relations to the natural world within environmental education,³ the next part of this chapter delves into reframing relations *to* the world as encounters *of* the world, and specifically *of* elements of the environment. As indicated in the epigraphs to this paper, there are (at least) two ways of thinking of our "relation to the world": that our relations are always constituted through a sensory encounter with otherness, as the quote from David Abram (1997) above suggests; or that relation *to* itself presumes that we are already disconnected and alienated from the world *of* which we are a part, as Bruno Latour (2017) intimates. Despite the apparent incommensurability of their positions (Abram positing a phenomenological approach to questions of our existence; Latour taking an immanent view of existence through relational ontology), I explore how the sensual dimension of our singular experiences are indeed also an important part of our human inseparability from the world and as such can inform the way we teach through encounters with elements of the environment. I then turn to a more in-depth exploration of Eliasson's climate installation *Ice Watch* and particularly focus on the way it holds two temporal dimensions together through the kinds of encounters it makes possible. Here, I discuss its relationship both to chronological time (*chronos*) and to living time (*kairos*), picking up on the themes introduced in chapter 5. Here I draw on Marianna Papastephanou's (2014) work on kairosophy and reflect on what teaching can learn from such an artwork temporally. In the third section I locate the time of environmental teaching at the juncture of *chronos* and *kairos* as a way of responding to our duty to educate about the future with our responsibility to do so in ways that contribute to students' living well in the present—that is, to create encounters *of* the world that educate about the climate emergency while also giving time for climate sorrow.

Relation to the "Natural" World in Environmental Education[4]

Many scholars advocate that one of the best ways for engaging students in sustainability issues is to create encounters that allow students to build a *living* relationship to the natural environment. Michael Bonnett (2007) for one notes how students' relationship to the natural world is often neglected in formal schooling curriculum in environmental education. Similarly, Anne Liefländer et al. (2013) observe that curriculum and pedagogy in sustainability education are frequently focused on "knowledge and attitudinal outcomes" and argue instead that developing feelings of connectedness with nature can lead to developing feelings of protection toward it (370). The development of such relationships has long been the aim of outdoor and experiential education, with which environmental pedagogy, especially with young children, has been intertwined (Dyer 2007). Encounters with plants, animals, and insects are regularly staged by teachers as a means to encourage children's curiosity, imagination, and wonder (Dyer 2007; Hauk et al. 2015; Jørgensen 2016), and many authors cite Rachel Carson's *Sense of Wonder* as an inspirational text in this regard. Thus, there is a broad, if varied, consensus that environmental education is not merely about the cognitive accumulation of facts about the effects of climate change, nor is it solely engaged with the domain of the intellect, but is dependent on developing relationships with the world that are both sensual and affective.

Hauk et al. (2015) speak of teaching in this regard as a form of "creative curation." For instance, in the activities collected in their extensive article, there is a strong sense of the aesthetic dimension as central to our experience with nature: each activity is designed around a form of embodied relationality through sound, scent, taste, touch, and vision. This turn to the aesthetic has not been lost on either environmental educators or climate artists who are also involved in staging sensory encounters with elements in the environment as part of augmenting awareness about sustainability.[5] For Hauk et al., environmental education is necessarily about "sensory entanglement" as a means for attending to and having compassion for the natural world.

In this respect, calls for environmental education indeed echo Abram's (1997) emphasis on the centrality of the sensual and perceptual dimensions of those relations. However, what constitutes this sensory "relation to the world" is far from straightforward since it is not always immediately clear what "relation" or "world" mean in these educational contexts. Is the "world" simply a substitute for "nature," for all that we hold outside of "culture"? And if so, where am *I* in that world? Moreover, is "relation" that which exists between an already defined self and an "other" from the realm of the "natural"? And if so, how do we conceive of ourselves as human within this more-than-human realm? I think these questions warrant further attention given that relationships with nature are seen to be beneficial both for students' present lives and for the future of the planet itself. Abram and Latour offer some conceptual distinctions that are useful for reframing what we are doing as teachers as we stage relational and aesthetic encounters with the world. It is to these that I now turn.

Reframing Relations through Sensory Encounters

For Abram our sensory entanglements are complex arrangements. Although drawing on a phenomenological heritage that can sometimes be construed as anthropocentric (Langer 2003) or colonial (Ahmed 2000) in its universalizing of singular experience, Abram (1997) seeks to utilize its perceptual framework to reconsider the kinds and qualities of relations we have to the world that respects the plural dimensions of more-than-human life forms. Indeed, he insists that we do not only receive the world (as one reading of the epigraph might suggest) but also that we *enter into* the world through our perception—a perception that is necessarily partial: "Yet it is also our insertion in a world that exceeds our grasp in every direction, our means of contact with things and lives that are still unfolding, open and indeterminate, all around us. Indeed, from the perspective of my bodily senses, there is no thing that appears as a completely determinate or finished object. Each thing, each entity that my body sees, presents some face or facet of itself to my gaze while withholding other aspects from view" (Abram 1997, 40). For Abram, the way I encounter the world is necessarily constantly shifting, as are the things and lives with which I come into contact. Our sensory relation to the world is not, therefore, only partial because of our subject positionality, but because as a living being among other beings and existents, I live in and through time: the time of continual flux and change. In this, our perception is something to be neither overcome nor perfected so that we may grasp the world in some all-encompassing gesture that freezes time. Instead, as Abram makes clear, our sensory encounters with elements of the environment enable us to attune to change and alteration, each encounter not quite like the one that comes before. He gives the example of looking at the seemingly static object of a clay bowl and is reminiscent of Dōgen's being-time, discussed earlier:

> Even a single facet of this bowl resists being plumbed by my gaze once and for all. For, like myself, the bowl is a temporal being, an entity shifting and changing in time, although the rhythm of its changes may be far slower than my own. Each time that I return to gaze at the outward surface of the bowl, my eyes and my mood have shifted, however slightly; informed by my previous encounters with the bowl, my senses now more attuned to its substance, I continually discover new and unexpected aspects. (1997, 40)

Abram (2011) is clear that our modern ways of conceiving of "nature" have ushered in a particular (negative) view of the senses. He attributes this initially to the heliocentric discoveries of Copernicus, Kepler, and Galileo that needed to hive off our sensory experience from thought and knowledge. As such, "sensory perception was increasingly derided as deceptive; only that which could be measured and analyzed mathematically could be taken as true" (2011, 293). Abram's point is not that we should return to a pre-Newtonian worldview, but that the stark division that devalued the ways we live our lives through our bodies and the senses has led to a distorted sense of ourselves and the environment, with calamitous results. Indeed, Abram suggests that even some environmental activists themselves keep at bay "creaturely sensations" in a bid not "to succumb to an overwhelming grief," (2011, 17) preferring instead to focus on statistics and abstractions to champion their cause. For Abram, this is yet another indication of how "we shelter ourselves from the harrowing vulnerability of bodied existence" (2011, 18)—and indeed, I would add, climate sorrow. Avoiding the senses becomes a way of averting the horror.

A remedy for this, as I read Abram, is to rethink the world not in terms of objects to be known and measured by a subject in a grand gesture of mastery, but in terms of encounters that bring me into commingling, connection, and tension with the things and lives around me. In other words, that bring me into *qualities* of relationship with the environment—and for Abram, particularly the "natural" or more-than-human environment. Drawing on Merleau-Ponty's (2012) idea of the "flesh of the world," Abram sees that it is not simply a singular body that perceives objects but that there is an exchange or interaction of flesh, a reciprocation in the encounter. "From within the depths of this encounter, we know the thing or phenomenon only as our interlocutor—as a *dynamic presence* that confronts us and *draws us into relation*" (1997, 43, emphasis added). Thus, our flesh is entangled, wrapped around one in the other, the folds of which are at times unclear. This does not mean we are one with the environment; rather that our very perception is a form of *participation* that takes on the rhythms of history as one of intrinsic plurality. "For these other shapes and species have coevolved, like ourselves, with the rest of the shifting earth; their rhythms and forms are composed of layers upon layers of earlier rhythms, and in engaging them our senses are led into an inexhaustible depth that echoes that of our own flesh. . . . They are all composed of repetitive figures that *never exactly repeat themselves*" (1997, 47). It is thus that our encounters are singular in the sense that while we might encounter a familiar object (for instance, a tree, rock, or bird in our local park), it is a nonrepeatable event, a moment of the variation in time that can never be replicated. Encounters are also, therefore, dynamic, since each one is solicited, active, and open. Abram writes: "To the sensing body *all* phenomena are animate, actively soliciting the participation of our senses, or else withdrawing from our focus and repelling our involvement. Things disclose themselves to our immediate perception as vectors, as styles of unfolding—not as finished chunks of matter given once and for all, but as dynamic ways of engaging the senses and modulating the body" (1997, 56). It is this unfolding of perception that suggests we are never in a static "relation to" something, but in a constant flow of relation, an immersion with a world which is itself vibrant, subject to alteration, differentiation, and endless variation. In this sense, our encounters are not merely *with* the world, but are *of* the world: moments of contact in the present that open up to the unfolding and shifting reality of the things and lives we meet.

Although Abram's position is rich in its depiction of the more-than-human world as it is *experienced*, I want to delve a little further here into a conception of the world that highlights even more significantly its relational qualities. I do this in order to probe deeper into the animate dimensions of the environment which do not simply offer themselves up to our sensory *experience*, but also exist as a network of interdependent relations that link me to life on this planet. Thus while Abram quite clearly sees that the more-than-human world shapes itself according to its own rhythms which "echo our own flesh," Latour actually takes this a step further to assert that our inseparability from the world as humans is not only an aspect of experience, but is part of an ontological condition of the world itself. As I argue below, this strengthens the idea that our sensory encounters are *of* the world in a manner that is both immersive and interdependent.

Reframing the World in Terms of Gaia

Latour (2017) asserts that the New Climate Regime has ushered in a "profound mutation in our relation to the world" (8). However, rather than placing relational qualities at the center of a phenomenological analysis as Abram does, he instead reconceptualizes the world itself *as* relation. This requires accepting that it is now no longer possible to think of nature as separate from culture (if it ever was) when we speak of the world itself.

> The difficulty lies in the very expression "relation to the world," which presupposes two sorts of domains, that of nature and that of culture, domains that are at once distinct and impossible to separate completely. Don't try to define nature alone, for you'll have to define the term "culture" as well (the human is what escapes nature: a little, a lot, passionately); don't try to define "culture" alone, either, for you'll immediately have to define the term "nature" (the human is what cannot "totally escape" the constraints of nature). Which means that we are

not dealing with domains but rather with one and the same concept divided into two parts, which turn out to be bound together, as it were, by a sturdy rubber band. (Latour 2017, 15)

Like Abram, Latour traces this division to the heliocentric discoveries of the sixteenth and seventeenth centuries; yet in distinction from Abram's critique, he emphasizes that this division has contributed to how humans live between two worlds: "One is where they have their habits, the protection of law, their deeds of property, the support of their State, what we could call the *world they live in*; and then, in addition, a second world, a ghostly one, often far remote in time and space, that benefits from no legal protection, no clear delineation of properties, and no State to defend its rights: let's call it the *world they live from*" (Latour and Weibel 2020, 15). Thus what the New Climate Regime ushers in is a reframing of the world that dispenses with the split itself and that reenvisions the world beyond the nature/culture divide. Latour speaks instead of a "Critical Zone": "We reside inside a thin bio-film no thicker than a few kilometres up and down, from which we cannot escape—and, 'Critical Zonists' would add, whose *reactions* (chemical alterations and geological mechanisms, as well as social processes) are still largely unknown" (Latour and Weibel 2020, 3). More importantly, this Critical Zone is neither a "chunk of space" (Latour 2014, 4) nor territory nor land, but depicts a spatio-temporal zone where life transpires on this planet. It is "critical," for Latour, in the engineering sense of feeling stress, signaling a structure's potential collapse under certain conditions. This Critical Zone is, in other words, the world of life itself, subject to stresses that are brought now to a point that does indeed threaten its ruin (2014, 4).

Underlying this formulation is Latour's reading of James Lovelock's Gaia hypothesis. In his Gifford Lectures, published under the title *Facing Gaia*, Latour (2017) argues that we need to "place ourselves inside this world" (36) in a way that understands the Earth in all its complexity and not simply as an effect of "Nature" or as that which is untouched by "Culture." He asks: "How to speak about the Earth without taking it to be an already composed whole, without adding to it a coherence that it lacks, and yet without deanimating it by representing the organisms that keep the thin film of the critical zones alive as mere inert and passive passengers on a physio-chemical system?" (86). For Latour, in line with Lovelock, we cannot understand the Earth, its behavior, or the way it works, without having a sense of the actions "accomplished by living organisms"; the Earth is teeming with the proliferation of life "between the top of the upper atmosphere and the bottom of the sedimentary rock formations"; it is a veritable "seething broth" (2017, 93). Living organisms are not, however, to be seen as "parts of a whole," for Latour, as if Gaia were one thing, one unified totality. In Latour's terms, Gaia represents an attempt to name the plurality of life not to mark yet another "organism" such as "Nature" with its own "laws" and "moralities" separate from the organisms that make up life in the Critical Zone.[6] Instead, Gaia is a multiplicity and "captures the distributed intentionality of all the agents, each of which modifies its surroundings for its own purposes" (2017, 98). In Latour's view, then, what Gaia, unlike "Nature," moves to encompass is the pulsing, ever-changing reality of liv*i*ng, not the context in which such living occurs. As Latour emphasizes, "Organisms . . . do not develop 'in' an environment; rather, each one bends the environment around itself, as it were, the better to develop" (2017, 98). As we have seen in chapter 2, with reference to Maxine Sheets-Johnstone's work, organisms are formed, deformed, and transformed through encounters with elements of their environments.

Importantly, this means that we cannot so easily distinguish where the action of an organism ends and the world begins; this is not merely a conceptual issue for Latour, neither is it a problem of perception, but is part of the facticity of the multiplicity of living. "Since all living agents follow their own intentions all along, modifying their neighbors as much as possible, there is no way to distinguish between the environment to which the organism is adapting and the point at which its own action begins" (2017, 100). This has a profound bearing on the ways in which we conceive the environment not only as a space which we inhabit or can have a *relation to* as though it is separate from us, but also as encapsulating a time of encounter; Gaia is a history of those encounters and relations that organisms, including human, viral, bacterial, atmospheric, animal, and vegetal, create through their own activity as living organisms. As Latour writes,

> There is nothing inert, nothing benevolent, nothing external in Gaia. If climate and life have evolved together, space is not a frame, not even a context: space is the offspring of time. Exactly the opposite of what Galileo had begun to unfurl: extending space to everything in order to place each actor

within it, *partes extra partes*. For Lovelock, such a space no longer has any sort of meaning: the space in which we live, that of the critical zone, is the very space toward which we are conspiring; it extends as far as we do; we last as long as those entities that make us breathe. (2017, 106)

What this means is that as humans we are neither at one with the world, nor are we separate from it. We are instead *of* the world as other organisms are: acting in ways that continually transform and change our environments, blurring the distinct edges between nature and culture we have created for ourselves. The problem of course is, for Latour, that we humans have not recognized ourselves as participating in this history of planetary life, and thus our actions (as culture) have been seen as separate from this history. Indeed, he sees that rather than trying to find our rightful place in nature (a spatial notion) we need to think more in terms of "learning to participate in the geohistory of the planet" (2017, 107), which Dipesh Chakrabarty (2009) discusses in terms of capturing humans as "geological agents" of history. Reconceiving of the world in this way suggests that our encounters with things, animals, and plants are an expression of our "of-ness"—an "of-ness" that challenges us to notice change as indicative of time: our inseparability is thus not only spatial but temporal. For Latour, Gaia is living history itself.

Following both Latour and Abram, encounters *of* the world, I would like to suggest, are thus not merely spatially oriented, as meetings that occur in a physical context, but are also temporally marked. They are occurrences that transpire from one moment to the next in an arc of *chronological time* that opens up to both history's precedent and the future's probable and potential consequences as well as in a *living time* of sensory experiences in the present. I turn now to explore how one rendering of these encounters *of* the world brings together these two temporal dimensions in ways that can inform educational encounters in environmental education.

Ice Watch and the Presence of Time

Olafur Eliasson worked with geologist Minik Rosing to create *Ice Watch*, which required the harvesting and transportation of thirty blocks of ice from the Nuup Kangerlua fjord in Greenland. As a participatory installation, *Ice Watch* stages encounters *of* the world by offering the public a spatial and temporal experience of glacial ice melting.[7] The installation outside the Tate Modern in London was set up in December 2018 and coincided with a then recent UN Intergovernmental Panel on Climate Change (IPCC) report. In fact, *Ice Watch* had been mounted twice before, both times coinciding with important climate meetings and events: once in Copenhagen in 2014 at the release of the IPCC's Fifth Assessment Report and once in Paris in 2015, during COP21 that led to the Paris Agreement.[8] The installation in London consisted of twenty-four blocks of ice arranged in the rough formation of a sundial on Bankside outside the Tate (while six were on display in front of Bloomberg's European headquarters in the City). People were encouraged to interact with them in any way they wished, inviting them into both an immediate sensory encounter with the ice and into a temporal zone that collapsed two worlds, to echo Latour: the one *in* which we live and the one *from* which we live.

The ice blocks themselves date back thousands of years, and Eliasson (2018) encourages the public to "witness the ecological changes that our world is undergoing." The *Ice Watch London* website (https://icewatchlondon.com) not only describes details of the project but contains scientific graphs and statistics about the significance of glacial melting, which themselves continue the installation in virtual form. However, Eliasson is concerned that facts alone are not enough to ignite action: "feelings of distance and disconnect hold us back, make us grow numb and passive." The main idea behind *Ice Watch* is to "arouse feelings of proximity, presence, and relevance." Eliasson (2018) particularly invokes the sensory dimensions of our encounters: "Put your hand on the ice and feel the cold, smooth surface against your skin. Put your ear to the ice and listen to the crackling noises it produces as it melts." The photos and videos documenting *Ice Watch* do indeed show children, youth, and adults interacting physically—and indeed intimately—with the ice and its slow transformation.

One might legitimately question whether Eliasson's work harkens back to an earlier romanticism (Barry and Keane 2019), which links *Ice Watch* to traditional invocations of the sublime and as such glosses over the multifaceted dimensions of the public's interactions with the ice. As environmental art critic Christopher Heuer (2018) notes in relation to the installation in Paris, the piece "maybe somewhat inaccurately universalizes the idea of the 'human' who is actually behind

Anthropocene warming" (302) in that it overlooks the corporate and capitalist element of the climate crisis as well as the way the Global South and impoverished peoples currently bear the brunt of ecological change. As part of a "neo-materialist turn in Arctic art practice," *Ice Watch*, according to Heuer, misses the climate crisis's "actually existing (and unevenly distributed) effects upon social spheres" (302). In other words, it is pitched, in Heuer's view, in a tenor that does not sufficiently interrogate the differential aspects of climate justice.

While these issues are not insignificant either to the actual *effect* the artwork might have to arouse action and to chart a course of change, or to the much needed, urgent critique of climate inequality, I do think the installation is nonetheless instructive for the way it pedagogically illuminates a chiasmic crossing of time that captures the complexity of living in the spatial and temporal presence of climate emergency within the Critical Zone. The piece is indeed marked by a "time of out of joint"; the presence of ice literally disrupts the flow of city life by their hulking and uncanny presence and introduces two rogue elements into the present: that of the sedimented weight of geological history and that of a vanishing future. In this, the ice is part of chronological time, a measured time, the time of marked events that have led up to its display in London, telling a condensed story of its beginnings in a Greenland ice sheet, its severance from that sheet due to warming temperatures, and its final resting place on the banks of the Thames. It also gestures to a future that is yet to be defined and which we cannot witness: the evaporation of the melted ice water into literal air. That is, while we can see and feel the transformation of ice into water, the final vanishing act is actually hidden from the powers of our perception. It is the predicted future of the climate emergency, obeying a logic of chronological time that is not completely within view.

Echoing my own discussion in chapter 5, Marianna Papastephanou (2014) writes critically of this view of time as *chronos* (past, present, future neatly laid out within a linear topography) which so dominates educational efforts, signaled by cultures of performativity and managerialism. We "know" the future and thus work backward not to change that future, but to live up to it; what I earlier referred to as an anachronistic sense of time. She understands chronosophy as "the discontent with mere empirical observation of the here and now and as the tendency and practice to make the future accessible, to make it an object of knowledge" (Papastephanou 2014, 722). For Papastephanou chronosophy is very much "reflective of a time-management logic" (722). Accordingly, if *Ice Watch* were a work solely in the time of *chronos*, its pedagogical trajectory would become the retelling of a narrative with a fixed ending (from ice sheet to vanishing ice), and it would be a statement of inevitability instead of a call to action. Instead, it intersects with another temporality, the time of *kairos*, or the living present, as a disruption of this linearity. As Papastephanou writes, *kairos* is "a qualitative sense of temporality, bearing associations of chance, opportunity, lived experience and relationality to time" (2014, 719). For Papastephanou, *kairos* is the time for thinking and reflection; it introduces neither finality nor certitude but openness to the vicissitudes of life itself. As such, it is a time of living and staying with our experiences—even in the face of a vanishing future.

First, we see in *Ice Watch* that the arc of chronological time, with its distinct linear phases of past, present, and future, can never simply disappear from view—rather it is held in a moment of engagement, providing a rich source of experiential reflection. However, as I explored in chapter 5, the time of the living present contains within it different temporalities due to the *presencing* of past and future through our encounters. Thus, secondly, the living present of *kairos* unfolds through the sensual experiences of our encounters with ice as well as through the ice's own interaction with its environment. From the vantage of the present, the ice we touch, smell, taste, and listen to is thereby caught within multiple lines of relationality: these blocks are not merely representatives of or stand-ins for ecological crisis but are material existents that are undergoing continual transformation under our eyes, ears, fingers, and tongues. In this sense, they are *of* the world, expressive of Gaia itself as living history, to follow Latour. Additionally, we are also caught up in this transformation: the warmth of our hands and breath, the saliva from our mouths, along with the infinitesimal particles and waves of heat, wind, and water in the surrounding atmosphere, contribute to the ice's shapes, textures, and rates of melting. As such, the ice (and its melting) is forged through a complex network of relations. Each block is singularly different from the next one, and each human interlocuter with each ice block senses something different and partial. As Abram suggests, we perceive not the thing in itself as complete, but in a flow of relation. The shifting light, temperature, and mood alters the conditions of interaction and therefore our attention. *Ice Watch* does not create a generalizable (or generic) encounter between glacial ice and the human but creates a series of living encounters that move to another rhythm than conventional, chronological time. Each encounter with the ice opens up both to our own human inseparability from the world by allowing us to sense, to notice, to reflect on the living dimension of time and to our own capacity to be *with*, to sit *with*, the world as it is in all its relationality. Thus to be with one of the ice blocks in an event of contact is not simply to witness its vanishing; this would turn *Ice Watch* into a predictable piece of theater, like a Greek tragedy. Instead, the cutting through of *chronos* with *kairos*, links the time of transformation (from solid to liquid to air; from ice sheet to harbor to Thames Embankment) to our own senses of the world as both vital and vanishing. It thus a poignant—if not shocking—entry into loss, and the ensuing sorrow, grief, and horror of the predicament we share as Earthbound beings[9] (who are unequally affected by the climate emergency) with the "living" ice itself.

Teaching in the Presence of Climate Sorrow

My primary focus has been to explore what relations with the world are possible in light of the enormity of climate issues facing youth today and to suggest that education needs to concern itself with creating contexts in which students' existential concerns can be faced in ways that fall into neither denial nor paralysis. I admit this is perhaps asking much of educators, but given that they make curricular and pedagogical decisions daily in order to curate student encounters with elements of the environment, then some clarity is needed to guide those decisions and to enable a reflection not only on the *kind* of encounters to choose (e.g., the design of the activities, the conditions in which they take place, the objects to be studied), but also the *quality* of those encounters teachers are enabling through their choices (e.g., do they give time and space to allow students to be with loss?; do they allow for complexity, openness and uncertainty?). As Affifi and Christie (2019) argue in their advocation of a "pedagogy of death," encounters with loss are central to creating opportunities for emotional and existential growth that contribute both to living well in the complex time of the present and to developing affective dispositions needed to deal with the future—the effects of which, to some degree, they are already living. The quality of encounter, therefore, is central to bringing students' present reality into contact with environmental destruction and alternative ways of formulating life in the future. Indeed, it is as Machado de Oliveira (2021) would put it, a form of hospicing.

The temporal dimensions of *Ice Watch* reveal what is possible to achieve when we do not merely reside in *chronos* but allow it to intersect with *kairos* (Papastephanou) or what I have referred to as the act of presencing. Chronological time is of course more familiar to us as educators; it sets the trajectory of development, breaks up the day into linear chunks of time, and structures lessons from start to finish. More importantly, it also often permeates our modernist narratives of human and more-than-human history—narratives which, to date, have been insufficient in addressing the interrelationality and interdependency of life on this planet. Like the story of the blocks of ice, there is a geohistorical (chronological) element to consider in teaching about the environment, whether this be in terms of evolution or geological epochs—all of which are fundamental to understanding the climate emergency as an issue of (urgent) time. Indeed, climate sorrow can be seen to arise from the sheer bombardment of information letting us know that within seven (or twelve, or fifteen years) we will reach a tipping point from which life as we know it cannot be saved. This is also part of *chronos*—the stretch between the first planetary life forms and a future without humans to mark the passage. As Eliasson, Abram, and Latour are all aware, however, it is not just our awareness of time *as it measured* that matters to life; indeed life itself occurs on another register: the traumatic past is lived in the present; the future is ever present in our unfolding. Bringing this complexity of living into our educational lives together with *chronos* requires a pedagogy that can work with the multiple time of the present.

From an educational point of view, the time of *kairos* is about students' bodily engagement with elements of the environment, forming sensations of connection, commingling and tension (Abram) that recognize their interdependence, while also acknowledging that the world itself consists in a multiplicity of living (Latour): the elements of the world that I encounter do not just comprise "my" world. The world is dynamic and animated, continually undergoing processes of change. *Kairos* as a living presence, we might say, *is* this incessant time of alteration and transformation—not in linear progression, but as proliferation, creation, and generation. As such, students' aesthetic experiences *of* the world tap into and become entangled with the teeming life of the Critical Zone. Encounters *of* the world, in my meaning here, are not entered into from some bird's-eye perspective through which I become a voyeur into processes of nature that are detached and alienated from me as a human, imitating the magisterial gaze of scientism. Instead, our sensory encounters as Earthbound beings can offer students an experience of the very interdependence of life—an immersion into the "seething broth" (Latour 2017, 93) of the Critical Zone, the offspring of living time.

Latour and Weibel (2020) call upon aesthetics "defined as what renders one sensitive to the existence of other ways of life" in order to help us deal with "the flood of terrifying news pouring in every day. . . . Artists are challenged to render us sensitive to the shape of things to come" (19). While, as we have seen, both in terms of Abram's phenomenology and Eliasson's artistic practice, the senses play a central role in this aesthetic endeavor, it is not only artists who bear this responsibility. Indeed, in line with what I see as teachers' educational and ethical responsibility to help youth live and lead fulfilling lives in a context that is responsive to their concerns and experiences, they are particularly well poised to consider how their staging of encounters can respond to climate sorrow in creating temporal encounters *of* the world located at the juncture of *chronos* and *kairos*. In this sense, the quality of those encounters that are staged can be seen as opportunities for sensory exploration in ways that neither dictate nor demand what feelings, sensations, and dispositions students "should" have by the end of a lesson or unit. This is not to say that we teach without purpose, factual information, or development, but that to allow *kairos* a place means also accepting—and indeed privileging—another quality of relationality with the world that is more about students' grappling with their place in it—a place that is not given or fixed but in flux and change. The striated texture of melting ice, the roughness of tree bark, the coolness of water from a brook or tap, or the smell of damp grass do not simply connect students to things that are external to them, but generate sensory experiences that become entangled in the emergence of who they are (a "me") in the present within an already existing relational world—a world which is composed not simply of solid objects (ice, trees, water, grass), but of variation and flow. Such fleeting sensations, coupled with the knowledge of climate change, the extinction of species, the threat to the air we breathe and the water we drink can indeed initiate feelings of loss, sadness, and despair. However, the work of education is not to teach as though they do not matter, but to teach in a way that allows students to attend to a mode of being that is not solely defined by factual knowledge (however important that knowledge may be). As such, teaching in the presence of climate sorrow is an aesthetic practice that says living time matters and that recognizes that what is difficult to bear can indeed be life-enhancing.

Afterword

The Touch of the Present and Education *as* Social Justice

Reflecting on where the touch of the present leaves us as educators means having to think about the intersections of the aesthetic and political aspects of our encounters. For those of us concerned with issues often roughly gathered under the term social justice, ranging from the project of decoloniality and global citizenship to sustainability and LGBTQ rights, there is, as I have argued here, a tangible aspect to our encounters that affects the very terms upon which we can stake our claims to transformation. Taking the singularity of sensation, feeling, and affect as central to the projects of enculturation and becoming means focusing on the ways bodies inter/intra-act, interrelate, and are interdependent with their environments—and that those environments are experienced locally while also being part of networks of relations that are informed by planetary life and global digital systems. In this way, there is no point from which we stand above and beyond our entanglements.

Yet, these very entanglements are also what allow us to become beyond the social determinants that work so powerfully to create the horizon of "common sense" through which we feel and perceive the world. Our encounters with the everyday are not only socially coded or lock us into the grid of identities and social positionalities. They also are the very condition of the movement of subjectivity and the movement of shared realities—shared spaced times and timed spaces. Sensory encounters are thresholds onto the world, they are membrane-like, porous, and liminal spaces of taking in, expelling, and holding in rhythms of fluid exchange. As such our encounters stand as testament to the fact that there is no aesthetic sphere separate from the political, at least in the terms that I have been outlining throughout this book. How we sense, the sense we make, and the sensations we feel are both fuel and fodder for the way we live our lives collectively and the social relations they support and challenge. Education is not a system or institution that serves society, its expectations, orders, and values. Instead, it is a force for an aesthetic politics, or to be more apt, its force of purpose lies in enacting the kinds of encounters that make enculturation and becoming possible *as* an aesthetic politics.

By exploring our encounters as practices that are central to what educators *do* we are able to better conceive of education as necessarily an open-ended process, and it is this very open-endedness that is crucial for practicing encounters that are transformative. As soon as one defines what the end should be, one is trying to stop the flow of time, to stop the act of presencing that is required if we are to make new communities of sense. We try to freeze the flow to prevent things from changing (particularly if they are not going in the direction we want). Divorcing education from a defined goal might seem highly problematic for some readers, since working toward greater equality, less environmental harm, and just treatment for others (not only ourselves) often means positing a future that places a specific aim in sight. What happens to our political visions and imaginations of alternative life when we keep the endgame open? Do we not risk promoting an education that is apolitical in the extreme, replicating practices that might be more sensual on the surface but do nothing to challenge what really matters?

My answer is that the open-endedness that the aesthetic brings to life is itself political. By open-ended, I mean those incipient potentialities that are necessary to acknowledge if any change is to come about—for it cannot happen through pedagogical relations that have already been prepackaged, designed, and simply delivered. Open-endedness is very much about not only resisting forces that would attempt to ensnare us into a mode of being already decided within the realm of the possible but is also a source of creating new connections and networks, new modalities for understanding and action—which can only emerge through new events of contact, of touching and being touched by. Open-endedness, like Braidotti's (2011) nomadic subject, is about mobilizing change by shifting the very modes of subjectivity in ways that respond to our entanglements with the now. New forms of subjectivity are only possible not by saying "Follow me. I know what we should do" but by creating encounters that allow students to move, act, and think about their profound implication in their contact with others, with things and objects, as well as with elements of the Earth itself. Education as a process of enculturation and becoming does not try to extricate the experience of singularity *from* the collective, and at the same time it does not define that singularity *by* the collective. This is not about trying to execute a balancing act, between what's inner and outer, what is sensed and what it socially coded, what is aesthetics and what is politics, but a consideration of the complex topography that lies in between, a topography that needs to be walked knowing that our paths through the terrain do not have a final destination.

Rather than see education as being aimless, however, its open-endedness is itself a direction, providing an opportunity to become *implicated in the path we are on*, the detours we take, those we walk with, and those we pass in the other direction. Educational encounters can never be about educating *for* a subject position for the simple reason that the very violences justice demands we work against, whether they are motivated by capitalism, homophobia, sexism, colonialism, ableism, or racism are not themselves objects or things but events and processes. To counter these violences politically means challenging the very processes through which they transpire and the bodily, sensory dimensions of experience that sustain them. And if challenging such processes is our aim, then a certain subject position or a specific way of being can never be an effective or appropriate response. Instead, the specifically educational response is to offer opportunities for becoming otherwise, always understanding that our implication in living a life means that we are relationally interdependent with the lives of others. If social justice means anything, it is precisely this idea that we are all in it together, whether we want to be or not.

Notes

Introduction

1. See the PhD thesis of Gry Worre Hallberg (2021), who is cofounding artistic director of Sisters Hope, for an elaboration of the collective's philosophy toward art and activism. See also Sisters Hope (2020) as well as the website www.sistershope.dk.

2. See Kyla Wazana Tompkins (2016) for a discussion of how "new" has been problematically appropriated, suggesting ways in which its use is deeply tied to ideas formulated not only by "old" materialism but also by indigenous and people of color's knowledges, which have at times gone unnoticed.

3. This work draws extensively on feminist philosophy. See Alaimo and Hekman (2008); Barad (2007); Braidotti (2011, 2013); Haraway (2016); Tuana (2001, 2008).

4. Iris van der Tuin (2008) has rebutted Ahmed's claims in terms of the overly broad brushstrokes with which Ahmed paints the field. In her article Ahmed focuses on Karen Barad's (2007) work. While I agree that Ahmed's focus on Barad cannot stand in the for the whole, I am sympathetic to Ahmed's concern about depoliticization.

5. I've put Andreotti in parenthesis here since Vanessa Machado de Oliveira has published primarily under this name. Machado de Oliveira is also part of the Gesturing Toward Decolonial Futures Collective, which runs educational-activist-aesthetic projects with indigenous and environmental communities.

Chapter One

1. All references to Pennac (2010) are to the location, not page number, of the Kindle edition of *School Blues*.

2. I alternate between the pronouns she/hers and they/them when referring to a person in the singular. The pronouns he/him have been over utilized in the history of thought, so I have not replicated that patriarchal tradition here.

3. As I discuss below, Masschelein and Simons's (2013) reading of Pennac is different from my own, since student bodies—their feelings and sensations—are left largely unaddressed in their work.

4. Becoming is therefore not to do with becoming a particular kind of person or having a certain identity; rather it is about an unfolding in which one is fully present. See my discussion in chapter 5.

5. See also Hanan Alexander's (2015) discussion of affiliation and tradition and their significance in liberal education.

6. Sometimes Biesta talks about the three functions, at other times the three purposes. In some of his work, he reserves the language of aim and purpose for "subjectification," making clear that qualification and socialization are not really "educational" purposes at all.

7. Rancière develops a political aesthetics in claiming that art works to provoke and interrupt dominant forms of sensibility. I discuss this in more detail in chapter 3.

8. This idea of egalitarianism within the Greek school has been viewed as a contentious part of their theory. See Friedrich (2014).

9. I also discuss this example in chapter 5 from the perspective of time.

Chapter Two

1. Stephen Batchelor, *Verses from the Center: A Buddhist Vision of the Sublime* (New York: Riverhead Books, 2000).

2. I will discuss art practices further in chapter 4 in relation to Nicolas Bourriaud's (2002) notion of "states of encounter."

3. Some of the feminist scholars on embodiment she engages with include Judith Butler, Elisabeth Grosz, and Moira Gatens.

4. Gibson's thesis draws extensively on systems theory to understand the senses not in terms of their individual functions, but how they combine to create active perceptual systems. He identifies them as: auditory, visual, haptic, taste-smell, and orienting. Some systems involve more than one sense while some senses participate in more than one system.

5. See Semetsky's (2004) discussion of this in relation to Jungian psychoanalysis.

6. See my (2015b) discussion of this within the context of Buddhism and education.

7. This is the basis for the well-known James-Lange theory of emotions in psychology.

8. I am not distinguishing here between a felt sensation and an affect. There is also some slippage between the terms in Massumi's work. Ultimately both are seen in terms of felt intensities.

9. See also Kearney's (2021) more recent discussion in *Touch: Recovering Our Most Vital Sense*, especially chapter 2.

10. In addition to the usual five senses, mind is a sixth sense within some eastern traditions, while Mark Paterson (2007) outlines some of the additional ones from psychology and neuroscience as including proprioception, kinesthesia, and the vestibular sense.

11. See Cronin (2017) and Hadlington (2008) for a description of how skin sees light. Noë (2009) also outlines a fascinating experiment whereby a man who is blind is able to see with the aid of stimuli from electrodes placed on his thighs.

12. The phenomenological position tends to focus on contact as something that is experienced by an already existing subject (however fluid that subject may be) and is less concerned with the dynamics of becoming through sensing/experiencing the flux of life itself.

13. Sheets-Johnstone is influenced by Husserlian phenomenology, and her philosophical project is marked by a robust interdisciplinarity, drawing on science studies, dance, and philosophy of language and mind.

14. Luce Irigaray (1985, 1993) has written extensively on the imaginary morphology that shapes patriarchal culture, for example, claiming that language, as well as experience, is rooted in a phallic figuration. Her project of inscribing a female morphology as an imaginary gesture to counter patriarchy raises some interesting questions regarding the relationship between morphologies and the imaginary underpinning political action. How might a decolonial or transgendered project, for example, move beyond sexed binaries in thinking through a morphological form of activism? A response to this lies beyond the scope of this book.

15. One is reminded here of the futurist sculpture by Umberto Boccioni, *Unique Forms of Continuity in Space* (1913), in which space is captured through movement in a static figure.

Chapter Three

1. When referring to the institutional or functional role of "education" in these opening paragraphs, I use scare quotes in order to distinguish it from the view of education I espouse throughout this book.

2. This is not Kant's *sensus communis*, about which Arendt (1982) writes as that which binds us together in common ways of understanding. See my discussion of this notion in chapter 8 of *Toward an Imperfect Education* (2009).

3. This cultural element of education is central in the work of Freire, as well as that of Raymond Williams. In their views, culture is conceived as a *set of practices* one enacts not a *uniform thing* one possesses. See my discussion in Todd (2018) for further elaboration of their positions.

4. She rightfully queries ideas about "bodily inscription" as though language literally acts on the body and its surface, or whether these are figurations we use to "establish the efficacy of language" itself (Butler 2015, 21).

5. This is an important point for Adriana Cavarero (2000, 2016) who sees the bodily aspects of subjectivity as having some power in formations of subjectivity outside its signifying or narrative function.

6. Sensations are referred to differently in the various texts under study. For Howes and Classen they refer to sense-feeling that is the result of perception, while for Massumi sensations are affects, generated out of our encounters with the world.

7. As many have commented on, the French *partage* is ill-served by its translation into English as "distribution." *Partage* means a share or portion that is brought about by division; it signals something is both part of and separated from that which it is divided.

8. Panagia discusses Butler's reading of the video footage of the murder of Rodney King in these terms. In his eyes, what she misses in her analysis of it on narrative and discursive terms is precisely the element of unrepresentability contained within the image itself, since it is intelligible only within a certain regime of readability. See Panagia (2009, 13).

9. See Granger (2015) for a more fulsome account of somaesthetics within the context of antiracist education.

10. An especial thanks to Seán Henry for pointing out certain connections that contributed to the shaping of my ideas here.

Chapter Four

1. Contemporary art practices are also less concerned with traditional aesthetic elements of form (composition, shape, contour) than one finds in sculpture, painting, and visual art and more concerned with generating new forms of relationship: between participant and art practice as opposed to viewer and artwork.

2. See my discussion of Marina Abramovic's work in Todd (2015a).

3. One can draw a parallel to the use of the circle form in dialogic pedagogies, which is dependent on the relational encounters of the students to generate the space of the circle itself in order for it to be truly dialogical.

4. The debate as to whether or not these artworks can be valued as art or not is not one I am pursuing here. Two theorists who have been involved in this debate are Claire Bishop (2012) and Grant Kester (2004).

5. There are a variety of positions that take up this educational aspect. See Pablo Helguera (2011) for example.

6. Claire Bishop's (2004) critique of Bourriaud's position centers on this very question. For Bishop artworks should not be held to the "dialogical" standard

but be an opening onto forming different kinds of conversations. She cites the work of Thomas Hirschhorn and Santiago Sierra as exemplary in this, contra to the artists Bourriaud draws on (such as Rirkrit Tiravanija, Liam Gillick, and Vanessa Beecroft).

7. This also speaks directly to the Situationist International art movement that emerged in the late 1950s. Proponents such as Guy Debord and Asger Jorn saw art as part of a revolutionary movement of changing fundamental social relationships. Artworks were therefore conceived as social situations that attempted to redistribute the sensible, to put it in Rancièrean terms.

8. In online photographs of conventional Western classrooms, students are frequently portrayed as either sitting still or sitting with their arms raised—a paradoxical form whose skyward trajectory belies their earthly presence in the room. Students seem to signal through such a gesture their anticipation of acceding to something the teacher already has access to.

9. Specifically, they conceive of these practices within notions of suspension and profanation (Masschelein and Simons 2013, 31–41), which I have discussed in chapter 1.

Chapter Five

1. Arendt discusses how "man" is inserted into time and as such disrupts it from its flow of linearity, occasioning a break, or gap, between the two forces of past and future. Jan Masschelein (2011) identifies this gap as the "time of education." My own take on the present here is less about construing it in light of the linearity any "gap" is based on and more concerned with its fluid and compound nature.

2. See my discussion of Marianna Papastephanou's (2014) idea of kairosophy in chapter 7.

3. See Rovelli (2018) for a fascinating discussion on quantum time, which in many surprising ways parallels the view of Dōgen I explore below.

4. See Thanissaro Bhikkhu's (1997) translation of the *Paticca samuppada-vibhanga Sutta*, and Bhikkhu Bodhi's (2000) translation of the *Nidanavagga* contained in the *Samyutta Nikaya* as well as his translation of the *Upanisa Sutta* (1980). I also consulted Rahula's ([1959] 2015) classic interpretation.

5. I have drawn on a few translations of this work. See Dōgen, Tanahashi translation (1985, 2013); Dōgen, Waddell and Abe translation (2002), and Dōgen, Nishijima and Cross translation (2006).

6. Purser (2015), Roberts (2018), and Stambaugh (1990) all comment on this act of presencing. Stambaugh discusses the shift Dōgen makes from horizontal time (chronology) to vertical time (dwelling within the moment), which holds different relations to past and future (50).

7. Educational discourses that focus on the hazards of "triggering" in teaching "controversial" issues are reminders of how this infusion plays out politically in education, often to preempt uncomfortable discussion for those who are already socially privileged. But there is a world of difference between creating discomfort in dealing with issues surrounding racism, homophobia, colonialism, and disability, which is necessary for facing and potentially addressing these issues, and "living" the past in the present in the way I'm discussing here.

Chapter Seven

1. As a term, "*the* world" keeps hidden the multiple relationships that coconstitute each of us with elements of our environment. Moreover it also conceals the colonizing relationships that have contributed to what John Law (2015) refers to as the "one-world world" and the way it has functioned to consolidate Western and Global North ideas about *the* world, in the singular. I have thus largely avoided its usage up until this chapter. However, I do so here in order to follow the language of Abram and Latour, and especially Latour's understanding of the world not as something that fixes reality into a singular entity or organism, but as a bio-cultural-political relation.

2. Orbach is clear to emphasize however that "facing feelings is not a substitute for political action, nor is it a distraction from action. Feelings are an important feature of political activity" (2019, 69).

3. I am not making any conceptual distinction between sustainability education, environmental education, ecological education, or education for sustainable development. My focus here is instead on investigating what is often a shared commitment to developing relationships to nature across these various strands of pedagogical thought and practice.

4. I use scare quotes around natural here since I take up Latour's critique of this usage below and argue that the living world cannot be simply captured by the term "nature."

5. See, for example, Marina Abramovic's new app *Rising*, the Kapu collective's transient murals, Mel Chin's *Unmoored* (2018), and Gemma Anderson's audio piece, *Observation and Operation: A Plant Meditation, 2020*, in addition to Olafur Eliasson's work *Ice Watch*, which I discuss below.

6. Bruce Clarke (2017) has referred to Latour's reading of Gaia as "secular." In his critique of both Latour and Stengers's positions on Gaia, he draws attention to their omission of the autopoetic nature of Gaia, which would bring nonduality into the picture and offer another "non-secular" language.

7. While Eliasson's artwork has drawn some criticism both in terms of its apparent "derivation" from process art of the 1960s and 1970s (Nechvatal 2015) and more importantly in terms of its own carbon emission levels (Nechvatal

2015; Barry and Keane 2019), his studio has worked closely with the NGO Julie's Bicycle who writes emission reports for cultural organizations in order to encourage sound environmental practices. According to their report, the offset contribution exceeded the installation's carbon footprint.

    8. In Paris, the installation also ended up coinciding with the Paris terrorist attacks on November 13–14, 2015. As Christopher Heuer (2018) notes, the Place du Panthéon where *Ice Watch* was mounted became a site of pilgrimage and "the ice accrued (for some) the poignancy of loss and tears" (301).

    9. This is a term used by Latour to move away from the "human" in order to highlight the boundedness of all life in the Critical Zone.

References

Abram, David. 1997. *The Spell of the Sensuous: Perception and Language in a More-Than-Human World*. New York: Vintage Books.
———. 2011. *Becoming Animal: An Earthly Cosmology*. New York: Vintage Books.
Adedoyin, Olasile Babatunde, and Emrah Soykan. 2020. "Covid-19 Pandemic and Online Learning: The Challenges and Opportunities." *Interactive Learning Environments*: 1–13.
Affifi, Ramsey, and Beth Christie. 2019. "Facing Loss: Pedagogy of Death." *Environmental Education Research* 25 (8): 1143–1157.
Ahenakew, Cash, Vanessa Andreotti, and Garrick Cooper. 2011. "Epistemological Pluralism: Ethical and Pedagogical Challenges in Higher Education." *AlterNative: An International Journal of Indigenous Peoples* 7 (1): 40–50.
Ahmed, Sara. 2000. *Strange Encounters: Embodied Others in Post-Coloniality*. London: Routledge.
———. 2008. "Open Forum Imaginary Prohibitions: Some Preliminary Remarks on the Founding Gestures of the 'New Materialism.'" *European Journal of Women's Studies* 15 (1): 23–39.
Alaimo, Stacy, and Susan J. Hekman. 2008. *Material Feminisms*. Bloomington: Indiana University Press.
Alexander, Hanan A. 2015. *Reimagining Liberal Education: Affiliation and Inquiry in Democratic Schooling*. New York: Bloomsbury Academic.
Alirezabeigi, Samira, Jan Masschelein, and Mathias Decuypere. 2020. "Investigating Digital Doings through Breakdowns: A Sociomaterial Ethnography of a Bring Your Own Device School." *Learning, Media and Technology* 45 (2): 193–207.
Andreotti, Vanessa de Oliveira. 2021a. "The Task of Education as We Confront the Potential for Social and Ecological Collapse." *Ethics and Education* 16 (2): 143–158.
Andreotti, Vanessa de Oliveira. 2021b. "Depth Education and the Possibility of GCE Otherwise." *Globalisation, Societies and Education* 19 (4): 496–509.
Appiah, Kwame Anthony. 2018. *The Lies That Bind: Rethinking Identity*. London: Profile Books.

Arendt, Hannah. 1982. *Lectures on Kant's Political Philosophy*. Chicago: University of Chicago Press.
Aristotle. 1986. *De Anima*. Translated by Hugh Lawson-Tancred. London: Penguin.
Bang-Larsen, Lars. 2006. "Social Aesthetics." In *Participation: Documents of Contemporary Art*, edited by Claire Bishop, 172–183. London: Whitechapel Gallery.
Barad, Karen Michelle. 2007. *Meeting the Universe Halfway: Quantum Physics and the Entanglement of Matter and Meaning*. Durham, NC: Duke University Press.
Barry, Kaya, and Jondi Keane. 2019. *Creative Measures of the Anthropocene: Art, Mobilities, and Participatory Geographies*. Singapore: Palgrave Macmillan.
Batchelor, Stephen. 2000. *Verses from the Center: A Buddhist Vision of the Sublime*. New York: Riverhead Books.
———. 2014. "Self-Reliance and the Present Moment." May 28, 2014. https://www.upaya.org/2014/05/qa-stephen-batchelor-self-reliance-present-moment/.
Bayne, Siân, Peter Evans, Rory Ewins, Jeremy Knox, James Lamb, Hamish Macleod, Clara O'Shea, Jen Ross, Philippa Sheail, and Christine Sinclair. 2020. *The Manifesto for Teaching Online*. Cambridge, MA: MIT Press.
Berardi, Franco. 2017. *Futurability: The Age of Impotence and the Horizon of Possibility*. London: Verso.
Bergdahl, Lovisa, and Elisabet Langmann. 2018a. "Time for Values: Responding Educationally to the Call from the Past." *Studies in Philosophy and Education* 37: 367–382.
———. 2018b. "Pedagogical Postures: A Feminist Search for Geometry of the Educational Relation." *Ethics and Education* 13 (3): 309–328.
Bhikkhu, Thanissaro. 1997. "Paticca-samuppadavibhanga Sutta: Analysis of Dependent Co-arising." *Tripitaka–Sanyutta Nikaya* 12.
Biesta, Gert. 2010. *Good Education in an Age of Measurement: Ethics, Politics, Democracy*. Boulder, CO: Paradigm.
———. 2014. *The Beautiful Risk of Education*. Boulder, CO: Paradigm.
———. 2015. "What Is Education For? On Good Education, Teacher Judgement and Educational Professionalism." *European Journal of Education* 50 (1): 75–87.
———. 2017. *The Rediscovery of Teaching*. New York: Routledge.
Bishop, Claire. 2004. "Antagonism and Relational Aesthetics." *October* 110: 51–79.
———. 2012. *Artificial Hells: Participatory Art and the Politics of Spectatorship*. London: Verso Books.
Biswas, Tanu. 2021. "Who Needs Sensory Education?" *Studies in Philosophy and Education* 40 (3): 287–302.
Bodhi, Bhikkhu. 1980. *Upanisa Sutta*. Kandy, Sri Lanka: Buddhist Publication Society.
———.2000. *The Connected Discourses of the Buddha: A New Translation of the Saṃyutta Nikāya*. 2 vols. Somerville, MA: Wisdom Publications.

Bonnett, Michael. 2007. "Environmental Education and the Issue of Nature." *Journal of Curriculum Studies* 39 (6): 707–721.
Bourriaud, Nicolas. 2002. *Relational Aesthetics*. Paris: Les presses du réel.
Braidotti, Rosi. 2011. *Nomadic Subjects: Embodiment and Sexual Difference in Contemporary Feminist Theory*. 2nd ed. New York: Columbia University Press.
———. 2013. *The Posthuman*. Cambridge: Polity Press.
———. 2019. *Posthuman Knowledge*. Cambridge: Polity Press.
Braidotti, Rosi, and Simone Bignall. 2019. *Posthuman Ecologies: Complexity and Process after Deleuze*. London: Rowman & Littlefield International.
Butler, Judith. 2015. *Senses of the Subject*. New York: Fordham University Press.
Cajete, Gregory. 1994. *Look to the Mountain: An Ecology of Indigenous Education*. Durango, CO: Kivakí Press.
Caruth, Cathy. 1996. *Unclaimed Experience: Trauma, Narrative, and History*. Baltimore: Johns Hopkins University Press.
Cavarero, Adriana. 2000. *Relating Narratives: Storytelling and Selfhood*. London: Routledge.
———. 2016. *Inclinations: A Critique of Rectitude*. Stanford, CA: Stanford University Press.
Chakrabarty, Dipesh. 2009. "The Climate of History: Four Theses." *Critical Inquiry* 35 (2): 197–222.
Clarke, Bruce. 2017. "Rethinking Gaia: Stengers, Latour, Margulis." *Theory, Culture & Society* 34 (4): 3–26.
Cronin, Thomas. 2017. "Seeing without Eyes." *Scientific American*. August 13, 2017. https://www.scientificamerican.com/article/seeing-without-eyes1/.
de Freitas, Elizabeth, David Rousell, and Nils Jäger. 2019. "Relational Architectures and Wearable Space: Smart Schools and the Politics of Ubiquitous Sensation." *Research in Education* 107 (1): 10–32.
Deleuze, Gilles. 1993. *The Fold: Leibniz and the Baroque*. London: The Athlone Press.
———. 2003. *Francis Bacon: The Logic of Sensation*. Translated by Daniel W. Smith. London: Continuum.
Dōgen, Eihei. 1985. *Moon in a Dewdrop*. Translated by Kazuaki Tanahashi. San Francisco: North Point Press.
Dōgen, Eihei. 2002. *The Heart of Dōgen's Shōbōgenzō*. Translated by Norman Waddell and Masao Abe. Albany: State University of New York Press.
Dōgen. Eihei. 2006. *Master Dōgen's Shōbōgenzō*. Translated by Gudō Nishijima and Chodo Cross. Book Surge Press.
Dōgen, Eihei. 2013. *The Essential Dogen: Writings of the Great Zen Master*. Translated by Kazuaki Tanahashi. Edited by Peter Levitt. Boston: Shambhala.
Dyer, Alan. 2007. "Inspiration, Enchantment and a Sense of Wonder . . . Can a New Paradigm in Education Bring Nature and Culture Together Again?" *International Journal of Heritage Studies* 13 (4): 393–404.

Eliasson, Olafur. 2018. *Ice Watch*. https://icewatchlondon.com.
Epstein, Mark. 2013. *The Trauma of Everyday Life*. London: Hay House.
Fanon, Frantz. 1982. *Black Skin, White Masks*. New York: Grove Press.
Field, Tiffany. 2001. *Touch*. Cambridge, MA: MIT Press.
Ford, Derek R. 2013. "Toward a Theory of the Educational Encounter: Gert Biesta's Educational Theory and the Right to the City." *Critical Studies in Education* 54 (3): 299–310.
Friedrich, Daniel. 2014. "Book Review: In Defence of the School." *Journal of Philosophy of Education* 48 (3): 510–512.
Fuchsberger, Verena, and Thomas Meneweger. 2019. "Experiencing Materialized Reading: Individuals' Encounters with Books." Human-Computer Interaction–INTERACT Conference. Cham, Switzerland.
Galloway, Sarah. 2012. "Reconsidering Emancipatory Education: Staging a Conversation Between Paulo Freire and Jacques Rancière." *Educational Theory* 62 (2): 163–184.
Gibson, James. 1966. *The Senses Considered as Perceptual Systems*. London: George Allen & Unwin.
Gilroy, Paul. 2000. *Between Camps: Race, Identity and Nationalism at the End of the Colour Line*. London: Allen Lane.
Granger, David A. 2015. "Funny Vibe: Towards a Somaesthetic Approach to Anti-racist Education." In *Art's Teachings, Teaching's Art*, edited by Tyson E. Lewis and Megan J. Laverty, 211–228. Dordrecht: Springer.
Grosz, Elizabeth. 2017. *The Incorporeal: Ontology, Ethics and the Limits of Materialism*. New York: Columbia University Press.
Hadlington, Simon. 2008. "Humans May See Light through Skin." *Chemistry World*. https://www.chemistryworld.com/news/humans-may-sense-light-through-skin/3002007.article.
Hallberg, Gry Worre. 2021. "Sensuous Society: Carving the Path Towards a Sustainable Future." PhD, Department of Arts and Cultural Studies, University of Copenhagen.
Hansen, David. 2008. "Curriculum and the Idea of a Cosmopolitan Inheritance." *Journal of Curriculum Studies* 40 (3): 289–312.
Hansen, Mark. 2006. *Bodies in Code: Interfaces with Digital Media*. New York: Routledge.
Haraway, Donna Jeanne. 2016. *Staying with the Trouble: Making Kin in the Chthulucene*. Durham, NC: Duke University Press,.
Hauk, Marna, Elise Baker, Rudina Petra Cekani, Kristy Gonyer, Ciarra Greene, Katelyn Hale, Linda Hoppes, Kimberley Kovac, Tess Kreosfky, Claire Lagerwey, Daniela Perez, Richard Presicci, Heidi Schmigdall, Jenka Soderberg, Kaileigh Westermann, and M. Zimdars. 2015. "Senses of Wonder in Sustainability Education, for Hope and Sustainability Agency." *Journal of Sustainability Education* 10.

Hayles, N. Katherine. 2012. *How We Think: Digital Media and Contemporary Technogenesis*. Chicago: University of Chicago Press.

Helguera, Pablo. 2011. *Education for Socially Engaged Art*. New York: Jorge Pinto Books.

Heuer, Christopher P. 2018. "A Post-Critical Arctic?" In *Ecologies, Agents, Terrains*, edited by Christopher P. Heuer and Rebecca Zorach, 292–309. New Haven, CT: Yale University.

Hickey-Moody, Anna, Helen Palmer, and Esther Sayers. 2016. "Diffractive Pedagogies: Dancing across New Materialist Imaginaries." *Gender and Education* 28 (2): 213–229.

Howes, David, and Constance Classen. 2014. *Ways of Sensing: Understanding the Senses in Society*. New York: Routledge.

Irigaray, Luce. 1985. *This Sex Which Is Not One*. Ithaca, NY: Cornell University Press.

———. 1993. *An Ethics of Sexual Difference*. Ithaca, NY: Cornell University Press.

James, William. 1912. *Essays in Radical Empiricism*. New York: Longmans, Green and Co.

Jørgensen, Kari-Anne. 2016. "Bringing the Jellyfish Home: Environmental Consciousness and 'Sense of Wonder' in Young Children's Encounters with Natural Landscapes and Places." *Environmental Education Research* 22 (8): 1139–1157.

Kearney, Richard. 2015. "What Is Carnal Hermeneutics?" *New Literary History* 46 (1): 99–124.

———. 2021. *Touch: Recovering Our Most Vital Sense*. New York: Columbia University Press.

Kester, Grant H. 2004. *Conversation Pieces: Community and Communication in Modern Art*. Berkeley: University of California Press.

Lander, Dorothy A. 2005. "The Consuming (No)body of Online Learners: Re-membering E-communities of Practice." *Studies in Continuing Education* 27 (2): 155–174.

Langer, Monika. 2003. "Nietzsche, Heidegger, and Merleau-Ponty: Some of Their Contributions and Limitations for Environmentalism." In *Eco-Phenomenology: Back to the Earth Itself*, edited by Charles S. Brown and Ted Toadvine, 103–120. Albany: State University of New York Press.

Latour, Bruno. 2014. "Some Advantages of the Notion of 'Critical Zone' for Geopolitics." *Procedia: Earth and Planetary Science* 10: 3–6.

———. 2017. *Facing Gaia: Eight Lectures on the New Climatic Regime*. Cambridge: Polity Press.

Latour, Bruno, and Peter Weibel. 2020. "Seven Objections against Landing on Earth." In *Critical Zones: The Science and Politics of Landing on Earth*, edited by Bruno Latour and Peter Weibel, 12–19. Boston: MIT Press.

Law, John. 2015. "What's Wrong with a One-World World?" *Distinktion: Journal of Social Theory* 16 (1): 126–139.
Levine, Peter A. 2015. *Trauma and Memory: Brain and Body in a Search for the Living Past.* Berkeley, CA: North Atlantic Books.
Lévy, Pierre. 1998. *Becoming Virtual: Reality in the Digital Age.* Translated by Robert Bononno. New York: Plenum Trade.
Lewis, Tyson E. 2012. *Aesthetics of Education: Theatre, Curiosity, and Politics in the Work of Jacques Rancière and Paulo Freire.* New York: Continuum.
———. 2017. "A Marxist Education of the Encounter: Althusser, Interpellation, and the Seminar." *Rethinking Marxism* 29 (2): 303–317.
Lieflӓnder, Anne K., Gabriele Fröhlich, Franz X. Bogner, and P. Wesley Schultz. 2013. "Promoting Connectedness with Nature through Environmental Education." *Environmental Education Research* 19 (3): 370–384.
Løvlie, Lars. 2007. "The Pedagogy of Place." *Nordisk Pedagogik* 27 (1): 32–37.
Machado de Oliveira, Vanessa. 2021. *Hospicing Modernity: Facing Humanity's Wrongs and the Implications for Social Activism.* Berkeley, CA: North Atlantic Books.
Manning, Erin. 2007. *The Politics of Touch: Sense, Movement, Sovereignty.* Minneapolis: University of Minnesota Press.
———. 2012. *Relationscapes: Movement, Art, Philosophy.* Cambridge, MA: MIT Press.
———. 2016. *The Minor Gesture.* Durham, NC: Duke University Press.
———. 2020. *For a Pragmatics of the Useless.* Durham, NC: Duke University Press.
Martin, Jane Roland. 2011. *Education Reconfigured: Culture, Encounter, and Change.* New York: Routledge.
Masschelein, Jan. 2011. "Philosophy of Education as an Exercise in Thought: To Not Forget Oneself When Things 'Take Their Course.'" *European Educational Research Journal* 10 (3): 356–363.
Masschelein, Jan, and Maarten Simons. 2013. *In Defence of the School: A Public Issue.* Leuven: E-ducation, Culture and Society Publishers.
Massie, Pascal. 2013. "Touching, Thinking, Being: The Sense of Touch in Aristotle's *de Anima* and Its Implications." *Minerva* 17: 74–101.
Massumi, Brian. 2002. *Parables for the Virtual: Movement, Affect, Sensation.* Durham, NC: Duke University Press.
———. 2015. *Politics of Affect.* Cambridge, UK: Polity.
Merleau-Ponty, Maurice. 2012. *Phenomenology of Perception.* Translated by Donald A. Landes. New York: Routledge.
Mignolo, Walter, and Catherine E. Walsh. 2018. *On Decoloniality: Concepts, Analytics, Praxis.* Durham, NC: Duke University Press.
Mika, Carl. 2017. *Indigenous Education and the Metaphysics of Presence: A Worlded Philosophy.* London: Routledge.
Mikulan, Petra, and Adam Rudder. 2019. "Posthumanist Perspectives on Racialized Life and Human Difference Pedagogy." *Educational Theory* 69 (5): 615–629.

Montagu, Ashley. 1986. *Touching: The Human Significance of the Skin*. 3rd ed. New York: Harper.
Nechvatal, Joseph. 2015. "Olafur Eliasson's Sundial of Melting Icebergs Clocks in at Half-Past Wasteful." December 9, 2015. https://hyperallergic.com/260217/olafur-eliassons-sundial-of-melting-icebergs-clocks-in-at-half-past-wasteful/.
Noë, Alva. 2009. *Out of Our Heads: Why You Are Not Your Brain, and Other Lessons from the Biology of Consciousness*. New York: Hill and Wang.
O'Donnell, Aislinn. 2018. "Spinoza, Experimentation and Education: How Things Teach Us." *Educational Philosophy and Theory* 50 (9): 819–829.
O'Loughlin, Marjorie. 2006. *Embodiment and Education: Exploring Creatural Existence*. Dordrecht: Springer.
Orbach, Susie. 2019. "Climate Sorrow." In *This Is Not a Drill: An Extinction Rebellion Handbook*, edited by Extinction Rebellion, 67–70. London: Penguin.
Pallasmaa, Juhani. 2012. *The Eyes of the Skin: Architecture and the Senses*. Chichester, UK: Wiley.
Panagia, Davide. 2009. *The Political Life of Sensation*. Durham, NC: Duke University Press.
Papastephanou, Marianna. 2014. "Philosophy, Kairosophy and the Lesson of Time." *Educational Philosophy and Theory* 46 (7): 718–734.
Paterson, Mark. 2007. *The Senses of Touch: Haptics, Affects, and Technologies*. New York: Berg.
Pennac, Daniel. 2010. *School Blues*. Translated by Sarah Ardizzone. London: MacLehose Press. Kindle edition.
Purser, Ronald. 2015. "The Myth of the Present Moment." *Mindfulness* 6 (3): 680–686.
Rahula, Walpola. (1959) 2015. *What the Buddha Taught*. Bedford, UK: G. Fraser.
Rancière, Jacques. 1995. *On the Shores of Politics*. London: Verso.
———. 2006. *The Politics of Aesthetics: The Distribution of the Sensible*. London: Continuum.
———. 2009. "Contemporary Art and the Politics of Aesthetics." In *Communities of Sense: Rethinking Aesthetics and Politics*, edited by Beth Hinderliter, William Katzen, Vered Maimon, Jaleh Mansoor, and Seth McCormick, 31–50. Durham, NC: Duke University Press.
———. 2014. "The Aesthetic Dimension: Aesthetics, Politics, Knowledge." In *The Aesthetic Turn in Political Thought*, edited by Nikolas Kompridis. London: Bloomsbury.
Ringrose, Jessica, Katie Warfield, and Shiva Zarabadi, eds. 2020. *Feminist Posthumanisms, New Materialisms and Education*. London: Routledge.
Roberts, Shinshu. 2018. *Being-Time: A Practitioner's Guide to Dōgen's Shōbōgenzō Uji*. Somerville, MA: Wisdom Publications.
Rovelli, Carlo. 2018. *The Order of Time*. London: Allen Lane.
Ruitenberg, Claudia. 2013. "The Double Subjectification Function of Education: Reconsidering Hospitality and Democracy." In *Education and the Political:*

New Theoretical Articulations, edited by Tomasz Szkudlarek, 89–105. Rotterdam: Sense.

———. 2015. "Toward a Curatorial Turn in Education." In *Art's Teachings, Teaching's Art: Philosophical, Critical and Educational Musings*, edited by Tyson E. Lewis and Megan J. Laverty, 229–242. Dordrecht: Springer.

Rytzler, Johannes. 2021. "Teaching at the Margin: Didaktik in the Sphere of Attention." *Ethics and Education* 16 (1): 108–121.

Säfström, Carl Anders. 2011. "Rethinking Emancipation, Rethinking Education." *Studies in Philosophy and Education* 30 (2): 199–209.

———. 2014. "The Passion of Teaching at the Border of Order." *Asia-Pacific Journal of Teacher Education* 42 (4): 337–346.

———. 2021. *A Pedagogy of Equality in a Time of Unrest: Strategies for an Ambiguous Future*. London: Routledge.

Schwartzman, Roy. 2020. "Performing Pandemic Pedagogy." *Communication Education* 69 (4): 502–517.

Sedgwick, Eve Kosofsky. 2003. *Touching Feeling: Affect, Pedagogy, Performativity*. Durham, NC: Duke University Press.

Selwyn, Neil, Thomas Hillman, Rebecca Eynon, Giselle Ferreira, Jeremy Knox, Felicitas Macgilchrist, and Juana M. Sancho-Gil. 2020. "What's Next for Ed-Tech? Critical Hopes and Concerns for the 2020s." *Learning, Media and Technology* 45 (1): 1–6.

Semetsky, Inna. 2004. "The Complexity of Individuation." *International Journal of Applied Psychoanalytic Studies* 1 (4): 324–346.

Seremetakis, C. Nadia. 1994. *The Senses Still: Perception and Memory as Material Culture in Modernity*. Boulder, CO: Westview Press.

Sheets-Johnstone, Maxine. 2009. *The Corporeal Turn: An Interdisciplinary Reader*. Exeter, UK: Imprint Academic.

———. 2011. *The Primacy of Movement*. 2nd ed. Philadelphia: John Benjamins.

———. 2016. *Insides and Outsides*. Exeter, UK: Imprint Academic.

Shusterman, Richard. 2008. *Body Consciousness: A Philosophy of Mindfulness and Somaesthetics*. Cambridge: Cambridge University Press.

———. 2012. *Thinking through the Body: Essays in Somaesthetics*. Cambridge, UK: Cambridge University Press.

Sisters Hope. 2020. *Sisters Academy: Education for the Future*. Copenhagen: I Do Art Books.

Stambaugh, Joan. 1990. *Impermanence is Buddha-Nature: Dōgen's Understanding of Temporality*. Honolulu: University of Hawai'i Press.

Stengers, Isabelle. 2005. "Introductory Notes on an Ecology of Practices." *Cultural Studies Review* 11 (1): 183–196.

Taylor, Affrica, and Veronica Pacini-Ketchabaw. 2015. "Learning with Children, Ants, and Worms in the Anthropocene: Towards a Common World Pedagogy of Multispecies Vulnerability." *Pedagogy, Culture & Society* 23 (4): 507–529.

Todd, Sharon. 2003. *Learning from the Other: Levinas, Psychoanalysis, and Ethical Possibilities in Education*. Albany: State University of New York Press.

———. 2009. *Toward an Imperfect Education: Facing Humanity, Rethinking Cosmopolitanism*. Boulder, CO: Paradigm Publishers.

———. 2015a. "Creating Transformative Spaces in Education: Facing Humanity, Facing Violence." *Philosophical Inquiry in Education* 23 (1): 53–61.

———. 2015b. "Experiencing Change, Encountering the Unknown: An Education in Negative Capability in Light of Buddhism and Levinas." *Journal of Philosophy of Education* 49 (2): 240–254.

———. 2016a. "Facing Uncertainty in Education: Beyond the Harmonies of Eurovision Education." *European Educational Research Journal* 15 (6): 619–627.

———. 2016b. "Education Incarnate." *Educational Philosophy and Theory* 48 (4): 405–417.

———. 2018. "Culturally Reimagining Education: Performativity, Voice and Publicity." *Educational Philosophy and Theory* 50 (10): 970–980.

Tompkins, Kyla Wazana. 2016. "On the Limits and Promise of New Materialist Philosophy." *Lateral* 5 (1). https://doi.org/10.25158/L5.1.8.

Tuana, Nancy. 2001. "Material Locations: An Interactionist Alternative to Realism/Social Constructivism." In *Engendering Rationalities*, edited by Nancy Tuana and Sandi Morgen. Bloomington: Indiana University Press.

———. 2008. "Viscous Porosity: Witnessing Katrina." In *Material Feminisms*, edited by Stacy Alaimo and Susan Hekman, 188–213. Bloomington: Indiana University Press.

van der Kolk, Bessel A. 2015. *The Body Keeps the Score: Brain, Mind, and Body in the Healing of Trauma*. New York: Viking.

van der Tuin, Iris. 2008. "Deflationary Logic: Response to Sara Ahmed's Imaginary Prohibitions: Some Preliminary Remarks on the Founding Gestures of the 'New Materialism.'" *European Journal of Women's Studies* 15 (4): 411–416.

Varela, Francisco J., Evan Thompson, and Eleanor Rosch. 1993. *The Embodied Mind*. Cambridge, MA: MIT Press.

Vlieghe, Joris. 2018. "Rethinking Emancipation with Freire and Rancière: A Plea for a Thing-Centred Pedagogy." *Educational Philosophy and Theory* 50 (10): 917–927.

Vlieghe, Joris, and Piotr Zamojski. 2019. *Towards an Ontology of Teaching: Thing-Centred Pedagogy, Affirmation and Love for the World*. Dordrecht: Springer.

Wall Kimmerer, Robin. 2013. *Braiding Sweetgrass: Indigenous Wisdom, Scientific Knowledge, and the Teachings of Plants*. London: Penguin. Kindle e-book.

Williamson, Ben, Rebecca Eynon, and John Potter. 2020. "Pandemic Politics, Pedagogies and Practices: Digital Technologies and Distance Education during the Coronavirus Emergency." *Learning, Media and Technology* 45 (2): 107–114.

Wilson, Helen F. 2017. "On Geography and Encounter: Bodies, Borders, and Difference." *Progress in Human Geography* 4 (4): 451–471.
Winnicott, D. W. 1974. "Fear of Breakdown." *International Review of Psychoanalysis* 1: 103–107.
Youdell, Deborah. 2017. "Bioscience and the Sociology of Education: The Case for Biosocial Education." *British Journal of Sociology of Education* 38 (8): 1273–1287.

Index

Abram, David, 12, 16, 171, 173–176, 177, 179, 182, 184, 185
aesthetics, 8, 10, 14, 91, 100, 102–103, 185–186; *see also* relational aesthetics
aesthetic politics, 14, 92, 104, 187–189
affect, 5, 8, 53, 56–60, 71, 85, 89, 92, 147, 187, 192n8
Ahmed, Sara, 6–7, 12, 13, 48–53, 62, 70, 173, 191n4
analog, 15, 158, 161–164; in teaching, 164–168
Arendt, Hannah, 23, 28, 124, 193n2, 195n1
Aristotle, 8, 60–61, 62
Assemble, art collective, 105

Bang Larsen, Lars, 103
Batchelor, Stephen, 132–133
becoming, as educational, 10, 11, 13, 14–15, 34, 38–39, 42–43, 46, 52, 54, 56, 60, 81, 82, 100, 102, 114, 187–189; future anterior of, 139–145; and movement, 115–120; and online education, 151, 153, 156, 158, 159, 162–164, 167; beyond socialization, 24, 29, 30, 32, 36; subjectivity and, 22–23,

57, 59, 66, 68–73, 84; in teaching, 3–5; and time, 123–147
being-time (Dōgen), 15, 131–133, 138, 140, 142, 144, 145, 174
Bergdahl, Lovisa, and Elisabet Langmann, 13, 28–29, 32, 107, 117; geometries of educational relations, 107, 112–113
Biesta, Gert, 13, 29–34, 42, 146, 152, 192n6
Bishop, Claire, 194n4, 194n6
bodies, abstract, 6–7; and change, 21–23; deformations and formations of, 65, 69, 84, 97; discursive constitution of, 5, 82–85; in education, 2, 20, 21, 32, 34, 39–42, 89, 94, 102, 122; in/of encounters, 34, 38, 53–54, 56, 59–60, 72; of the environment, 101; and future time, 141–145; liminality of, 67, 118; living bodies of sense, 13, 14, 15, 46, 53–60, 62–68, 82, 92, 97, 109, 134; and materiality, 5; in online education, 153, 155, 156; and past time, 135; as racialized and sexualized, 7, 48–52, 78; as relational, 24, 41, 72, 97, 119, 187; in relation to culture, 70, 82; in relation

bodies *(continued)*
  to devices, 157–158; in relation to nature, 174; as socially coded, 85–88, 96; as territories, 58; as virtual, 162; *see also* somaesthetics
body-subject, 22, 28, 34, 71
Bourriaud, Nicolas, 12, 14, 99, 102–105, 106–107, 109, 118, 120–122, 194n6
Braidotti, Rosi, 6, 10, 12, 188
Buddhism, 12, 54, 61, 95, 115, 125, 135, 145; conception of time, 128–134, 141; pedagogy of, 14, 110–111; *see also* codependent arising
Butler, Judith, 14, 82–85, 87, 90, 91, 96, 194n8

Cavarero, Adriana, 112, 194n5
change: and bodies, 21–23, 32, 57, 70, 162, 174; cultural and social, 24–26, 42, 139–140; in relation to climate emergency, 171, 172, 179, 180, 181, 185; and time, 123–124, 141, 179, 185; and transformation, 3, 5, 8, 32, 34, 42, 60, 71, 79, 87, 184, 188
choreography of education, 14, 110–111, 115, 118, 122
chronological time, 124; *chronos*, 171, 181–182, 184–18; limits of, 125–128
climate sorrow, 15–16, 170–171
codependent arising, 128–133
coloniality, 4, 7; in education, 69, 78, 107; of encounters, 48, 50, 57, 60, 85; organizing time, 161
colonization, 13, 23, 33, 40, 47, 48, 49, 124, 196n1; in online education, 154, 168
common sense, 7, 14, 75, 76, 77–78, 80–81, 83, 87–92, 94, 97–98, 187

communities of sense, 8, 14, 77, 91, 97, 98, 101, 167, 188
contact: with elements of the environment, 51, 70–71, 84, 147, 158, 170, 173, 189; in encounters, 47, 109; events of, 46, 52, 53, 57, 62, 71, 141, 183, 188; moments of, 59, 60, 143, 176; sensory and bodily forms of, 5, 9–10, 24, 53, 54, 55, 61, 63–64, 66, 68, 69, 70, 72, 73, 129, 130, 138, 144, 157, 158, 193n12
contemporary art practice, 99, 102, 103, 194n1
Critical Zone, 177–179, 181, 184–185
cultural inheritance, 26–29, 32, 70
cultural translation, 13, 28–29, 32, 93, 104; *see also* translation and Lovisa Bergdahl and Elisabet Langmann
curating encounters, 2, 8, 15, 98, 99, 100, 107, 121–122, 152, 165, 166; as teaching, 102, 167, 168, 170, 183; *see also* staging encounters

decolonial project, 4, 7, 15, 124, 139, 187; decolonizing online education, 154–155, 167, 168
digital encounters, 10, 15, 101, 151–168; bodily aspects of, 156–158; with e-readers, 157–158; *see also* online education
"distribution of the sensible" (Rancière), 90–93, 96
Dōgen, 12, 131–133, 140

ecology of practices, 11–12, 108, 119; *see also* Isabelle Stengers
education: as distinct from schooling, 76; as mechanistic system and

social institution, 77–81; proper, 21, 23, 29, 32, 34, 35, 81; purpose of, 23, 25, 68, 165, 192n6; *see also* enculturation, becoming, and educational encounters

educational encounters, 7, 11, 12, 13, 14–16, 51, 52, 54, 100, 102, 106, 107, 113, 115, 120, 121, 124, 146, 167, 179, 189; as acts of presencing, 145, 166; digital, 152, 155, 167; as embodied, 19–43; as living, bodily, 53, 60, 68, 128; political and aesthetic dimension, 8, 93, 97, 98, 99, 102, 165; time and, 134, 138, 139, 147s

educational processes, 10, 46, 88, 151

elements of the environment, 10, 16, 22, 24, 53, 54, 59, 60, 62, 63, 66, 68, 70, 73, 77, 83, 97, 98, 118, 120, 134, 143, 159, 171, 174, 183, 184

Eliasson, Olafur, 15–16, 102, 169, 171 179–180, 185; *Ice Watch*, 16, 169, 171, 179–183, 184, 196n7, 196n8

emancipation, 21, 29, 30, 33–34, 70, 71, 103

encounters, 3–4; colonial and racialized, 48–53; in context of climate emergency, 183–186; cultural encounters, 25; with the environment, 46, 63; as forms and formations, 99–122; as interruptive, 96–98; living bodily encounters, 46, 53; normative demands of, 4; in the plural, 9; troubling encounters, 47–53; *see also* educational encounters, sensory encounters, and staging encounters

enculturation, as educational, 10, 11, 13, 14, 26, 34, 38, 39, 43, 46, 52, 53, 54, 60, 69, 72, 93, 97, 127, 151, 153, 188, 189; as distinct from socialization, 33, 42, 69; and the politics of the senses, 75–98; and translation, 28–29, 32, 41, 70, 88

Epstein, Mark, 12, 15, 125, 135, 136, 138

Field, Tiffany, 55

formations, 70, 106, 115, 140; bodily, 65, 69, 97; as distinct from form, 100–101, 106, 108; of educational encounters, 8, 14, 99–122, 145, 163; relational, 117, 128, 133, 137, 157, 165, 167, 168; subject, 21, 82–84, and teaching, 107–115, 119, 153, 155; virtual, 158

flux of life, 56, 70, 72, 193n12

future, 10, 14, 15, 22, 123, 136, 139, 146, 171, 173; in amnesiac time, 127; in anachronistic time, 127; as defining education, 35; as future anterior, 125, 139–145; linear, chronological sense, 128, 181, 182; between past and, 124, 125, 134, 195n1; present connection with, 132, 133, 134, 147, 182, 184, 195n6

Gaia, 176–179, 182, 196n6
Gibson, James, 54–55, 192n4
Greene, Maxine, 3
Gross, Lisa, *League of Kitchens*, 105

Hansen, David, 26–29, 31
Hayles, H. Katherine, 157, 158, 163, 165
Heuer, Christopher, 180–181
Howes, David and Constance Classen, 14, 85–88, 90, 91, 96

identity positions, 21–22, 59, 77, 143, 146, 147; grid of, 22, 23, 52
individuation, 59, 71, 118, 141–142, 144
interdependency, 6, 10, 12, 96, 129, 133, 140, 176, 184, 185, 187, 189; of body, materiality, and the senses, 12
instrumentalism of education, 23–24, 35, 78, 108, 127, 139, 140
Irigaray, Luce, 158, 193n14

Jacoby, Russell, 76
James, William, 51, 55–56, 57, 58–59, 72

kairos, 16, 124, 171, 182–183, 184–185
Kearney, Richard, 61, 62, 65

Lacy, Suzanne, *Silver Action*, 106
Latour, Bruno, 12, 16, 171, 173, 176–180, 182, 184, 185, 196n1
Lévy, Pierre, 153, 156, 159–161
Løvlie, Lars, and "pedagogy of place," 41

Machado Oliveira, Vanessa (Andreotti), 7–8, 184
Mammalian Diving Reflex, *Nightwalks with Teenagers*, 105
Manning, Erin, 10, 12, 14, 15, 140, 145; on future-anterior, 141–143; on movement and stillness, 115–118; on touch, 107, 119, 143
Martin, Jane Roland, 24–26, 27, 29, 30, 31
Masschelein, Jan, 13, 195n1; and Maarten Simons, 13, 35–40, 41, 42, 108–110, 112
Massie, Pascal, 61
Massumi, Brian, 9, 12, 13, 65, 165; on affect and sensation, 56–60; on the analog, 161–163; on change and bodies, 21–23; on the virtual, 158, 159, 162
membranes, 51, 62, 63, 68–73
microperceptions, 58–59, 72, 94, 166
Montagu, Ashley, 55
morphology, 64, 67, 68–73, 193n14
movement, 14, 22, 34, 46, 65, 124; bodily experience and touch, 51, 53, 54, 58, 60, 63, 68, 69, 98, 113, 119, 120, 124, 141, 163; inclination, 113–114; pointing, 113–114; of potentiality, 160; reaching out, 118, 142–143, 159; space created by, 67, 97; and stillness, 115–117; of teaching, 112, 115–117, 118, 119, 122, 133

Nagarjuna, 12, 46, 53, 59, 137
new materialism, 5, 6, 191n1, 191n4

O'Loughlin, Marjorie, 52
online education, 15, 47, 49, 151, 156, 161; advocates of, 153; critique of, 153–155; naming of, 152–153; and teaching 164–168
Orbach, Susie, 170–171

Pallasmaa, Juhani, 66–68
Panagia, Davide, 75, 76, 89, 92, 194n8
pandemic, 3, 9, 10, 15, 152, 154
Papastephanou, Marianna, 171, 181–182, 184
past, 10, 14, 18–29, 69, 133, 141; leaving behind, 36, 40, 42; neurotic, 126; nostalgic, 127; presencing, 15, 139, 145–147; relation to present and future, 109, 123–125, 128, 132, 134; traumatic time of, 15, 134–139

Pennac, Daniel, 19–20, 22, 35, 37, 39; and Jocelyne example, 39, 138
perception, 2, 20, 33, 46, 51, 53, 54, 56, 60, 62, 65, 70, 75–77, 81–82, 86, 88, 89, 91, 92, 93, 105, 147, 163, 173–175, 178, 181; and aesthetics, 8; Aristotle on, 61; Gibson's theory of perceptual systems, 54–55; social ordering of, 85–87; *see also* microperceptions and regimes of perception
"perceptual shock" (Rancière), 14, 33, 91, 97, 167, 170
politics of the senses, 14, 33, 53, 75, 77, 85, 91, 94, 96, 97; biopolitics of the senses, 86
posture, 112, 115, 117; of inclination, 113, 116; of pointing, 102, 113; of rectitude, 113, 115, 116; in teaching, 107, 116; *see also* Bergdahl and Langmann, and Cavarero
presencing, 10, 14, 15, 131, 132, 134, 141–143, 166, 167, 184, 188; the future 142, 144, 182; the past, 138–139; as time of education 145–147; *see also* present
present, 9, 10, 16, 22, 28, 53, 82, 124, 125, 145, 166, 169, 171, 179, 183, 187; as flow, 132–133; fluidity of, 15, 128–134; as incarnated, 19–20, 34, 40, 42; moment, 132; relation to past and future, 113, 123, 124, 128–129, 134, 140, 142, 143, 147, 182, 184; six framings of in education, 125–128; tense of education, 35–37; and trauma, 135–139; and translation, 69, 88, 93; as unfolding, 124, 128–129, 133, 134, 141, 176, 184; *see also* being-time, *kairos*, and chronological time

profanation, 13, 37–41
"pure experience" (James), 51, 55–56, 57, 69, 132; as flux of life, 56

racialization, as embodied process, 6, 13, 50, 120
Rancière, Jacques, 7, 8, 12, 14, 23, 33, 76, 78–79, 89–92, 96–97, 106, 167, 170; *see also* "distribution of the sensible," "perceptual shock," and "regime of perception"
Raphael, *School of Athens*, 107
"regime of perception" (Rancière), 7, 14, 33, 75–76, 78, 80–81, 89–94, 100, 106, 167
relational aesthetics, 14, 99, 102–107; relational art, 105–106
"relationscapes" (Manning), 119, 120, 165
relations of sensation, 101
relational ontology, 6, 12, 96, 129, 171; world as relation, 176–179
relations to the world, 15, 170–173; as alienation, 171, 185
Rembrandt, *Two Women Teaching a Child to Walk*, 114f
Ruitenberg, Claudia, 107, 121–122

Säfström, Carl Anders, 76
Sedgwick, Eve Kosofsky, 14, 115; "pedagogy of Buddhism," 110–111
Sensations, 1, 2, 6, 7, 40, 51, 55, 70, 76, 81, 138, 184, 185, 187–188; and analog, 162–164; aesthetics of, 100; and becoming, 34, 118; and codependent arising, 129–131; directness of, 56–57, 60–61; event of, 9, 14, 46, 53, 61, 64, 68, 69, 72, 73; and perception, 55; beyond social scripts, 70, 71, 76, 81, 83, 84, 87–89, 92–94, 101; socially coded, 85–86, 95

senses, 6, 7, 9, 13, 14, 21, 33, 53, 80, 81, 96, 117, 151, 165; Abram on, 173–175; Aristotle on, 60–61; Buddhism and, 129–132; Butler on, 84; in encounters, 53–56; *Ice Watch*, 182, 183, 185; meaning of, 8; Pallasmaa on, 66–67; socially coded, 85–87; *see also* politics of the senses, touch, perception
sense-scape, 2, 3
sensory encounters, 2, 7, 13, 46, 52, 83, 102, 134, 151, 159, 173, 174, 176; *see also* educational encounters
sensory experience, 7, 8, 14, 46, 47, 53, 66, 77, 174, 176, 193
Sheets-Johnstone, Maxine, 12, 14, 62–69, 97, 178
Shusterman, Richard, 51, 60, 94–96
Sisters Hope, 1–2, 98, 100; Sisters Academy, 1; *The Boarding School*, 1–2, 5, 100
Skin, 50, 51, 60, 67, 71, 72, 118, 119, 169, 180, 193n11; epithelial sensitivity, 61; as surface sensitivity, 63, 64, 66
social justice, 4, 11, 16, 22, 79, 139, 187–189
socialization, 13, 14, 21–24, 26–35, 38, 42, 59, 69, 70, 75–85, 97, 145–147
somaesthetics, 94–96
spaced times and timed spaces, 10, 118, 142, 187
Springgay, Stephanie, *Artists' Soup Kitchen*, 105
staging encounters, 2, 3, 5, 8, 32, 98, 99, 105, 106, 120–122, 126, 133, 155, 170, 172, 173, 180, 185; digital encounters, 167, 172
states of encounter, 105, 107, 109, 118, 120
Steen, Jan, 107

Stengers, Isabelle, 11–12, 75, 76, 108
stillness, 113, 115–117
subjectification, 13, 21, 23, 29–34, 38, 52, 70–72
subjectivity, 10, 22, 30, 46, 56, 58, 59, 60, 68, 69, 71, 73, 77, 80, 106, 127, 187–188; colonial forms of, 64; discursive, 82–85; on grid, 28, 42; modernist assumptions, 103; posture and, 112, 116; senses central to, 53
suspension, 13, 35–42, 109–110, 127

teaching, 5, 10, 68, 107–122, 133, 145, 155, 161, 170, 171, 184; aesthetics of, 100–101, 186; as curation, 107, 170; as formation, 119; as inclination, 112–115; online, 152–153; as pointing, 107–115; as rectitude, 112–113; reframing, 23, 35; virtual, 164–168
time, 12, 15, 16, 35, 72, 122, 123, 155, 158, 161, 167, 174, 181–186; being-time (Dōgen), 131–133, 174; "free time," 35–36; six framings of in education, 125–128; as unfolding, 123–147; *see also* present, past, future, chronological time, *kairos*, presencing, traumatic time
Tiravanija, Rirkrit, *pad thai*, 105
Touch: as all the senses, 61, 118; bodily in education, 68–73; as event, 9; as movement, 115–120; and the future, 141–145
touch and touched by, 2, 9, 14, 15, 59, 60–73; 76, 81, 83, 88, 113, 118, 119, 120, 122, 124, 125, 134, 142, 144–145, 157, 164, 188
translation, 34, 38, 39, 41, 42, 52, 69, 70, 81, 82, 83, 85, 88, 93, 104, 126, 156, 162, 163, 164; *see also* cultural translation and Lovisa Bergdahl and Elisabet Langmann

van der Kolk, Bessel, 135–136
virtual, the, 15, 158–164;
    virtualization, 159–161; virtual
    teaching, 164–168
Wall Kimmerer, Robin, 120–121

Wilson, Helen, 47–48
Winnicott, D. W., 12, 15, 125, 136–138

yoga, 95, 96, 116

www.ingramcontent.com/pod-product-compliance
Lightning Source LLC
Chambersburg PA
CBHW030650230426
43665CB00011B/1029